Gerhard Falk

Football
and American Identity

Football
and American Identity

THE HAWORTH PRESS
Contemporary Sports Issues
Frank Hoffmann, PhD, MLS
Martin Manning
Senior Editors

Minor League Baseball: Community Building Through Hometown Sports by Rebecca S. Kraus

Baseball and American Culture: Across the Diamond edited by Edward J. Rielly

Dictionary of Toys and Games in American Popular Culture by Frederick J. Augustyn Jr.

Basketball in America: From the Playgrounds to Jordan's Game and Beyond edited by Bob Batchelor

Football and American Identity by Gerhard Falk

Football
and American Identity

Gerhard Falk

The Haworth Press®
New York • London • Oxford

For more information on this book or to order, visit
http://www.haworthpress.com/store/product.asp?sku=5227

or call 1-800-HAWORTH (800-429-6784) in the United States and Canada
or (607) 722-5857 outside the United States and Canada

or contact orders@HaworthPress.com

PUBLISHER'S NOTE
The development, preparation, and publication of this work have been undertaken with great care. However, the publisher, employees, editors, and agents of The Haworth Press are not responsible for any errors contained herein or for consequences that may ensue from use of materials or information contained in this work. The opinions expressed by the author(s) are not necessarily those of The Haworth Press, Inc.

The Haworth Press, Inc., 10 Alice Street, Binghamton, NY 13904-1580.

Cover design by Kerry E. Mack.

Library of Congress Cataloging-in-Publication Data

Falk, Gerhard.
    Football and American identity / Gerhard Falk.
        p. cm.
    Includes bibliographical references and index.
    ISBN 0-7890-2526-4 (hard : alk. paper)—ISBN 0-7890-2527-2 (soft : alk. paper)
    1. Football—Social aspects—United States. 2. Football players—United States—Social conditions. 3. Social values—United States. 4. National characteristics, American. I. Title.

GV951.F25 2005
796.332'0973—dc22
                                                                                    2004012740

CONTENTS

Preface

xi

Introduction

1

Chapter 1. The School and American Football

7

The Social Psychology of Football

7

The Academic Achievements of Football Players
   and Other Athletes

12

Children's Football

17

Football and Aggression

19

Death and Injury on the Playing Field

25

Football As an Alternative Status System

27

Summary

32

**Chapter 2. College Football—The Professionals' Minor
League**

33

Football Develops a Subculture

33

Recruiting College Football Players

35

Money and Greed—The College Football Business

44

The Race Issue in College Football

51

Who Plays College Football?

52

The College Football Coach—Role Model for All Seasons

53

Football Injuries and Football Deaths

56

Cheerleaders

58

Summary

59

Chapter 3. Football As a Profession

61

A Brief History of Professional Football

61

The Coming of Television

64

Race and the NFL

71

Football Fanatics

73

The Domestic Lives of Football Players

76

Professional Football Players As Victims

79

Professional Football and Social Class 81
Summary 82

Chapter 4. Football and Social Stratification 85

The Status of Football Players 85
Wealth, Income, and the Football Business 86
Race and Football: A "Mixed Marriage" 87
The Jewish Football Experience 91
Pennsylvania, Ohio, and Texas: Mothers of American
    Football 93
Gender and Sexual Orientation 98
Retired Football Players 100
Summary 108

Chapter 5. They Also Serve 109

Coaches 109
Scouts 112
Trainers 113
Officials 114
Cheerleaders 116
Football Doctors, Injuries, and Drugs 119
General Managers 122
Owners 123
Summary 132

Chapter 6. Fanatics 133

The Football Hall of Fans 133
Female Football Fans 134
The Football Culture 135
Regional and Generational Differences Among Football
    Fans 137
The Tailgate Party and the Football Diet 139
In Groups and Out Groups 141
Fan Violence 144
Fantasy Football 147
The Influence of Gender on Human Conduct 149
Catharsis 152
Summary 154

Chapter 7. Football and the Media   155

Announcers and Analysts   155
Football and the Written Word—Print Journalism
    Supports the Game   161
Women Enter the Locker Room   163
Magazines   164
Football Books   166
Football in Film   170
Football Songs and Lyrics   173
Football Jokes   174
Summary   175

Chapter 8. The Football Business   177

Money, Money Everywhere   177
Film Production   178
Advertising   179
Merchandise   182
Contract Advisers/Agents   186
Lawyers   189
Stadium Construction Profits   191
Gambling   194
Small Business Contracts   197
Summary   197

Chapter 9. Crime and American Football   199

The Benedict-Yaeger Research   199
Felonies and Misdemeanors: The Football Culture
    of Crime   200
Super Bowl XXXIV   209
Understanding Criminality Among Football Players   210
Gambling and Drugs   213
The Sociology of Crime   217
Summary   219

Chapter 10. The National Football League   221

Football Politics and the South   221
College Football Politics   224

The Commissioners   226
The NFL Machine   232
Urban Warfare   233
The International NFL   235
From Football to Politics   237
The NFL Community   240
Summary   242

Epilogue   **243**

Notes   **245**

Index   **267**

ABOUT THE AUTHOR

Gerhard Falk is Professor of Sociology at the State University College of New York at Buffalo. He has authored forty articles in journals as diverse as *The Journal of the American Bar Association, The Journal of Educational Sociology,* and *Mankind Quarterly.* He has also written twelve books, including *Man's Ascent to Reason, Grandparents, Stigma—How We Treat Outsiders, Sex, Gender and Social Change,* and *The Life of the Academic Professional.*

Preface

Almost 3,000 books are available that deal with football, both American and European. Many of these books address the lives of famous coaches and players. Others concern the history of the sport or are devoted to strategy or other aspects of playing the game. Some books denounce one or another aspect of the game. Some are for children; others have a regional appeal.

The purpose of the present study is to consider the social conditions and cultural implications of American football. This book deals with the football subculture as a reflection of some of the most important American values, including competition, conflict, diversity, power, economic success and fairness, respect for others, and patriotism.

It is my contention here that all of these values are found in football and that football serves largely to preserve these values. I find that football exemplifies all that is great in America and therefore have titled this book *Football and American Identity*. This does not mean that I hid some of the ugly aspects of the game. It does mean, however, that, in my judgment, football is the essence of the American spirit which has made the United States the leader of the world and given immigrants such as myself more opportunities than anyone could dream of or achieve anywhere but here. For that I shall always be grateful and therefore have dedicated this book to the United States. May it prosper forever.

I thank my son Clifford Falk for the many hours he spent dealing with my computer problems and for reading the manuscript several times. I also thank my wife Ursula for the same effort.

Introduction

Every human society includes a system of values that distinguishes it from all other human societies. Therefore, we can understand a society best by studying these values, which are made concrete by the activities a society enjoys the most. These activities reflect the beliefs, attitudes, and concerns of those who promote them, as well as giving an outsider the opportunity to discover what is important to those who practice the preferred activities of their society. Values may therefore be defined as preferences for a line of action or "statements from the standpoint of a culture as what ought to be." Yet another way of defining values is to say that "values are socially shared ideas about what is right."[1]

Among the numerous activities that serve to define American society, sports ranks high. The value Americans place on sports, and football in particular, can be seen in the salaries paid to players; the average football player's salary in 2004 was $1,1640,000. The thirty-two teams of the National Football League (NFL) surpassed $1 billion in signing bonuses paid to players.[2] In contrast, American physicians, who constitute the most prestigious occupation in the United States, earned an average income of $140,500 in 2004.[3] Similar incomes and even more are available to the top athletes in other sports such as basketball, baseball, and hockey. Therefore, it is legitimate to claim that sports is a principal concern of the American people and that football ranks high among the sport activities that Americans choose to support.

I contend that the reason for the great support football has enjoyed in America for the past century is that football encompasses all the values that make American society unique. Of course, all human societies are unique and all have an ethos, which I define here as the personality of any society. This means that every society differs from all other societies in the same fashion as all individuals differ from all other individuals.

It is necessary to begin by listing the principal characteristics of the American value system. Such a list will demonstrate that the values which define the game of football are also the values which define American life; therefore, the football subculture overlaps the values held generally in American life.

Sociologist Robin M. Williams identified several core values important to the people of the United States. Among these are individualism, achievement or success, activity, work, material comfort, and efficiency. These seven values are all found in the football subculture, thus one could understand the American value system in an encapsulated form by following the U.S. football schedule.[4]

I will begin with individualism and achievement. Although football is a team sport, individual football players and coaches have been idolized and elevated to mythological status in a manner previously reserved for persons of religious significance or military prowess. Two examples are Amos Alonzo Stagg and Harold Edward "Red" Grange.

Stagg was the first football coach employed by the University of Chicago when it opened its doors in 1892. Stagg had been a baseball and football star at Yale University. He was at once given tenure as head of the Department of Physical Culture and Athletics and chief coach of the football team. As such he literally ruled the University of Chicago until 1929, when Robert Maynard Hutchins became president of the university. Stagg repeatedly won the Big Ten title and several unofficial national championships. In the 1920s he was so popular with alumni and other supporters of the Chicago football team that Chicago was called "Stagg's University." The university profited greatly from this success, so football players became exempt from attending classes, were given license to conduct themselves in a variety of atrocious fashions, failed numerous courses, and graduated just the same. All that came to an end after Hutchins became president. Coach Stagg was then seventy years old, and the university refused to renew his contract. He therefore accepted a coaching position at the College of the Pacific, where he remained until he was eighty-four years old. The football program at the University of Chicago was abolished altogether in 1939 after Stagg's successor lost numerous games and interest in the football program at Chicago sunk to an all-time low.[5]

Grange is another football legend. His permanent fame rests on his achievement during the Illinois/Michigan football game on October 18, 1924, as well as on the definition of the situation provided by the media and the values his success illustrates. Grange accomplished so great a sports feat on that October day that it ranks with such other legendary attainments as Jesse Owens's record-setting track and field achievements and Don Larsen's pitching in the 1956 World Series. Owens broke three world records and tied a fourth in only seventy minutes during the 1935 Big Ten Conference Championships and went on to win four gold medals at the 1936 Olympics. Yankee pitcher Larsen threw ninety-seven pitches during the World Series against the Brooklyn Dodgers without allowing one runner to reach base.

Grange did no less for football in 1924 than Owens and Larsen did for their own sports later. He scored five touchdowns, four in the first twelve minutes, passed for another touchdown, rushed 402 yards, and completed six passes for another 64 yards.[6]

The achievements of Grange, Owens, and Larsen were of course not attained in a vacuum. On the contrary, they were the product not only of the athletes who performed them but also of the media who recorded them. Prior to the rise of the mass media, other athletes equaled the performances of those who have been in the public eye since the 1920s. Those athletes, however, could not hope to reach the fame that Grange attained almost instantaneously.

Activity is of course the very essence of football. The evidence that work and activity are most important to Americans can be seen by looking at any study of prestige rankings in the United States. These rankings, based on public opinion, always use occupation as the most important index of prestige because occupation is the most important indicator of social class ranking in this country.[7]

Material comfort refers to making money and spending it. Football players earn more in a year than most Americans earn in a lifetime. More specifically, in 2000, Ruben Brown, of the Buffalo Bills, was paid $1,330,600; Sam Rogers, also a "Bill," was paid $2,142,000; and Jeff Burris of the Indianapolis Colts was paid $4,002,800. Some players receive a signing bonus of as much as $5 million.[8]

The consequences of earning such vast sums include lavish spending on luxuries the players never knew existed. Another consequence of earning so much money is that a good number of players are cheated by unscrupulous business managers or investment counselors.[9]

Efficiency, which may be defined as the ability to achieve results, is important to succeed in any sport but particularly in football. The career of football coaches depends on their efficiency, as visible in the number of their winning seasons.

The value of equality is certainly visible in the ethnic makeup of American football teams. A large contingent of American football players is of African descent. Furthermore, it can be said that ethnic origin, religion, or race are all ignored within the setting of American sports. Men of every religion or ethnic origin are involved in football. Therefore, we can be confident that equality and ethnic integration are well entrenched in American football today. This is true for players but not for coaches. Considering that more than half of all football players are black, it is noteworthy that in 1995 only 5.5 percent of all head football coaches at American colleges were of African descent. Since then, this number has slightly increased but is by no means equal to the contribution to football on the part of black players.[10]

If we define humanitarianism as the belief that humans can reach perfection through their own efforts, then football most certainly exemplifies that attitude. Football, like so many human endeavors, requires a great deal of self-discipline, determination, and endurance. These qualities are necessary to achieve success in all kinds of activities. Added to this list is the need to get along with other players on the team. Here again is an important American virtue, since teamwork and getting along with others are vital characteristics for anyone seeking a career in American industry.

Finally, the core values liberty and freedom, which are called upon at all patriotic events, apply to football as well. Football sends a message to Americans which non-Americans are not likely to recognize. That message is that any person has the right, in a free society, to gain fame and money if he or she is willing to take the risks necessary to bring about such success. In fact, football is an expression of the capitalist system upon which our freedoms rest. Obviously, very few would be willing to take the arduous road to football fame and fortune if it did not pay off. Likewise, hardly anyone would engage in business or risk capital or labor if the possibility of success were not at hand. It is the very root of freedom and liberty to allow citizens to make any effort to achieve success. The fall of the Soviet Union has shown conclusively that government-operated societies remove all incentive from working people so that bureaucracy and lack of effort ruin the land. Football teaches the opposite. It teaches that anyone can achieve and that the democracy of capitalism supports the efforts of those who try.

Football is not only an economic enterprise. It is also part of the educational experience of almost all Americans, including those who do not play football but who are affected by the high status which football players and their coaches enjoy in American schools. I first examine the educational aspects of football by showing how that game originated in an English school, only to become America's favorite sport.

Chapter 1

The School
and American Football

THE SOCIAL PSYCHOLOGY OF FOOTBALL

The relationship between education and American football is symbiotic. Football and schooling have lived together since 1823 when William Webb Ellis, a student at Rugby School in England, violated all the rules of British football. Ellis put the ball under his arm during a football game and ran to the goal in order to beat the five o'clock bell which was to end the game. "His schoolmates looked on dumbfounded and aghast at this maneuver that outraged all the proprieties."[1]

Some thought carrying the ball was a good idea, while others viewed that move as "heretical." Consequently, the English organized two kinds of football, one to be known as soccer and the other as rugby. Soccer was a neologism derived from the abbreviation of the word "association," as in "Assoc. Football." The London Football Association formed in 1863 and decided to exclude rugby from their games. Hence the British game, now played all over the world, is called soccer.[2]

When a Canadian team visited Harvard College in 1873 and introduced rugby to America, American football was born. It took a century to develop the present game of football, including its heroes, its villains, and profits. It all began, however, in an educational setting, where it has remained despite the rise of professional football after the invention of television.

The reason for the great attraction football has had for young, college-age men and those in high school and below is chiefly its appeal to masculinity. Of course, aspects of sports other than football are prized by Americans and others because they contribute to physical fitness, because they are enjoyable, and, most important, because they bring participants together with others, thereby inducing many friendships.

For adolescents, sport has additional functions. Because adolescence is a subculture derived from the difference between physical and social maturity, adolescents suffer from the lack of power over their own lives, which are generally controlled by adults. All the physical, mental, emotional, and social difficulties adolescence implies are blocked out by competitive sports. Football and other sports can be an escape from the realities of schoolwork, sexual problems, peer pressure, failure to understand one's identity, and parental control.

Football, and undoubtedly other sports, contributes greatly to the construction of a sense of self for those who participate. Because football allows boys to compete with one another, free from parental supervision, it is a key experience for those who engage in it. Unlike the demands of teachers concerning scholastic efforts, football brings immediate rewards of recognition and status. This, of course, is of immense importance to college and high school students who are otherwise excluded from the rewards of the adult world. Adults can gain the attention and approval of others by conspicuous consumption, as Thorsten Veblen called it. Adults also have power and are in control of all social institutions as well as the home and the school in which adolescents live.[3]

The sports field, however, is the territory of the adolescent himself. There he rules and parents, teachers, and others sit on the sidelines. It is on the football field that boys can earn the adulation of others, particularly that of girls as well as their families. Furthermore, football permits boys to bond with their fathers, who are likely to give them considerably more attention for playing football than for any other activity in which they may engage. Football, certainly on the college level and among professionals, also serves as a gateway to recognition in the business, professional, and political arena. Witness the careers of "Whizzer" White and Jack Kemp.

White was a Supreme Court Justice from 1962 to 1993. He was appointed by President Kennedy, who knew him as a Rhodes Scholar when both lived in England in 1939. White gained his law degree at Yale but was far better known as a football player than as a lawyer. He played for the University of Colorado, where he became the first All-American player in the history of that university. In 1938 he became the Most Valuable Player (MVP) at the Cotton Bowl, moving on to professional status with the Pittsburgh Steelers of the National Football League. He was paid $15,800 that year and thereby became the highest-paid professional football player for a one-year contract. Thereafter he joined the Detroit Lions where he was the leading rusher (a player who runs with the ball).[4]

Undoubtedly, White was an outstanding student and lawyer. Nevertheless, his fame as a football player also gave him considerable prestige and contributed greatly to his appointment to the Supreme Court. White was confirmed by the U.S. Senate twelve days after his nomination, after staying in the witness chair only eleven minutes, because his football prowess was viewed as sufficient evidence that he could be a Supreme Court justice.[5]

Another example of the strong appeal of football to the American public is the career of Jack Kemp. Kemp was a college football hero at California's Occidental College, where he earned three letters and a number of other athletic honors. Unable to land a quarterbacking job in the National Football League, he joined the newly formed American Football League (AFL), playing with Los Angeles and San Diego from 1960 to 1962. He then came to the Buffalo Bills, where he stayed as quarterback from 1962 to 1969. During those years he contributed to making the Bills one of the elite teams in the AFL. In 1965, after the Bills beat the San Diego Chargers 23-0 for the championship, he was awarded the AFL's Most Valuable Player Award. Kemp retired from football in 1970, the year in which the AFL merged with the NFL. In 1984 he was elected to the Buffalo Bills Wall of Fame.

Thereafter Jack Kemp entered politics, winning a seat in the House of Representatives by a landslide victory in 1971. He remained a member of the House until 1989. He became a member of the cabinet of President George H. W. Bush in 1989 as Secretary of Housing and Urban Development. Kemp was repeatedly urged by his friends in the Republican party to seek the nomination for president, and did so briefly in 1988, and additionally was nominated for the vice-presidency in 1996. He has been a member of innumerable boards, mainly concerned with advancing conservative causes.

Kemp earned a degree in physical education at Occidental College. It is almost certain that without a football career he would never have been able to achieve the prominence he holds today, because he was elected to Congress on the basis of his football fame.[6]

Numerous other life stories demonstrate that football can be the catalyst for success in American politics, business, and industry. Every society has heroes. In some cultures, military achievements are most important. In others, business ability is most honored. Actors and religious leaders gain great admiration in other societies. All of these accomplishments are viewed with favor in America. However, the greatest heroes are famous athletes.

Because sports achievements are so important to male students at all levels of the school experience, many are blind to the danger that is inherent in a total absorption into the football subculture. Although there are indeed those who profit greatly from their exceptional ability as football players, there are also those for whom that very ability in their younger years becomes an albatross around their necks.[7]

The inclusion of football and other sports in schools is most positive for those who are capable of participating. Those boys receive great applause from their families, particularly from fathers. In addition, they achieve considerable acclaim from their peers. By age nine, most boys know whether they are good at sports. Those who are, commit themselves to continuing participation. There are those, of course, whose sports abilities are limited and whose athletic competence is overshadowed by others the older they become. Some boys cannot or will not involve themselves in any sport. This does not mean that anyone who is not a sports participant is therefore unable to relate to the status system in schools. The schools offer several alternative status systems. Certainly, excellence in scholarship is valued in some schools but not in all. Among the black population an excellent student may even be ostracized and rejected because of his or her good grades.

Sports, and particularly football, are seen as sources of masculinity in American culture. Winning is so highly prized that the phrase "winning isn't everything; it's the only thing," attributed to famous football coach Vince Lombardi (1913-1970) and others, is repeated again and again in schools, in the media, and in social situations. Boys have this drummed into them so that losing becomes a real trauma for those who cannot win. Losing in this context does not only mean losing one or more games. Losing means being a loser in the sense of failing to gain the attention and applause of those who define the situation in which football is played.

The definition of the situation decides a great deal of human action and experience. This means that an act may have a number of meanings, depending on how it is defined by the audience observing it. For example, a man who shoots another person may be defined as a hero by the army in which he serves. He may also be defined as a cold-blooded killer by a prosecutor in a criminal trial in civilian life. Likewise, someone who accepts the definition of "winner" in the Lombardi sense will view himself as a loser if he cannot "play the game." Nevertheless, numerous other students care nothing for sports and instead excel in theater, journalism, or mathematics and are satisfied. However, many other students feel they are left out, unwanted, and failures because they cannot excel in any of the alternative status systems available in schools and because this is important to them.

Sports, and in particular football, segregates boys from girls, men from women. Football does of course promote social bonding for men. However, it also excludes men from women. Sexism is virulent in the sports world and most extensive among those who play football. Derogatory language concerning women is common in locker rooms, and men who appear weak or incompetent in sports are called "girls." The outcome of these learned behaviors is male domination in the sense that these sexist attitudes rehearse conduct in later life.[8]

It has been a major complaint of female athletes that the sports facilities available to them are far inferior to those available to men. This is of course true of facilities available to adults as well as children, as visible by looking at the football stadiums, gymnasiums, number of spectators, and money spent on female sports as compared to male sports. Men also have the most exciting opportunities in the sports arena, an opportunity hardly ever available to women. In addition, it can hardly be overlooked that football and some other sports are married to violence, which is the antisocial aspect of masculinity.[9]

Acceptance of physical pain and the concomitant need to portray men as powerful are also taught by football and other sports. The outcome is to teach boys that "real" men bear pain in silence, that "real" men do not complain, and that "real" men do not cry. Evidently, the infliction of pain on others is therefore also seen as an important male attribute, so that hurting others is acceptable conduct. Surely, the victims of violence are expected to conform to the same ethos as those who inflict it, particularly because these are the same men. The will to win in a contact sport depends on the ability to dominate others, so that the determination to succeed can easily lead to hostile aggression. We can therefore support the view that football is a form of warfare.[10]

The warfare analogy is widely supported by the media and becomes a part of every American's worldview. Football players who are unusually aggressive and ruthless are praised highly with such labels as "killers," "murderers," "butt kickers," etc. Because violence is so highly prized and so many Americans attend football games because they want to see violence, many players use illegal acts of violence on the opponents because they know that this is approved by the fans and the huge television audiences, as demonstrated in the book *Fighting Fans: Football Hooliganism As a World Phenomenon,* by Eric Dunning and colleagues.[11]

THE ACADEMIC ACHIEVEMENTS OF FOOTBALL PLAYERS AND OTHER ATHLETES

Because football originated in the arena of higher education and because it is now of major importance in secondary schools, it is vital that we be concerned with the relationship between football performance and academic achievement.[12]

Anyone who reads the popular press, watches television, reads magazines, listens to the radio, or otherwise pays attention to the media must come to the conclusion that the only purpose of education in America is to conduct sports events. Indeed, there are occasional remarks made in the media about failed school budgets, large gifts given to universities, or medical breakthroughs by professors which promise to defeat this or that disease. Nevertheless, these stories are easily overshadowed by the enormous coverage given to high school and college football alone. Almost all daily newspapers have sports pages which recite the accomplishments of college and high school sports as well as professional sports. No regular newspaper feature deals with the academic achievements of students except for a few stories about graduations.

All this has been criticized again and again by numerous observers. Nevertheless, these media-driven "heroics," first developed in the 1940s and 1950s, are with us to stay despite the half-hearted effort of the National Collegiate Athletic Association (NCAA) to introduce some academic requirements into eligibility rules for participation in college sports.[13]

These requirements demand that any freshman wanting to participate in a Division I sport must be a high school graduate who successfully completed thirteen academic courses, including mathematics, English, social sciences, physical sciences, and either a foreign language or a computer language. A reasonable grade average is also demanded by these rules.[14]

As soon as these rules were published, Tai Kwan Cureton and three other minority athletes sued the NCAA on the grounds that their poor performance in high school should not prevent them from playing in NCAA sports. They claimed that the academic requirements under Proposition 16 of the NCAA constitute racial discrimination because minorities failed to meet the required academic standards more often than is true of white students. They further contended that minority students were the victims of discrimination because their SAT scores were generally too low to meet the requirements of the NCAA. They contended that these requirements had a "disparate impact," meaning that the same requirement applied to majority students should not be applied to minority students.

In March 1999, U.S. District Judge Ronald J. Buckwalter of Philadelphia ruled in favor of the minority students. However, in December 1999 the U.S. Court of Appeals for the Third Circuit in Philadelphia overturned the ruling of Judge Buckwalter, so the minimum scores on standardized tests and a minimum grade point average remained in effect.

Thereupon President Clinton signed an executive memorandum that expanded the rules under Title IX of the Civil Rights Restoration Act of 1987 to the effect that any federally funded school activity would have to avoid the NCAA rules and therefore allow minority students to participate in NCAA sports without meeting minimum academic qualifications. The NCAA claimed that Clinton had redefined the presidency as a monarchy.[15]

In 1993, economists Michael T. Maloney and Robert E. McCormick published a study of course grades for all undergraduate students enrolled at Clemson University in South Carolina during 1985 to 1988. This study was designed to discover whether intercollegiate athletic participation affects scholarly classroom success. Their findings were these: first, they found that college athletes do not perform as well as nonathletes in academics. They found that athletes perform one letter grade worse than other students in three out of ten classes. This means that although 35 percent of students fail to achieve graduation standards, 42 percent of athletes fail to meet such standards.

Maloney and McCormick also found that a student's high school performance also has a big impact on his or her subsequent college career. "Good grades breed good grades" and therefore, say Maloney and McCormick, the NCAA requirements make sense because they would encourage high school students interested in college athletics to prepare themselves academically.

The third finding of the Maloney and McCormick study is of great importance to football. They discovered that the worst students are those participating in revenue sports such as football and basketball. The study showed that male basketball players have a lower grade point average than any other players and that football players are not much better. These athletes have a 53 percent graduation rate with a grade point average of 2.12.

Maloney and McCormick also found, not surprisingly, that grades of revenues-sport athletes are lower during the season than out of season, meaning that the exploitation of athletes in big-money sports extends into the classroom. It should be added that athletes in nonrevenue sports, such as tennis, achieve as much academically as other students.[16]

The exploitation of athletes by universities and colleges is particularly visible with reference to minority students. Exploitation of black athletes by universities has gone on for years, although that exploitation is also fostered by the athletes themselves. Many of the young athletes who attend sports-minded universities agree to a "contract," i.e., an unofficial agreement that they will perform in exchange for an education. The contract, however, appears to be one-sided. The athletes do their part. The universities gain huge gate receipts, television revenues, a national reputation, and donations from alumni. Meanwhile the athletes seldom get an education.

The reasons for the failure of athletes to succeed academically are not hard to recognize. Many of the top black athletes come to wealthy universities on football scholarships. These "scholarships" have nothing to do with being a scholar. They have everything to do with being an athlete and enhancing the university that recruited the athlete. This tells the young man that academics are of no importance but that he must perform well if he is to stay at that college and perhaps go on to professional football.

Many people believe that superior athletic ability is genetically race related, but no evidence supports this view. In fact, such beliefs, now associated with blacks, were at one time associated with other ethnic groups of European descent.

One excellent example of the belief that an ethnic group is genetically more competent than others to engage in a sport was the widespread conviction in the 1920s and 1930s that boxing was a Jewish sport and that Jews were somehow "born" boxers. The reasons for this belief were the numerous young Jewish boxers who dominated that sport in those decades. The following boxers were active in the years indicated: Benny Leonard (1911-1931), Barney Ross (1931-1938), Joe Choyinski (1888-1904), Louis "Kid" Kaplan (1925-1927), "Slapsie" Maxie Rosenblum, Rube Goldstein, Issy Schwartz and many others.[17]

These were the children of recent immigrants who fought their way out of the poverty and misery of the New York slums. So did other children of recent immigrants who also had to use the most risky road to fame and fortune. This was so because established Americans did not compete in those areas and because the immigrants and their children had few avenues of escape from the horrors of early urban life other than sports, crime, or new industries.

The evidence is that those whose economic opportunities are limited and whose children for any reason live in dire straights are more likely than others to use their talents to enter the entertainment world. Football is part of that entertainment. Therefore, African Americans now, and others at other times, steer their talented children into those avenues which promise rather quick success. The black athletes who are now the heroes of the college gridiron or basketball courts are there for the same reason that "Two-Ton Tony" Galento and Rocky Marciano were there a generation ago.

The relationship between sports ability and ethnicity is cultural and social and in no way biological. In the African-American community it has only been recently, and in limited fashion, that blacks are seen in high-prestige, high-earning occupations, except for sports. Hence African-American children tend to model themselves after the successes they see among basketball and football players.

The African-American family tends to reward sports achievement more than academic attainment. In fact, masculinity in both the African-American and white communities is associated with sports success. Furthermore, academically competent black students are often teased and ridiculed by other black students, so that academic success is hard to attain or maintain in that community. Of course, many African-American students cannot accept athletic scholarships because their grades are too low.

The result is that these athletes become the victims of what is sometimes called "the slave trade." This refers to the practice of having "scouts" find these boys and enroll them in two-year colleges where their grades often improve enough to go on to a four-year college or university. This can be done because U.S. two-year colleges are generally academic disaster areas. About 35 percent of these athletes graduate from college. Of these, 75 percent have degrees in physical education or some other major held in low repute by other students and in the job market. Therefore, the vast majority of black athletes have no employment opportunities outside of sports. These athletes become unemployed more often than nonathlete college graduates. The ex-athletes also earn less and have less job satisfaction than non-athlete graduates.[18]

The employment opportunities for black ex-football players are not good. Since blacks make up more than half of all football players on athletic scholarships at the largest colleges and universities, it should be reasonable to expect a proportionate number of experienced black players to be named head coaches at these schools.

This is by no means the case. For example, in 1995, 4,527 scholarship athletes at major college football programs were black. Yet in that year only six, or 5.5 percent, of head coaches in such programs were black. In that same year 3.7 percent of offensive coordinators were black and blacks constituted 6.5 percent of defensive coordinators.[19]

By 2002 the situation for black head football coaches had become worse. Shortly before Thanksgiving in 2001, Oklahoma State fired coach Bob Simmons and Wake Forest fired coach Jim Caldwell. That reduced the number of black coaches at major colleges to six out of 115, or 5.2 percent of the total. Observers of this situation claim that the reason for this discrepancy is racism and not competence. In fact, Richard E. Lapchick, a foremost football reporter, writes that "not only are blacks not getting the jobs, they weren't even being interviewed." Lapchick points out that during the fifty years ending in 2001, the one hundred colleges that play football had approximately 750 openings for head football coaches and that fewer than twenty of these appointments went to blacks.[20]

CHILDREN'S FOOTBALL

In 1929, a Philadelphia football coach, Glenn "Pop" Warner, loaned his name to an effort by Joe Tomlin, a Philadelphia writer, to organize a football league for children. This league was named the Pop Warner Youth Football League. During its seventy-fifth season, that league also included girls, who are taught dance and cheerleading in the summer camps organized for both sexes. The league has changed its name to Pop Warner Little Scholars, claiming that "its goals are to inspire youth, regardless of race, creed, religion, or national origin, to practice the ideals of sportsmanship, scholarship and physical fitness, as reflected in the life of the late Glenn Scobie 'Pop' Warner."

Nationwide, this league enrolls more than 350,000 children, 40,000 coaches, and 750,000 parents and friends. The children enrolled are five to fifteen years old with the majority in the eight- to thirteen-year-old range. The league does allow girls to play football and boys to be cheerleaders. The league claims that a child must have demonstrated a sufficient amount of academic progress to be allowed to compete. The league also awards scholarships for higher education. To ensure safety, the children compete with children of similar age and size.

The league is divided into eight national regions. These regions compete against one another for eight regional championships. In 1995 a "superbowl" for this league was held for the first time in Orlando, Florida. Pop Warner Little Scholars awards are given to children based on their school performance, not on their football performance. These awards are provided by corporate sponsors and include scholarships to institutions of higher education. Adult volunteers are also recognized.[21]

In view of these high-minded goals and actions it is unfortunate that children's football and other sports are accompanied by some parental conduct that is the exact opposite of the goals of Pop Warner football. Between 1999 and 2002, forty-two cases of adult violence at youth sporting events have been documented.[22]

Much more such violence is likely not documented or reported in the media. Such violence occurs in all children's sports. Here are some examples relating to Pop Warner football:

- In Port Orange, Florida, a Pop Warner football game ended in a brawl involving more than 100 parents, coaches, and players. Police filed charges against a thirty-one-year-old mother for resisting arrest and a fifteen-year-old player for battery on a law enforcement officer.
- In Villanova, Pennsylvania, about 100 parents from two youth football teams fought in a melee at the end of a championship football game. Parents from South Philadelphia and Springfield in Delaware County had to be restrained by police. A number of arrests were made.
- In Jacksonville, Florida, a football coach threw a ten-year-old player to the ground. The coach was charged with aggravated assault because both of the child's arms were broken.
- In Westport, Connecticut, a fight broke out after one coach slapped the other coach in the face after a youth football game.
- In Coppell, Texas, the fifty-six-year-old father of a football player was arrested for felony injury to a child after he knocked his son's teammate to the ground during football practice.
- In Nebraska a parent was sentenced to thirty days in jail and fined $500 for punching a sixteen-year-old referee at a football game involving six- and seven-year-old children.[23]

Another example of the intensity with which football is pursued in some high schools is the experience in Odessa, Texas. Odessa has slightly less than 96,000 people, who buy 5,000 season tickets to the high school football games every year. The high school stadium seats 20,000 people, and these seats are sold out at every game. Odessa is an oil town whose people do the blue-collar work, while twenty-five miles away Midland, Texas, live the white-collar bankers and engineers who make the "real" money in the oil business. In this situation the high school football team gives the Odessa citizens a reason to live there.

In 1990, H. G. Bissinger published a book about Odessa football called *Friday Night Lights.* This book not only exhibited the positive side of the football craze that grips Odessa each fall. It also describes the despair of those boys who don't measure up to playing football together with the academic failures that are given scant attention in Odessa. This is well illustrated by the $81,000 salary paid to the Permian High School football coach. Teachers with twenty years experience in that school earn only $44,000.[24]

The anxiety with which parents are pursuing child football and other sports is the consequence of the enhanced rewards that go to those who eventually graduate into "big time" sports. Using the most expensive and best equipment, children as young as five are forced into organized sports by parents hoping to push them into lucrative sports careers.[25]

FOOTBALL AND AGGRESSION

Aggression against others before, during, and after an aggressive sports event is a well-known phenomenon. Aggression as a function of collective behavior is well understood. Sociologists have identified the conditions under which spontaneous aggression occurs. These conditions apply to many sports events, including American football. Such aggression or violence is produced by crowds.

Sociologists recognize a variety of crowds. A crowd is said to be *casual* if those who happen to be physically close do not interact with one another and have nothing in common other than their temporary proximity. A crowd waiting for a bus is an excellent example. A second type of crowd is called a *conventionalized* crowd. It is the product of deliberate planning. A public lecture, a concert, or a funeral are examples. Here the crowd acts according to the norms or expectations the situation dictates. An *expressive* crowd is one which is provided with an emotional appeal. A New Year's Eve celebration in Times Square, a religious revival meeting, or the onlookers at a hockey game may serve as examples. Expressive crowds shout, yell, jump up and down, and express a variety of emotions. Finally, sociologists speak of the *acting* or *aggressive* crowd. Such crowds are motivated by an intense, single-minded purpose such as seeking to hear a rock concert or participating in a riot. The best current example of an acting or expressive crowd is a crowd of onlookers at a football game who use violence during or after the game.[26]

For example, a violent riot occurred on June 9, 2001, in downtown Denver, Colorado, after the Colorado Avalanche, the local hockey team, won the Stanley Cup and thereby became national hockey champions that year. That riot included fire setting, damaging parked cars, fistfights at various levels, and police using tear gas.[27]

In December 2001, the NFL began a review of its security policies after fans at Giants Stadium in East Rutherford, New Jersey, threw bottles into the field during two games on the same weekend. That same week Browns fans in the Cleveland, Ohio, stadium threw plastic bottles at the referees and players because they disagreed with a fourth-quarter call by a referee. In New Orleans, Louisiana, Saints fans threw plastic bottles into the field after a referee called pass interference against the Saints during the fourth quarter. In earlier years even more dangerous incidents occurred because fans were then still allowed to bring bottled drinks into the stadiums.[28]

Similar scenes and worse occur regularly after European and South American soccer matches. In this connection we can cite the riot that occurred in England on January 24, 2002, because a popular player was traded by the manager for someone not as popular or not as competent as the ousted player. Violent fans assaulted the premises of the soccer club and damaged equipment to demonstrate their unhappiness with the manager's decision.

On June 10, 2002, Russian soccer fans rioted in Central Moscow. In this riot one person was stabbed to death. Cars were overturned and set on fire and windows were broken after Japan defeated Russia in the World Cup finals. The crowd, mainly composed of teenagers, attacked pedestrians and the police, leading to the hospitalization of thirty people. Firefighters and camera operators were also beaten.[29]

Bill Buford wrote a whole book about European soccer violence. Here he details the fighting that accompanies European soccer matches throughout the continent. Evidently, the violence of soccer "supporters," as the fans are known in England, is institutionalized in that it is expected and part of every game involving England.[30]

Likewise, soccer has led to violence in South America. For example, a referee's decision led to a riot in Lima, Peru, which resulted in the deaths of a number of spectators. In 1985, 400 million people were watching a televised soccer game between Italy and Great Britain. Sixty thousand spectators watched from the bleachers. In the course of the game the English and Italian fans began to shout epithets at each other. Then someone threw a bottle at the other side, leading to a short "bottle war." This finally escalated when a wave of British fans surged toward the Italians. In minutes thirty-eight people were dead and over 400 injured.[31]

The most extreme outcome of a soccer riot occurred in 1969 when El Salavador invaded neighboring Honduras after a qualifying soccer game. More than 3,000 people died in that war. The use of farmland was the underlying cause of this "soccer war," which was not settled until 1992 when the International Court of Justice divided the disputed land between these countries.[32]

Some observers of violent behavior claim that viewing aggression leads to a form of catharsis, thereby leading to a lessening of aggression among spectators. The belief is that vicarious hostility catharsis will reduce the hostility among spectators to an aggressive sport. Zoologist Konrad Lorenz supported this view in his famous book *On Aggression,* which deals with animal behavior.[33]

However, a well-founded study by sociologists Jeffrey Goldstein and Robert Arms concluded that "hostility data collected at football games indicate that, regardless of team preference and the outcome of the game, subjects were significantly more hostile after observing the game than before."[34]

The hostility generated by football games and other violent sports is by no means confined to the fans who view these games from the bleachers. As any high school student can testify, football in particular creates a whole culture of violence and hostility in schools which can have terrible consequences. Two events in American high school history demonstrate how bullying has become the norm in schools, leading to suicides, rape, and murder in a few cases and to a general atmosphere of contempt almost everywhere. These examples exhibit the most extreme consequences of the football culture in U.S. high schools and will demonstrate the manner in which bullying can lead to tragic consequences for some and a miserable school experience for thousands.

In 1989, four popular football players at the Glen Ridge High School in Glen Ridge, New Jersey, were accused of raping a seventeen-year-old retarded girl. The high school seniors had lured the girl into the basement of one of their homes and there used a baseball bat, a broomstick, and other instruments while numerous other boys cheered them on. This gang rape became a public scandal only after the rape was exposed by the only black football player, whose race did not permit him to be part of the "in" crowd. The journalism professor Bernard Lefkowitz wrote this, concerning that episode: "You either wormed your way into the 'in' crowd or you spent the next four years in social Siberia. And you really got into trouble if you thought or acted differently. For such kids, Glen Ridge High School could be torture."[35]

Lefkowitz brought this case to national attention in his book *Our Guys: The Glen Ridge Rape and the Secret Life of the Perfect Suburb*. That book exposes an attitude toward so-called football heroes which largely permeates all of American society. According to Lefkowitz, the rape provoked no community introspection in Glen Ridge. Instead, adults and fellow students rallied around the accused athletes. The community dismissed the victim of the rape but collected $30,000 for the defense of the accused. No doubt, Glen Ridge, New Jersey, reflects the values of American communities across the country.

At the graduation ceremony at Glen Ridge High School in 1989, many female graduates wore yellow ribbons to remind the onlookers of the four boys who had been charged with rape and were therefore not allowed to attend graduation. The wearers of these ribbons thought of the victim as a "slut" and felt sorry for the perpetrators of this crime.

Lefkowitz's investigation revealed that one football player regularly masturbated in class in the presence of female students and teachers. The girls believed that they had to endure that and all kinds of other horrendous bullying because they would not be accepted in that school unless they submitted to this conduct by football players.

Academic achievement hardly counts in such schools. The parents of high school students in Glen Ridge had little interest in scholarship. Their interest was in seeing their sons attain a touchdown instead of gaining academic recognition.

On April 20, 1999, two students at the Columbine High School in a suburb of Denver, Colorado, called Littleton, shot and killed twelve students, a teacher, and themselves. Eric Harris, eighteen, and Dylan Klebold, seventeen, used a number of weapons to achieve this massacre. The two boys were members of a group of students who called themselves "the trench coat mafia." Wearing these coats they sought to belong to a group capable of withstanding the bullying which is part of almost every high school experience for those many students who are not athletically inclined and who do not play football or are in the good graces of those who hold that distinction.

It is no exaggeration to say that U.S. schools from grade school through college are generally anti-intellectual. This means that American culture is generally unimpressed by scholarly achievement or so-called "eggheads" while giving considerable credence to accomplishments in sports and particularly football success. This is a nearly universal aspect of American culture and not unique to Colorado or Columbine High School.

Therefore, football players in almost any American high school are singled out for praise and admiration from other students, teachers, administrators, and parents. This adulation for those who happen to be physically large and competent in football often leads to bullying in the schools. Bullying in turn may well lead to revenge shootings on the part of the bully's victims, as was the case in the Columbine tragedy.

On June 12, 1999, *The Washington Post* published an article by Lorraine Adams and Dale Russakoff. These reporters described the Columbine "jock culture," which is by no means different from thousands of other high schools around the country where athletes are glorified to the detriment of everyone else. For example, Adams and

Russakoff reported that "football players were allowed to tease girls about their breasts in class without fear of retribution by the teacher, also the boys' coach." At Columbine High School the homecoming king was a football player on probation for burglary. The two killers, Harris and Klebold, knew that athletes convicted of crimes went without suspension from games or expulsion from school. Harris and Klebold, as well as thousands of high school students around the country, knew that athletes were permitted to torment other students while school authorities did nothing to help the victims of this bullying. For example, at Columbine the state wrestling champion, Rocky Hofschneider, shoved a girl into a locker in front of teachers who did nothing about this. In fact, Hofschneider, now a construction worker, continually teased a Jewish boy, Jonathan Greene, in the presence of the wrestling coach and gym teacher Craig Place. Even after Hofschneider was sentenced to probation by a court for harassment, kicking, and striking, he continued in both football and wrestling at Columbine High School.

It is well known that people who give the impression that they are powerful will attract a following who seek to identify with power. School bullies generally assemble such cliques around them. This also happened at Columbine High School, where Hofschneider assembled a gang of school toughs who took control of the school. The athletes associated with this gang wore white hats as a badge of honor. To combat their "outcast" standing, students who were usually harassed by the Hofschneider gang began to wear trench coats leading to the nickname "the trench coat mafia." The jocks taunted everyone, including Harris and Klebold, who planned to revenge themselves on their brutal persecutors even at the cost of their own lives. As reported by Adams and Russakoff, the two boys shouted "all the jocks stand up" as they began firing, killing one teacher and twelve students.[36]

Both the Glen Ridge rape and the Littleton murders occurred in the suburbs of big cities. Like many other American upper middle-class towns, the citizens viewed their town as their "Valhalla" and wanted to protect the reputation of their town at all costs. Thus, conduct of athletes and other bullies were not given any attention by adults. The mistreatment of young women and weak boys by the "jocks" in our schools is of course a reflection of American culture generally. American culture extols winners. These need not be football players. The rich businessman, his fashionable wife, and his big-spending children are the elite in every town. This contrasts with the poor, the dowdy wife, the inconspicuous underpriveleged kids. In all the world, and certainly in our small towns, the "losers" have few rights and fewer privileges. In fact, our culture tends to make objects out of subjects and thereby create victims for those who have power, money, and influence. A human "object" is seen as a nonperson who can be used by those who have the opportunity to do so. Such "objects" are devoided of their humanity and their feelings, needs, and hopes. They exist only as foils for the exploitation of the "jocks" or other dominators. The consequences, as we have seen, can be horrible when a victim of bullying strikes back. Yet, the consequences of bullying are also hideous when the victims of the bullies suffer indignities every school day for years. Therefore the time has come for our schools to use any and all methods to prevent bullying in the future and to make schools friendly places in which to learn rather than nightmares in which to suffer the torments of bullying.

DEATH AND INJURY ON THE PLAYING FIELD

According to the National School Safety Center, fifteen school associated deaths were caused by violent crime during the school year 1999-2000. Likewise, fifteen high school football players died during the regular season and during playoff games in 1999, according to the National Federation of State High School Associations. In August 2001, two high school football players were killed as a result of football practice in Houston, Texas. Leonard Carter, then only fourteen years old, and Steven Taylor, fifteen years old, both died at home where they collapsed approximately two hours after practice. On that same day a thirteen-year-old boy died during football practice in Monticello, Georgia. Earlier that year two boys at Jackson High School in Stevenson, Alabama, died after football practice. In 1999 a total of seventeen high school football players died. Five of these died from head injuries during a game and the others from heat stroke or exhaustion. These cases raised the total high school deaths from football to 616 during the past seventy years. These deaths are exceeded by deaths associated with college and professional football.[37]

In addition, seven high school boys were paralyzed by playing football in 1999.

Commenting on these deaths and the numerous spinal injuries and other injuries endured by high school football players, the coach of Seneca Valley High School in Pennsylvania said, "You have to be tough on them. You have to push them to the brink and either they are going to break or they are going to stand up and be a man."[38]

That comment could hardly concern eighth-grade student Andrea Wood, a Lubbock, Texas, girl who was paralyzed after being tackled by a boy outweighing her by forty pounds.

Looking now at a summary of football fatalities from the fall of 1982 to the fall of 1996, we find that sixty-one direct and eighty-nine indirect fatalities were associated with football during those years. The number of high school students playing football during that time was estimated at 21,302,203. Therefore, the incidence of fatalities per 100,000 football players was less than one. It is of course unlikely that the parents of the dead football player children were concerned with these statistics.

We need to add to these numbers the nonfatal, but serious injuries inflicted on football players. During the years 1982 to 1996, 313 such injuries occurred.[39] In 2000, ten high school students in this country suffered catastrophic head injuries, including injuries to the brain. Over the years there have been thousands of football players who were not seized and forced to play football but who chose to do so despite the dangers inherent in the game.

The use of drugs, particularly steroids, among football players has been widely discussed ever since the girth and weight of football players has increased dramatically during the generation ending in 2000. An anabolic steroid is a synthetic derivative of testosterone which has masculinizing effects. Men who use these drugs display changes in hair and libido. Most important, these drugs increase muscle mass. Therefore, about 8 percent of males of high school age use these drugs. Among athletes the use of steroids appears to be cyclical in that boys who use them do so only during the sports season. Some athletes use several drugs, a method called "stacking," which involves the use of a combination of different steroids. This is also called "megadosing." Evidently, the dangers of using large amounts of steroids are not detectable for months, years, and even decades after use.[40]

Some athletes increase the dose through a cycle called "pyramiding," which is designed to promote body bulk. Some consequences of using such drugs are erratic mood swings, irrational behavior, increased aggressiveness, depression, and finally, dependency. In some cases liver dysfunction may also occur. Therefore, the U.S. Supreme Court ruled that public schools can subject students in extracurricular activities to mandatory drug tests.[41]

In view of the dangers associated with playing football we can conclude that the possible rewards for risking one's life, body, and health must be very great. And so they are. Football is an alternative status system in the United States and it is this which attracts so many to that all-American sport.[42]

FOOTBALL AS AN ALTERNATIVE STATUS SYSTEM

Status is defined by sociologists as the sum of rights and privileges that anyone has in any social arrangement. Therefore, husband and wife are both statuses. The same is true of teacher and student or employer and employee. It is evident that normally any and every status also demands that the status holder play the role assigned to that status. We therefore define a role as the sum of the obligations that must be discharged if the status is to be maintained. Statuses are distinguished by the manner in which they are acquired. An *ascribed* status is one that is given us at birth. Female and male are ascribed statuses. Black, white, or Asian are also ascribed statuses and so is age.

Some statuses are achieved and are seen as having been earned by the incumbent. One such *achieved* status can be athlete or football player. Of course, all of us occupy many statuses. Student, son, part-time waiter, and athlete can all devolve on one person. Therefore, sociology teaches that one of our statuses is our master status. That is, the status which is not only most important to us, but which determines a person's social position. For women, traditionally their master status was that of daughter, wife, and mother. For men, occupation was and is their master status in the United States. Among adoles-

cents attending high school that may well be student. However, athletes and particularly football players attain so much adulation in our
competitive, anti-intellectual schools that their master status is football player.[43]

I have repeatedly referred to American schools as anti-intellectual.
That may seem a contradiction within the frame of an institution devoted to learning. However, the history of American education reveals that anti-intellectualism was always part of educational efforts.
The reason for this lies in the pioneering experience of the European
settlers who came here between 1620 and the closing of the frontier in
1890. These Americans, although of European descent, were, according to historian Frederick Jackson Turner, the world's first free
men. Whatever one may think of Turner's frontier thesis of American
history, it is hardly feasible to overlook its lasting effect on our
understanding of the American west.

According to Turner, Americans in the first three centuries of European settlement were confronted with conditions along the American frontier which made practical, here-and-now solutions to everyday problems vital. There was little room for "book learning" during
the frontier years. Those who had gained formal schooling were
viewed with suspicion by frontiersmen who needed a "practical and
inventive turn of mind" in order to survive. Therefore, intellectuals
became outsiders in America and remain so to this day. Indeed, the
majority of work now done in the United States is of an intellectual or
at least non-physical kind. However, the concept of culture lag tells us
that people will continue to believe outdated views long after their
usefulness has been exhausted. Therefore, anti-intellectual attitudes
continue to flourish in this country even though 25 percent of Americans are college graduates.[44]

This anti-intellectualism is very much part of our educational system. Students in the American school or college want to know
whether a course they are expected to take will make a positive contribution to their vocational aspirations. History majors see no reason to
learn mathematics and accounting majors care nothing for history
courses. We want immediate results and practical advantages in and
out of school.

In this situation, football is far more appealing than academics. Innumerable students in high school and in college are easily convinced

that the next football game is far more important to them than distant academic goals. Furthermore, those who actually play football can hardly be expected to free themselves from the constant cheering, the perpetual adoration, and praise of their "great contribution to the glory of the school." Football trophies, not books, are displayed in the hallways of our high schools. Indeed, acknowledgment is weak for outstanding academic achievement and there is no all-school rally for scholarship. In addition, it is well known and even commonplace that colleges and universities exempt athletes, particularly football players, from the entrance requirements imposed on all other applicants.

Admission to most American colleges and universities depends on scholastic aptitude tests, augmented by the American college testing program. These tests are usually known as the SAT/ACT tests and claim to foretell whether the applicant can succeed in higher education. For example, at the University of California at Los Angeles, a SAT score of 1300 is required for admission. Yet UCLA and other universities enroll athletes with far lower SAT scores than required of all other applicants. Some of these athletes achieve scores on the SAT in the vicinity of 850, or less than 65 percent of the score needed by everyone else. Since a grade of 65 percent or less than that achieved by other students usually means failure of a course at any American college or university, it is evident that these schools are willing to admit students to their institutions whose aptitude for higher education predicts failure. Yet they are admitted because they are athletes. Surely, such policies must be most discouraging for all other students. It is also well known that at some large universities some professors deliver advance copies of examinations to football and basketball coaches so that players can be given advantages that allow them to remain on the teams. The pretense in these schools is that only those who meet minimum academic standards may play. The facts, however, are otherwise.[45]

American social statuses are determined mainly by occupation. Therefore, the attitudes just described fit the expectations that students and others have of our schools. Schools are seen as preparatory institutions designed to help graduates "get a good job." Making money is the ultimate purpose of schooling in America. Nevertheless, occupational prestige studies have shown that the manner in which one makes money is given a great deal of consideration by the Ameri-

can public. This is the reason why physicians exceed all other workers in occupational prestige on every National Opinion Research
Center study of occupational prestige. Physicians are of course not
highly respected for their scholarship but for their income and because they help people attain good health. The fact that the dispensa-
tion of an occupation has a great deal to do with its public acclaim is
easily seen because college professors and/or lawyers generally attain the second place in the occupational prestige studies conducted
at intervals by the National Opinion Research Center. Professors are
not known for their wealth. Professors, however, dispense college ed-
ucations and are therefore given high occupational ratings. I emphasize that professors do not enjoy considerable occupational prestige
because of their reputed intellects, but because they are seen as a
means of attaining the needed symbols, such as the BA degree leading to a high income for the eventual graduates.[46]

It is of course true that those few professional football players who
earn vast salaries and gain much publicity in the media also enjoy
considerable occupational prestige. These athletes are very few. The
best high school football players have little chance of ever becoming
professional, a statement that is also true for almost all college athletes. Therefore it is evident, or should be evident to high school athletes, that it would be in their interest to learn something useful in
high school so that they can compete in the job market after graduation. Yet many football players, basketball heroes, and other sports
enthusiasts deny the need for a practical education useful in later life.
Many athletes are so heavily influenced by the acclaim they receive in
school and in their families and among their friends that they convince themselves that they will become professional players, earn
millions, and live in the limelight forever. Such beliefs are fostered by
adults, including teachers and administrators of schools who benefit
by football victories even if they know that the players involved face
an uncertain economic future.

Not all observers agree that athletes are less competent as students
than nonathletes. Some individuals claim that high school athletes
perform better academically than their nonathletic peers because athletes, particularly in football and basketball, feel accepted, admired,
and secure. These feelings, say the sociologists Vogler and Schwartz,
lead to a positive self-image and therefore to better academic perfor-

mance. Little evidence supports these claims despite the fact that so many high school athletes are given college scholarships.[47]

Contrary to the Vogler-Schwartz argument, the National Assessment of Educational Progress for 2001 indicates that a large segment of high school graduates and even college graduates cannot compute a simple account charge and that an even higher percentage of 26,000 students interviewed could not read and understand simple directions.[48]

Many high school football stars get athletic scholarships with which to go to college, but these scholarships only postpone the agony in most cases. Colleges and universities allow athletes to gain income and publicity for their school, only to dump the senior athlete into a job market he cannot master while exploiting the next generation of boys for the sake of alumni contributions and high salaries for coaches and college presidents.

In small towns all over America, except those that are home to a university, the high school football team often consumes the entire community. This all-consuming football passion centering on high school athletes may be gleaned from small town newspapers anywhere. However, these passions are not restricted to small towns. Ethnic pride in large cities led thousands of Chicago or New York or Cleveland residents to watch football games between high schools representing ethnic neighborhoods in the decades from the 1920s to the 1950s. Thereafter, ethnic enclaves began to decline in large American cities, so that a high school located in a particular neighborhood no longer represented only Polish or Italian or Jewish or Irish immigrants.[49]

Football, then, is not only a sport; it is also an alternative status system. This means that those who are not born to wealth, those who do not excel academically, those who are not otherwise "celebrities" can and do attain attention, money, and approval by playing football. It is therefore to be expected that football will continue to have a great future in American schools and in particular in institutions of higher learning, which are not only dispensers of social honor and prestige for athletes but which also provide the training grounds for the few who become professionals.

Violence, bullying, and even murder can be the product of an overemphasis on football in high schools. Of course, extreme violence is a rare but widely publicized occurrence. Much more common is the production of disdain for academic achievement on the part of the majority of high school students, who are told over and over again that athletics are important and that everything else is of minimal significance. This teaching has consequences for higher education in which sports and in particular moneymaking spectacles such as football and basketball occupy the center of attention, at least in the major American universities.

SUMMARY

American football is the product of English Rugby and English Association Football. In this country it is closely linked to education and serves the needs of adolescents in several ways. Outstanding football players open doors to future careers because of the immense publicity they receive from the media. However, most football players are far from outstanding and suffer from considerable academic deficiencies. The deficiencies are covered up by athletic scholarships resulting in mostly negative consequences.

Aggression by spectators is common in Europe and America. Football also leads to bullying in schools together with some revenge aggression by the victims. Big-money college football exploits talented boys who learn little academically and are therefore in danger of being unable to earn their livelihood after their football career ends at a young age. This is best illustrated by college football, which is the topic of the next chapter. The next task is to review the role of football and football players in the training grounds of the professionals, i.e., institutions of higher learning.

Chapter 2

College Football—
The Professionals' Minor League

FOOTBALL DEVELOPS A SUBCULTURE

We have already seen that college football developed at the end of the nineteenth century. During those years the media, almost always newspapers, created the popularity of the game by emphasizing its brutality and the possibility of seeing a player get hurt. At first, college football received a great deal of criticism because of its violence and the evidence that both players and spectators were at risk of getting hurt as a result of an altercation between players or because of riots caused by the fans. In fact, before World War I, the controversy concerning the brutality of the game led several universities to cancel participation in football. Nevertheless, by the 1920s, intercollegiate football was well established in the American college or university.[1]

The main reason for the entrenchment of football in American colleges by the 1920s was the immense amount of newspaper coverage college football received before the advent of television. It is evident that the big circulation newspapers did for college football in the first half of the twentieth century what television did for professional football in the second half of that century.[2]

These developments led to the promotion of football as a subculture in America. A subculture is a group of people within a larger culture who are set apart from the larger society by participation in a minority religion, or in involvement in an occupation or in the use of a foreign language. In fact, the use of a separate language is the most important criterion of membership in a subculture. This language is very much in evidence in the sports world particularly with reference to football. An entire football vocabulary grew over the past one hundred years, invented by sportswriters and football professionals to describe football experiences and football requirements.

Football, and other sports, have not only created heroes on the playing fields, but also famous sportswriters and broadcasters who live with the athletes they "cover" in a symbiotic relationship. Each needs the other to succeed since sport without the media would not have any fans and vice versa. This symbiosis has led to language developed in the football subculture. The late Tim Considine published a book called *The Language of Sports,* which illustrates the extent to which subcultural language is used in all sports. Football is included in this dictionary of sports expressions, some of which are well known and have entered the daily American vocabulary. Others are confined to football use only. For example, to "blindside" someone is derived from tackling a right-handed quarterback unable to see one side as he is prepared to pass. A "bench warmer" is a reserve player who may never see action, while a "cornerback" is a defensive player who lines up behind and outside the linebackers. Other expressions include a "down" which activates the ball, an "end zone," a "flea-flicker," which is a double hand-off followed by a pass, a "gridiron" or a football field, and a "hike." We can go to the end of the alphabet and find that a "zone" is an area to be covered by a defender. These and other football expressions let us recognize that football players, their coaches, their followers, and those who publicize them have created a subculture which is effective in segregating the football world from those not involved. Football, like any profession, allows only "insiders" to be at home and understand the meaning of it all.[3]

Every human society develops "in-groups" consisting of peers and "out-groups" which are those outside the bounds of intimacy. An "in-group" may also be viewed as a group commanding a member's esteem and loyalty while an "out-group" may be defined as a group toward which one feels competition and/or opposition. This is certainly true of football teams and becomes most enhanced by the manner in which football is raised to disproportionate importance on college campuses.[4]

Disproportionate importance means that the immense emphasis given college football in many American institutions of higher learning has led many football players to believe that they will become professional football players with the National Football League and will earn millions while also collecting the admiration and social honor that comes with success. Disproportionate importance also means that the vast majority of college students who are not football players are coerced into believing that college consists of "beer and circuses," only to find after four years that employment opportunities go to all those who earned high academic averages and all those who have private "connections," but not to those whose only concern in college were football games.[5]

Many college football players are enticed into believing they will have a momentous career in football and are the victims of a system that promotes the interests of college presidents, alumni, sportswriters, spectators and the general public, but not those of the players themselves. This is particularly true among those who temporarily succeed in becoming Saturday-afternoon heroes at big-time football universities. It is less true at other colleges and seldom visible among the many "run-of-the mill" colleges in America. The illusion that a boy may become "great" at football exists in the heads of almost all who participate because the temporary adulation, particularly of the opposite sex, is such a great aphrodisiac and miasma or delusional fog leading to many academic failures. At the same time, we must guard against claiming that any and all college football players are poor students or victims of exploitation.

RECRUITING COLLEGE FOOTBALL PLAYERS

Anyone who seeks information about the recruitment of college football players can find ninety-eight places under the category "football recruitment" on any search engine. These Web sites include numerous commercial recruiters who will, for a fee, submit a high school student's academic record to schools in which the prospective player (student) may have an interest.

Included in this effort to use the Internet for recruiting purposes is a magazine called *Superrep: America's Recruiting Magazine.* This magazine informs the reader about the "big-time" recruits in the country. This magazine, among others, illustrates the attitudes, expectations, and values of high school football players intent on continuing their football career in a college or university. Here the reader learns "the real truth about who the college coaches think the finest prospects are. . . ." For $155 a subscriber is also furnished with the "Premium Recruitin' Trail" which promises to tell the reader the best information from *America's Recruiting Magazine.* This is followed by a long list of paragraphs, each describing a young man's self-evaluation as a football player with a view of finding a college willing to offer the applicant a football scholarship. The paragraph includes the applicant's height and weight, his favorite college, his reasons for favoring a particular school, his strengths and weaknesses as a player, and his willingness to commit to a team. Nothing in any of these advertisements concerns the applicant's scholarly ability. Possibly that is considered irrelevant in connection with the competence to play the game. It is also possible to interpret this total lack of information about the scholastic achievements of the applicant as a sign that no intellectual competence is expected and that colleges will accept a good football player as a pseudo-student.

Such pseudo-students may be found on every campus and include many who are not athletes. According to the well-known study by sociologists Burton Clark and Martin Trow, there is a "collegiate subculture" on the campuses of our colleges which is distinguished from the academic, vocational, and rebel subculture. Clark and Trow wrote that the collegiate subculture is

> a world of football, fraternities and sororities, dates, drinking and campus fun. A good deal of the student life on many campuses revolves around this culture. It (the campus culture) is, however, indifferent and resistant to serious demands emanating from the faculty for an involvement of ideas and issues over and above that required to gain the diploma.[6]

Even worse for the academic reputation of any university is the conduct of some football players. For example, DeShaun Foster, who was once a leading candidate for the Heisman trophy, was suspended from playing football at the University of California at Los Angeles because he accepted a sport utility vehicle from a television producer. In addition, players at the University of Nebraska and the University of Colorado have been accused of criminal behavior. Several University of Georgia football players were involved in a barroom brawl in the summer of 2001. A survey by the Institute for International Sport found that one-fifth of 202 college athletes surveyed said they had been involved in off-campus violence. This kind of misconduct is explained by "experts" to be caused by the adulation of college athletes, by their isolation, and because college athletes who misbehave are judged by the athletic department and not the normal judicial process in effect in all colleges. In addition, the macho atmosphere surrounding male athletes contributes to some of the aggression displayed by them. In an effort to reduce the violence associated with college football the Mentors in Violence Prevention program was started by Northeastern University in 1993. That program has training sessions in over 100 schools, with particular emphasis on preventing violence against women.[7]

During the past several years student rioting after sports events has become so common that it resembles the conduct of British soccer fans, who are notorious for violent rioting. Much of this rioting is attributed to alcohol abuse. Reporter Sally Jenkins claimed that more than 600,000 students are assaulted annually by another student who had been drinking and that one-third of all college students meet the criteria of alcohol abuse. While conventional wisdom attributes violent "after football" riots to poverty, racism, poor family life, etc., the truth is that many of the rioters come from affluent homes who can afford to send their children to expensive universities. These rioters are seldom apprehended because of the anonymity of the crowd and the generally permissive attitude of adults concerning the misconduct of young people. Recent riots in Minnesota and Maryland found police standing idly by while students burned furniture, smashed car windows, jumped on passing cars, smashed street lamps, and finally injured several officers. Only then did the police intervene.[8]

Another reason for rioting after football games is that some individuals do not view colleges as institutions of higher learning but as training grounds for football glory. This is easily illustrated by looking at one of the many football recruiting Web sites available on the Internet. For example, Don Campbell's *Texas Football* displays a front cover depicting "Four of the State's most prolific football stars." These are by no means football stars who are also great writers. Instead, these are the pictures of football "greats" who came from Texas and then graduated to the NFL. The magazine also features a section listing high school students who have verbally committed to a college. This list gives the name of the high school athlete and the name of the college he will attend. No commitment is made to study or learn anything.[9]

On February 6, 2003, "decision day" or National Signing Day came as it does every year for those high school football players seeking to sign a letter of intent to play football for a college. Prior to the arrival of National Signing Day the players and their parents suffer considerable anxiety as they wait to discover which college will give the high school athlete a football scholarship. The best football players are in a position to decide which college they want to attend among the many making offers. Recruitment, then, is a two-way street for those who are outstanding athletes.

Sometimes football players decide to enter a college because they want to play for a particular coach. For example, Brandon Tobias, who had already committed to play forward for Arkansas in 2000, changed his mind and went to the University of Alabama to follow his high school coach Mike Anderson to that school.[10]

Because recruitment of the best high school players is so important to large football-oriented universities, the coaches who succeed in winning because of their recruiting success earn large, even outlandish salaries. For example, Larry Coker, coach of the University of Miami football team, earns $900,000 plus incentive bonuses and a $100,000 raise each year. Compare that to the salaries of professors, whose existence makes the university possible. The average annual faculty salary in 2001 was only $58,400. Professors earned an average of $76,200 that year and associate professors less. Even college presidents, whose appointments and salaries are determined mainly by political considerations, seldom earned more than $200,000, although there are some who take home over $1 million a year. It is significant that football coaches usually are paid more than professors in any other department and that some coaches earn more than the president of the college. The meaning is clear. Football is important, administration is also important, but teaching and learning are unimportant sidelines justifying the sports program.[11] It is therefore not surprising that some football coaches are tempted to use unethical means to gain appointment to some of the better coaching jobs. Perhaps the best known example of such unethical conduct was that of coach George O'Leary, who was most successful at Georgia Tech and then sought his dream job at Notre Dame University. He was in fact appointed head coach at Notre Dame in 2001 but lasted only two weeks when it was discovered that he had lied on his application. He claimed to have played varsity college football. This was not true. He also claimed that he had a master's degree in education and that too was a lie.[12]

A study by social scientist Lee Sigelman showed the extent to which football players' admissions standards were lowered at "big time" football universities in comparison to normal admissions policies. Sigelman also studied the extent to which such deviation from normal admissions procedures paid off. The results of this study indicate that more selective schools recruit more academically qualified football players, although newly admitted football players have substantially lower entrance scores than all new students. He further found that the more selective the school, the wider the gap between all entering freshmen and football players. Sigelman found no connection between a team's success and football players' scores. Finally Sigelman concludes that a school's academic quality constitutes a decisive recruiting advantage.[13]

Recruitment into football is a rite of passage from childhood to adulthood in many American communities. It is an initiation rite into masculinity that contains all those elements which anthropologists have recorded in the masculinity rites of cultures around the world. First is the man-boy relationship. This includes continuous interaction between older men, or "offiants," and younger men, or "initiates." The "offiants" recruit and motivate selected initiates to engage in appropriate behaviors, beliefs and values.[14]

The recruitment of young men into football includes conformity to the rules and requirements of football playing. Like other initiations, conformity to ritual is enforced on football players even as it is enforced on military recruits, college freshmen, apprentices of all kinds and anyone seeking to join anything. Isolation from women, or at least a disparaging attitude toward everything feminine, is another aspect of the initiation rite associated with entering the world of football. In fact, the issue of manliness has been a prime motivation for the involvement in football for over a century. The ethnographer Michael Oriard recorded comments concerning football manliness, beginning with 1885 when a magazine called *Outing* featured this sentence: "Football is the most manly and scientific sport in existence." According to Oriard, the *Illustrated Weekly* commented in 1892 that "to bear pain without flinching and to laugh at the wounds and scars of a body contested game, is very good discipline, and tends to develop manliness of character."[15]

Similar rites of initiation are found in all cultures. Anthropologists have repeatedly documented the initiation rites of so-called primitive men. According to students of these rites, tribal initiation is a severe ordeal. These ordeals can include sprinkling of human blood, head biting, loss of teeth, and, most often, circumcision. Also included in these initiation ceremonies are sleep deprivation, constant excitement, and other "long-continued torments."[16]

These initiation rites, whether used in American football or among the most primitive of men in the outback of Australia or the jungles of Africa or South America, always include the teaching of respect for older men. We may call this "Deference to Male Authority," leading to an understanding of the hierarchical rank of the men, which is as often maintained by the football fraternity as the business community or the academic establishment.

Among primitive peoples and also among the street gangs of American cities, the willingness to suffer pain without complaint is an important signal of achieved masculinity or manliness. For example, Yuni boys in New Mexico are flogged with yucca whips, Nandi boys in East Africa are circumcised in a most tortuous manner, and in some North American tribes it was customary to self-inflict pain. The ability to endure pain is used to set apart the initiates uninitiated males, i.e., non-football players, and women. Although no longer fashionable, the term "sissy" was used until about the 1960s to describe men not willing to accommodate football-style conduct.[17]

Although the demeaning of women is one of the principal characteristics of the football subculture, the use of sex appeal as a recruiting device is very much in evidence among college football coaches eager to enlist a talented young man. Almost all recruiting efforts involve the mediation of college girls promising smiles and more. An example is the experience of a prospective football recruit who visited an Ohio campus where he and three other recruits were met by four girls who entertained them in a Winnebago camper until early the next morning. The boys were promised more such entertainment if they decided to play football there.[18]

Concomitant with the allure of sex is the willingness of college administrators, professors, and certainly coaches to overlook any and all academic deficiencies among talented football recruits. The history of college football clearly demonstrates that failure to achieve academic adequacy is as old as college football itself. This does not mean, of course, that every college football recruit is a "dumb jock." Some football players do attain both academic and football success. A current example is Jay Fiedler, quarterback of the Miami Dolphins, who holds a degree in engineering from Dartmouth College. There are also W. Brad McGonagle, PhD, who was an offensive lineman at Texas A&M University, Dr. Roger Hughes, head coach at Princeton University and former tight end at Doane College in Nebraska, and Michael Oriard, PhD, author of a number of books, former Notre Dame football player, and professional football player for the Kansas City Chiefs from 1970-1973. Dr. Oriard is now professor of literature at Oregon State University.

A far better example of the academic standing of the vast majority of college football players, however, is Dexter Manley. Manley, who learned to read at the age of thirty, stunned a Congressional committee when he told them that he graduated from the University of Oklahoma although he could not read. Perhaps there are as few college football players who resemble Fiedler as there are those who resemble Manley. However, poor academic performance among those recruited from high school to colleges around the country is almost routine.[19]

Evidently, this has been the tradition for some time. James Hogan, who played football for Yale University from 1901-1904, began his football career at the age of twenty-seven. He came to Yale after he received a ten-day vacation in Cuba, was moved into the most luxurious dormitory on campus, ate at the University Club, received free tuition, a $100 scholarship, and a monopoly on the sale of game programs. He was also made an agent of the American Tobacco Company, receiving a commission on every package of cigarettes sold in New Haven. His scholarly ability was negligible but was also held to be unimportant.[20]

The introduction of the outstanding athletes who were academically inept led to numerous jokes and stories concerning this campus phenomenon such as story about the "jock" who is given a French test. The "test" consists of five questions, all in English, which the "jock" answers with "oui" and therefore "passes" the French test.[21]

For underpriveleged boys who were the sons of immigrants or who were members of racial minorities, football was and is a means of emerging from the ghettos and gaining access to the wealthier and educated segments of American society. Little doubt exists that football provides a bridge allowing those otherwise excluded to enter the best colleges and universities. That exclusion was at one time based almost only on social class. However, with the expansion of American higher education to everyone after World War II, academic ability rather than social class has made higher education accessible to many whose finances would not allow their participation in higher education in earlier years. The "GI Bill of Rights," or Servicemen's Readjustment Act, allowed millions of American men to enter expensive colleges and universities after World War II.

Consequently, good students without money were able to enter American universities and benefit from those experiences by entering the professions and leading business and government jobs in greater numbers than had ever been anticipated before World War II.

The end of World War II released several million men from the armed services. Of these men, 2.2 million attended colleges and universities between 1945 and 1950 and made up over 50 percent of college football players. The next players, regardless of academic ability, were then lured to various colleges by all kinds of deals available to recruiters. Here we learn about an offer to one player of $15,000, the use of a car, a $300 per month vacation job, and employment after graduation at a high starting salary (remember that $300 a month in 1945 is equivalent to $3,000 a month in 2002).[22]

Perhaps the most extreme effort to profit from the recruiting mania among college football coaches was the "selling" of Albert Means, a 6-foot-4-inch-335-pound high school football player to a University of Alabama "booster." Means was an all-American defensive lineman at Trezevant High School in Memphis, Tennessee, when the head coach at that high school, Lynn Lang, accepted $200,000 to steer Means into the University of Alabama, where he played one season. When news of this "sale" became public and coach Lang was indicted for conspiracy, bribery, and extortion, Means enrolled at the University of Memphis. There he was declared academically ineligible in the summer of 2002 so that he was obliged to attend summer school with a view of rejoining the football team for the 2002 season. It is noteworthy that Means and his mother did not receive one cent of the $200,000 collected by the coach.[23]

The most recent study of the role of football in American higher education is the work of Murray Sperber. Writing in 2000, Sperber demonstrates that so-called "special admissions" allow those with low SAT scores to be admitted. Sperber gives this example: "At the University of North Carolina at Chapel Hill, a school that accepts only 35 percent of all applicants, men's basketball players average 905 out of a possible 1600 on their SATs, and regular undergraduates average 1220."[24] There is no reason to believe that football players are asked to do more than basketball players.

All football players, even at "big-time" football schools, do not fail. It is therefore of interest to understand the differences between those football players who achieve academic success and those who fail. The paradox university administrations usually create in the major football playing colleges is that the universities claim that they exist to promote learning and scholarship, even as they cannot raise sufficient funds from alumni and legislatures unless they win football games with players who have no interest in academics. Yet, all athletes do not fail academically.

Lang and colleagues have identified some factors that are related to academic failure of football players. They found, not surprisingly, that high school grade point averages and the need to repeat a year in high school are the most important predictors of college academic success or failure. Academic motivation is of course another important predictor of academic success in college. Lang and colleagues found that some football players who failed academically had the "feeling like I'm majoring in eligibility." "History of trouble" is the next variable influencing academic failure in later years. This refers to the number of times a football player was disciplined by the coach. The next two variables influencing failure in college for football players are mother's education and graduation from a private high school. It is well known that students who come from a home whose adults have little education are much more likely to fail in academia than those whose parents could afford a private high school and who are well educated. This would mean that students from minorities who furnish an extraordinary proportion of football players to our colleges and universities are most likely to fail academically. The solution to this problem cannot be the exclusion of minority football players. Therefore, programs need to be devised by universities which will make it possible for minority and disadvantaged football players to succeed academically.[25]

MONEY AND GREED—
THE COLLEGE FOOTBALL BUSINESS

The National Collegiate Athletic Association was founded in 1906. It is made up of 977 schools classified in three divisions. Division I has 321 schools, in turn divided into I-A and I-AA; Division II has 260 schools, and Division III has 396. The NCAA sponsors eighty-seven championships in twenty-two sports, in which 24,500 students compete.

There are now slightly less than 1 million high school football players in the United States. Approximately 250 of these make it to the NFL, which means that a high school football player has a chance of one in 6,000 to ever get a professional contract. Even that does not provide him with a career.

In 2002, the Division I colleges and universities associated with the National Collegiate Athletic Association gave out an estimated $1 billion in grants-in-aid to 360,000 college athletes at approximately 320 institutions of "higher learning."[26]

Since there are also Division II and Division III schools it is evident that the support of athletics in American colleges is far greater than $1 billion, as is the amount spent by Americans on all leisure activities. In fact, Americans spend hundreds of billions of dollars on leisure activities every year and sports occupy a large share of this amount. Included in this spending are the intercollegiate athletic programs at major universities with big-time athletic programs. It is estimated that such universities budget $15-$20 million per year for athletics. This would mean that the athletic department is either the most expensive department in such a university or is second behind the medical school, if the university has a medical school. Since the budgets of big-time athletic departments in the early 1970s were only about $1 million, this growth is indeed phenomenal despite the inflation in the entire economy since then. Nevertheless, about one-half of the athletic programs at major American universities had operating expenditures which exceeded income.[27]

The staffs of athletic departments in large universities include seventy-five to 200 coaches and assistants as well as support personnel such as academic tutors, physicians, and cheerleaders. The economic surge involving big time college sports also includes the commercial sponsorships of such sports. This increasing commercialization of college football is visible to anyone who ever looked at a televised college football game. Corporate sponsors advertise widely, as best illustrated by the Tostitos Fiesta Bowl. The principal consequences of this sponsorship of college football are: college football is now subordinate to its commercial function, sponsorship perpetuates the kind of elitism already discussed, and college football has become a television spectacle.[28]

This television spectacle became possible when the U.S. Supreme Court ruled in 1984 that the property rights to college telecasts belong to the college and not the NCAA. Beginning with that ruling, colleges were able to negotiate contracts for telecasts. This led to greater recruiting success for colleges whose games were telecast so that non-football powers lost the ability to compete with football powers.[29]

Television is the greatest contributor to university income derived from sports. Billboards and advertisements are also displayed in football stadia. It is for this reason that some small colleges have nevertheless fielded football and basketball teams, looking to become eligible for the profits in division I sports. As we have already seen, academic standards for athletes involved in football and basketball in big sports universities have been relaxed to such a point that a number of weak "cover-up" efforts were made by the NCAA to raise these standards. These efforts have been largely ineffective. As a consequence of the immense growth of athletic departments in our major universities, some have called these departments "the front porch" of the institution. The media, seldom interested in academic performance, give college football and basketball teams far more publicity than any other endeavors by a university. The preeminence of football and basketball at most colleges is also certified by the salaries of sports coaches, leading to separation between athletic departments and the other parts of the university. Because these programs cannot be funded out of taxes at public universities and must be self-supporting at private universities as well, the need for commercial sponsors and the influence of television income leads athletic departments to make decisions based on the needs of their financial supporters.[30]

Because university administrators are generally academics who know little if anything about television and sports bowl contracts, these matters are usually left in the hands of the athletic directors, who thereupon become almost independent of the university.

In 1902, Stanford University played the first ever Rose Bowl football game against the University of Michigan. Michigan won 49-0. Thereafter, numerous other college championship games were played in various "bowls" spawned by the Rose Bowl and designed to increase attendance, enthusiasm, and income for college football. Twenty-five bowl games were played at the end of the 2001 season. Many of these bowls such as the Gallery Furniture Bowl, the Orange Bowl, and the Cotton Bowl are sponsored by corporations. No doubt, these spectacular football games draw attention to the products there advertised. Included in these advertisers are Ford Motor Co., Honda, General Motors, Dodge/Chrysler, Charles Schwab, Morgan Stanley, Budweiser, Pepsi, Sears, and others. These advertisers paid $1.9 million for a thirty-second TV spots in each of the four most popular bowl games played at the end of each football season.[31]

All the money generated from these activities make athletic personnel dominant on campus and free to run their own affairs without much contact with anyone else in the academic community. Similar to many medical schools which have more money and influence on the public than other academic programs, athletic departments "lord it over" the universities in which they function.

This independence from the university can often be seen in the salary structure of the institution. In years when academic professors receive little or no increase in salaries, coaches and other employees of the athletic department may, and often do receive increases in salaries far in excess of the earnings of professors. This too contributes to the cleavage between the athletic departments and the university. In fact, university athletic directors are valued for their ability to raise funds and to evade the rules of the NCAA, thereby rising to real power on the campus. These conditions are mainly predicated on the assumption that they relate to basketball and football with lesser impact derived from other sports such as swimming or tennis.[32]

Even as the NCAA makes rules designed to rein in the financial adventures of athletic departments on the campus, some individuals accuse the NCAA of fostering the very greed they claim to limit. That accusation stems from the recent NCAA legislation allowing schools to play twelve games in years in which the calendar provides one more Saturday in August than usual. The college football season starts the last Saturday in August and ends the last Saturday in November. Therefore there will be twelve Saturdays in 2003, 2008, 2013, 2014, and 2019. In all these years schools will be able to schedule twelve games. The reason for extending the college football season is money. The twelfth game will undoubtedly inject extra cash into the college athletic departments even as the longer season means less practice, less players, and more games. In addition it is easy to speculate that in years containing no additional Saturdays, the athletic departments will miss the money they were able to earn in 2003 and demand the installation of a twelfth game as a permanent feature of the college football season. It is also evident that those teams who play in the championship play-offs will be playing fourteen games, with the exception of Nebraska, who also play a "preseason classic" and therefore could potentially demand that the football players play in fifteen games.

The twelve-game season also changes bowl eligibility from 6-5 to 7-5. Also, it should be considered that in view of the August heat it may be particularly hard on the players to begin the season earlier than usual. In addition to these changes, the NCAA will also include bowl games in its statistics, beginning with the 2003 season. Therefore, a 1,000-yard-rushing season may well be less impressive, as the benchmark for rushing could reach 1,500 yards.[33]

The most important outcome of this extended schedule is that it will make it even less possible for student-athletes to achieve academic success even as coaches and athletic directors and college administrators collect more money than ever before.[34]

It may be well to berate the poverty of academic achievement among student athletes, yet it can be shown that universities which win a lot of football or basketball games will increase the *quantity* of applicants wishing to enter that university.[35]

All of this leads some college and university officials to use unethical persons or procedures to gain advantages. The most infamous case of malfeasance by a university concerning its football program occurred in 1987 at Southern Methodist University. The NCAA banned SMU from competing in collegiate football that year after it became known that the university had a "slush" fund used to pay football players. The so-called student players were in fact professionals paid and supported by wealthy alumni, including the governor of Texas. Although SMU had been a true football powerhouse, the program was eliminated by that suspension and the subsequent failure of SMU to continue football in 1988. Additional restrictions led some observers to call the action of the NCAA against SMU a "death penalty."

Similar violations have since occurred in other colleges and universities. For example, in 1989 Memphis was penalized for unethical conduct by the football coach in giving a student athlete extra benefits. Texas A&M was placed on five-year probation in 1994 for giving players extra benefits and using impermissible recruiting contacts. The school was not allowed any televised or bowl games for one year. In 1996, Michigan State was placed on four years probation, lost its scholarships, and forfeited a game because of unethical conduct with reference to recruiting. Likewise, Texas-El Paso in 1997, Wisconsin in 2001, and Alabama in 2002 were placed on probation and suffered other penalties for improper recruiting, distributing extra benefits, or violating academic eligibility rules.[36]

Colleges that have won the national championship in one of the important sports are seen as winners and their applications increase as do donations by alumni and others. The opposite is true of universities whose football teams are losers, no matter what academic achievements the players may have. This is best illustrated by the dismissal of football coach Cam Cameron from the Indiana University football program in 2001. Commenting on that dismissal, the sports writer Bill Benner wrote, "it would not have mattered if Cameron's players had a 100 percent graduation rate, perfect GPA's and . . .

staffed homeless shelters and volunteered at senior citizens center."[37] He is right, of course. "Winning isn't everything, it's the only thing."

A further illustration of the divorce of big-time college football from the announced purposes of universities and colleges concerns the major college football spectacles, which are big moneymakers unrelated to any scholastic purpose the college may have had at one time.

When, after the September 11, 2001, attack on the World Trade Center, football-related income declined, this was reported at length in business journals of all kinds. *The Memphis Business Journal* worried that the annual football game between Tennessee State University and Jackson State College had lost 42 percent of revenues in 2001 because the game had to be postponed to the Thanksgiving weekend. It had originally been scheduled for September 15, only four days after the attack on the World Trade Center. Calling this football game "one of Memphis' most lucrative sporting events" the business journal reported that "the event pumps $9 million into the local economy annually."[38]

Likewise, the Ohio State University administrators sold suites at $70,000 each to corporate entertainers who sought to impress out-of-town visitors with the spirit of the community on football Saturdays.[39] Is it conceivable that any corporation would invite a business visitor to see the Ohio State University library or meet with its honor students or attend a lecture by a professor? The answer is self-evident and the lesson is that Ohio State University is a school attached to a football team, not the other way around.

The football careers of two Ohio State Heisman Trophy winners illustrate this. Archie Griffin was awarded the trophy in 1974 and in 1975. At a time when Woody Hayes was the "Buckeye" coach, Griffin achieved a rushing record of 1,577 yards in 1974 and 1,620 yards in 1975. He went on to play in the NFL for eight years. In 1995 Ohio State's Eddie George was awarded the Heisman Trophy. He had rushed for 1,927 yards and twenty-four touchdowns and became the NFL's "rookie of the year" in 1996. During all that time, not one academic attainment at Ohio State University gained even a modicum of publicity, nor did anyone contribute financially for the sake of the academic program.[40]

Business success depends in part on advertising. This is true of the college football business as well. Therefore the University of Oregon and Oregon State University both conducted publicity campaigns in the fall of 2001 in an attempt to gain the Heisman Trophy for their candidate. Neither school succeeded because the trophy, indicating the best college football player of that season, went to another college. Meanwhile, the University of Oregon spent $250,000 to set up a 100-foot-tall mural of "Joey Heisman" in downtown New York. This led to a great deal of notoriety for both West Coast schools and a good deal of coverage in magazines, newspapers, television, etc. The expense is evidently worth it since sports generates about $250 billion in the United States every year. The college football share of this money is big. For example, Oregon State University earned $250,000 when ABC aired their game against the University of Oregon nationally. A team that competes in the Bowl Championship Series can gain between $500,000 and $1 million. Of course, the money earned goes only to the athletic departments of these universities even when there is a budget shortfall in the academic program. Donations to the Oregon State University foundation increased 30 percent because of the success of the football team.[41]

In view of all these advantages, the State University of New York (SUNY) at Buffalo has recently succeeded in upgrading its football program to Division I of the National College Athletic Association's twenty-nine-year-old system of categorizing athletics. The 321 colleges associated in this division usually offer more scholarships, sponsor more sports, and have more demanding game schedules than schools in Division II or III.[42]

When the SUNY system was first organized in 1948, the trustees decided not to offer football scholarships on the grounds that athletics would become more important than academics. In 1986, however, the trustees voted to overturn that policy. Consequently, the four major campuses of the SUNY system—Albany, Buffalo, Binghamton, and Stony Brook—are now into fund raising, recruiting, and marketing. The motivation for moving into Division I was of course the opportunity for these four schools to attract more applicants and more money from alumni and put the university "on the map" with the media. SUNY at Buffalo moved into Division 1A, the top division, in 1999. Buffalo has an athletic department budget of $12 million a year and a new stadium seating 30,000. Buffalo now spends $3.5 million on 220 full-time athletic scholarships although the average attendance at football games was only 11,000, leaving nearly two-thirds of the stadium empty. Losing seasons caused the poor attendance. Buffalo was 0-11, 2-9, and 3-8 during the past three seasons.[43]

THE RACE ISSUE IN COLLEGE FOOTBALL

Prior to the Civil Rights Movement of the 1960s, racism was so prevalent in American culture that few found it objectionable that many southern colleges would not play against a team including black players. The number of black players was small. An outstanding example of the atrocities of racism during the 1950s was the failure of the University of San Francisco football team to receive any invitation to any bowl game because it included two black players on the team. This, despite their undefeated record in 1951. The team rejected the idea of playing in a bowl game without the two black players, Ollie Matson and Burl Toler. Their decision was unanimous. They held the view that either everyone goes or nobody goes. Fifty years later, the University of San Francisco celebrated that attitude with the slogan, "Undefeated, untied and uninvited."[44]

It is obvious even for someone who has not studied the racial composition of American football players that African Americans are overrepresented in revenue-generating intercollegiate sports. This is visible to anyone attending a college football or basketball game. Yet, it is easily determined that the graduation rates of African-American college students are below those of Euro-American and Asian-American students. Because this racial divergence has been true for some time, some institutions of higher learning have attempted to strengthen their academic support system for athletes. However, the athletic enterprise, consisting of the athletic department personnel and their supporters, seldom give academics any support.

It has been mentioned that in the 1920s many Americans believed that Jewish sports success was the product of racial inheritance, despite the fact that Jews are not a race. The effort to link race to sports ability is best illustrated by the Hollywood film *White Men Can't*

Jump (1992) and the (April 1989) telecast by NBC, "Black Athletes: Fact or Fiction?".

Numerous observers such as Sperber, Telander, Wiley, and Hatchett have repeatedly shown that athletics are worth more to major sports universities than academic programs. The argument that athletic scholarships help blacks to upward mobility is not borne out by experience. Although a few athletes, black and white, gain lucrative contracts with major teams in football and other sports, usually athletes, both black and white, do not gain access to the NFL. This vast majority of college athletes are then unlikely to earn a livelihood outside of sports because they never learned a useful skill in college. Most of all, they did not learn how to think and that should be the most important product of a college education. However, media propaganda and the entire sports culture of the United States led many a student-athlete to delude himself that he will be "rich and famous" when in fact he is most likely to be poor and ignored. The truth is that blacks are led to believe that they have a better chance of success as athletes than lawyers, accountants, doctors, or teachers despite the fact that only one in 12,000 makes it as a professional athlete.[45]

It has been a perennial complaint by black football players that there are very few black football coaches in proportion to the number of blacks who excel at that game. It is therefore noteworthy that Notre Dame University appointed Tyrone Willingham head football coach in 2002. Willingham is black.

WHO PLAYS COLLEGE FOOTBALL?

In 1988, psychologist Daniel Garland administered the Sixteen Personality Factor Questionnaire (developed by Raymond Cattell) to 272 football players from three universities. This study discovered a number of characteristics of football players which were associated with high levels of performance. Included were extroversion, emotional stability, and democratic decision making instead of dependence on autocratic coaches and socially supportive behavior.[46]

Another study compared sixty students who had lettered in high school football with sixty students who had not lettered in any sport. This study showed that successful football players were less de-

pressed, fatigued, or confused than nonplayers. The study also showed that football players were more "other" oriented than nonplayers
and were much more authoritarian than former athletes who in turn
were more authoritarian than those who never participated in a competitive sport. The suggestion here is that football selects or nurtures a
narrow-minded, conventional, and conservative personality.[47]

A further study, conducted at Notre Dame University, discovered
that football players came from much lower socioeconomic backgrounds than "regular" students. That study also found that only 29
percent of college football players earned advanced degrees while 44
percent of "regular" students achieved this.[48]

THE COLLEGE FOOTBALL COACH— ROLE MODEL FOR ALL SEASONS

A role is defined by sociologists as the sum of our obligations with
reference to our status. A status is any position in any social relationship and includes our rights and privileges. Hence a role is a performance which is obligatory for those wishing to maintain a status. The
most common and most important American status/role is occupation.

Americans rank occupations by prestige, meaning social honor
associated with the work we do. According to the National Opinion
Research Center (NORC), Americans view most important those
occupations that demand extensive training and provide a high income. Physicians and lawyers are best examples of these high-rank-
ing professions.[49]

Coaching football is an occupation, although it is unusual and
therefore not included in the surveys concerning occupational prestige conducted by the NORC each year. Nevertheless, there can be no
doubt that college football coach is a very prestigious occupation, not
only because football is regarded by so many as the very essence of
the American identity, but also because it is so lucrative. For example,
Ralph Friedgen, head football coach at the University of Maryland,
earned more than $1 million in 2002. His base salary at the University
was $183,820 that year. In addition, Friedgen receives $762,000 from

footwear contracts, personal appearances, and an automobile allowance. Yet other sources of money drive his income past the $1 million mark.[50]

Approximately sixty head football coaches at Division I institutions earn such vast incomes. This is true of Larry Coker, head coach of the University of Miami football team. Because his team won the national championship in 2001 he was given a $5.25 million contract in February 2002. This includes a salary of $850,000 for 2002 and a pay increase of $100,000 through 2006.[51]

Sports Illustrated reported that Tyrone Willingham, newly appointed head football coach at Notre Dame University, would receive between $2 and $3 million per year in that position.[52]

Lou Holtz, head coach at the University of South Carolina, received a $25,000 raise in 2002 to reach a base salary of $200,000. Including all provisions in his contract, Holtz will earn upward of $1 million in 2002. In addition, Holtz hired his son "Skip" Holtz as assistant coach at $155,000. Holtz has six additional assistant coaches whose salaries range from $87,000 to $124,000.[53]

The highest college football coach salary paid in 2002 is $2 million per year, which goes to Bobby Bowden, head coach at Florida State University. Endorsements, personal appearances, and other opportunities will likely boost his income into the stratosphere. These salaries may well be viewed as obscene if we consider that coaches earn such sums by exploiting young college students who get nothing for their efforts except hope. Such an income leads to the belief that the education professors provide must be worth very little when compared to the entertainment delivered by football teams. Since the bulk of the money received by football coaches comes from booster clubs, speaking engagements, and sports equipment manufacturers, it is evident that none of these football promoters think very much of spending money on scholarships for the poor who really want an education. In fact, the young football players who are given athletic scholarships are led to understand that football is more important than school and that they ought to devote themselves to it without pay and without consideration of their future. Coaches know that very few college athletes ever become professionals. In most large sports oriented schools, less than one-half the athletes graduate. This then teaches that we value coaches and defensive tackles more than we value research scientists and that it is highly prized for coaches to make millions from the efforts of those who get next to no pay.[54]

About twenty of the head football coaches at Division I institutions earn $1 million or more each season. Others earn less, and yet a great deal more than professionals in other endeavors. Since athletics programs do not operate on university budgets but run their own finances, head coaches are generally well-versed businessmen. Such coaches are well acquainted with ticket sales numbers and the incomes of rival coaches. Above all, football coaches know how to recruit football players. As we have seen, recruitment generates a great deal of revenue in preseason ticket sales, renewing options on preferred seating, luxury suites, big donor contributions, and summer camps.

It is evident that football and basketball drive most athletic departments in higher education. In view of Title IX of the Education Amendments of 1972 to the 1965 Higher Education Act, and the Equity in Athletics Disclosure Act of 1994, it is mandatory that colleges and universities spend as much on women's athletic programs as on men's in the areas of recruitment, scholarships, and budgeting. This evidently reduces the contributions a school can make to its football teams. In fact, by 2003 there were 600 more women's teams than men's teams in the NCAA. Because of the controversy Title IX has engendered for over thirty years, the Commission for Opportunity in Athletics has held public hearings concerning Title IX in Atlanta, Chicago, San Diego, and Colorado Springs. It remains to be seen whether the program will be altered to reduce the number of women's teams now supported by higher education nationwide.[55]

Meanwhile, football teams in many colleges and universities have tried to eliminate men who "walk-on," i.e., students who want to play football but are not the recipients of a football scholarship. At some of the bigger football programs such as Ohio State, Michigan, or Texas A&M, expansive team rosters for men and women are affordable. However, smaller, nonrevenue-generating sports and colleges that are not among the top moneymakers cannot afford to allow such walkons. In short, many young men who want to try out for the football team or other sports are no longer given an opportunity to do so because there is no profit in their participation. This has come about mainly because thousands of women's teams have been added to the athletic offerings in almost all colleges in order to comply with Title IX. Many men seek to walk-on even if they never play in any game because they want to add membership on the football team to their résumé and/or seek only to brag about their football prowess even if it never happened. A few colleges have now added some "recruited walk-ons." These are high school players who have not received a scholarship but are included in the team and are allowed to play. Therefore, the average size of NCAA football teams was 94 in 2002.[56]

It would be a mistake to believe that the NCAA is all-powerful in the area of college football. This is hardly possible because the real power in college football lies in the "Top Six." The Top Six are the Big Ten, the Big 12, the Pac 10, the Big East, Conference USA, and the Atlantic Coast Conference, all of which include about seventy-five colleges who are Division I A and appear on television, thereby making big money.[57]

FOOTBALL INJURIES AND FOOTBALL DEATHS

The National Center for Catastrophic Sport Injury Research (NCCSIR) publishes an annual report concerning major injuries and deaths resulting from playing the game. These reports have been conducted since 1931. The 1990 report was unique because it was the first year in which no direct fatality occurred in football at any level of play. The NCCSIR divides fatalities into direct and indirect. The direct fatalities are evidently those which occur during a game or during practice. The indirect are "those fatalities which are caused by systemic failure as a result of exertion while participating in football activity or by a complication which was secondary to a non-fatal injury."[58]

The report lists seven high school football fatalities in 2001 and estimates that 1,800,000 individuals participated in football on all levels in 2001. The rate of direct fatalities for high school was 0.44 per 100,000 that year. It was 0.00 for college fatalities. In 2001 one fatality happened during recreational play. The seven high school fatalities occurred during regularly scheduled games. Six of these fatalities were the result of a brain injury.

Fifteen indirect football fatalities occurred in 2001, ten of which were associated with high school football and were heat related. Three fatalities occurred in college football, and two in professional football. Since heat-related deaths can be prevented, they should be of major concern to coaches and team physicians. In the nine years from 1994 to 2003, twenty young men died from heat stroke while playing football.

Here are some examples of high school football fatalities:

1. A seventeen-year-old high school football player suffered a severe brain injury while trying to break the wedge on a kick-off. The player had a previous concussion. Cause of death was second impact syndrome brain injury.
2. A sixteen-year-old high school running back was injured while being tackled. Cause of death was a fractured cervical vertebra.
3. A seventeen-year-old high school quarterback fell on the ball and died the same day from a ruptured spleen.
4. A seventeen-year-old defensive end was injured during a game. Cause of death was a subdural hematoma.

Examples of college football fatalities include these:

1. A twenty-two-year-old college football player collapsed during summer conditioning drills. He was six feet tall and weighed 212 pounds. Cause of death was exercise-induced asthma.
2. An eighteen-year-old college football player died during summer conditioning drills. Cause of death was heatstroke. He was six feet and two inches tall and weighed 255 pounds.
3. An eighteen-year-old college player died after morning workout. Cause of death was sickle cell trait.[59]

Those who defend the manner in which football players are injured at games use such trivializing language as "having your bell rung," "being knocked around," "dinged," or "shaking it off." The truth is that many of the concussions football players suffer are equivalent to a car accident occurring at a speed of twenty-five miles an hour.

A concussion is an alteration of consciousness ranging from amnesia to unconsciousness. It has been estimated that during any one football season 63,000 concussions occur among all sports, with football accounting for 63 percent of these concussions. Included in these injuries are "second-impact syndromes," which are defined as "rapid irreversible brain damage."[60] Patients with second-impact syndromes develop memory loss, dizziness, insomnia, lethargy, back pain, "fogginess," labile emotions, and constant migraines.

An additional danger to football players is "toxic cascade." This condition results in accumulated damage in the brain stemming from two or more concussions. Such football players exhibit a decline in the "executive" brain functions.[61]

Because coaches and others who profit from football prefer not to discuss injuries and deaths incurred by football players, these matters are seldom given much publicity. In addition, it should not be forgotten that the team physician's relationship to the players is quite different from that of a doctor to his or her patient for several reasons. In the first place, team physicians are paid by the team and not the player. Therefore it is in the interest of the doctor to minimize injuries and have the player return to the game quickly. The pay the physician collects is not only fiscal, but lies also in the prestige a team doctor can use to enhance his reputation and therefore his practice.

In many cases a team doctor is appointed because he knows the coach or the college president even if sports medicine is not his specialty. It is unlikely that football coaches have sufficient knowledge of medicine to evaluate whether a team doctor really understands the needs of the players. In view of all this, it is legitimate to ask whether players have much confidence in team doctors.[62]

CHEERLEADERS

The introduction of female cheerleaders into the college football scene occurred sometime during the 1920s. Prior to that decade, young men, usually college students, led the fans in cheering for their team.

The first female college cheerleader was Marion Draper, who led the cheers for Tulane University during a 1925 game against Northwestern. Girls had already done the same in a few high schools. Draper was a former Ziegfeld Follies beauty. By the 1940s female cheerleaders had become established and were part of the sex appeal boosting the game. Some of the early cheerleaders received a good deal of publicity in magazines and sports pages and some married the star quarterbacks, to the acclaim of the football fanatics of the day.

The Rose Bowl and the twenty-seven additional bowl games increased the visibility of female cheerleaders whose sex appeal was now enhanced by tight-fitting costumes, bare legs and boots, and dance routines which became ever more complicated and demanding. Sports writers now indulged in descriptions of sex appeal, which in the third millennium would be called gross sexism but was never criticized in the 1950s and later decades. Even now, despite women's liberation and constant warnings against making women sex objects, the exhibition of female appeal at the Orange Bowl in particular has not ceased but has become a principal sales pitch for these spectaculars. *Sports Illustrated* and other magazines devoted to football display the cheerleader beauties who may be seen at college games throughout the country. Most appealing seem to be pictures of a cheerleader between two giant football players with captions such as "Beauty and the Beasts," "The Big Bears and little Miami cutie," etc.[63]

An organization for cheerleaders called Cheerleaders of America runs summer camps for girls wanting to improve their acrobatic skills. Cheerleaders of America also sponsors a number of cheerleader competitions in ten locations throughout the country. One of these competitions awards a $2,250 college scholarship to the winner of the stunt competition held in Orlando, Florida, each year.[64]

American Cheerleader Magazine deals with such topics as cheerleader training, outstanding cheerleaders, fundraising, various means of accomplishing acrobatic stunts, and, of course, "Big Men on Campus" and how to meet them.[65]

In sum, college football, like all occupations, is a subculture exhibiting its own language, values, and loyalties. It encompasses men and women, and attracts millions of Americans who view the sport as an expression of the American identity only surpassed by professional football, which appears to have become the focus of more interest among Americans than politics or economics or even Hollywood. That profession will be explored in depth in the following chapter.

SUMMARY

In its infancy, college football led to a great deal of controversy concerning the brutality it engendered. However, newspapers of the day glorified the game and added a special football language which led to the development of a college football subculture. That subculture includes the all-important recruitment of new talent each year. This in turn has led to much criticism concerning the majority of college football players who either do not ever graduate or who do poor academic work.

College football has led to much commercialism in that large corporations advertise at football games. Television is most responsible for this commercialism, as it has created a tremendous following for the game.

Injuries, and even fatalities, are common among football players. These are minimized by both team doctors and management.

Football is enhanced by the introduction of female cheerleaders, who have been employed by the game since the 1920s. Today, cheerleaders can expect the adulation of the fans and a great deal of publicity. In fact, television has promoted the cheerleader as the image of a sex symbol. Television is also the driving force behind professional football, for which it raises enormous revenue each year.

Chapter 3

Football As a Profession

A BRIEF HISTORY OF PROFESSIONAL FOOTBALL

"Pro-football is paid poorly, attracting mostly collegians who could do no better in the depressed job market." That is indeed a strange sentence in view of the immense amount of money that football attracts at the beginning of the twenty-first century.[1]

A professional, whether in football or any other sport, is someone who gets paid for participating in the sport. Therefore, William W. (Pudge) Heffelfinger was the first American professional football player because he was paid $500 for playing a game in November 1892. At that time, $500 was the annual income of a rural family or a public school teacher.[2] Subsequently, Heffelfinger and his teammates were paid $100 per game while playing for the Allegheny Athletic Association from 1892 to 1896. The Allegheny Athletic Association then went out of business for lack of money. The Pittsburgh Athletic Club also paid football players at the end of the nineteenth century. Lason Fiscus was paid for playing football for the Greenburg (Pennsylvania) Athletic Association in 1894, as was John K. Brallier, who received $10 plus expenses from the Latrobe, Pennsylvania, YMCA for playing on its team. In later years the great athlete Jim Thorpe participated in paid football games, thus gradually moving the game into a professional stance.

It wasn't until August 20, 1920, however, that a professional football league was first organized in this country. On that day, a Canton, Ohio, auto dealer, Ralph Hay, and several businessmen from Canton, Cleveland, Akron, and Dayton formed the American Professional Football Conference. Shortly thereafter teams from Buffalo and Rochester, New York, also joined. One year later the group changed its name to the American Professional Football Association. Subsequently, the 1921 meeting included George Halas, a baseball and football player and an engineer from Chicago, as well as Jim Thorpe, who was appointed manager.

Then, in 1922 the team managers, meeting in Cleveland, Ohio, changed the name of the organization to the National Football League (NFL). By then the league had established itself in a number of smaller midwestern towns such as Green Bay, Wisconsin, but also in Chicago. There were no teams west of Kansas City because train travel was too slow to permit expansion into the West. In the 1930s the inclusion of "Red" Grange brought a number of fans to the games played as far east as New York City, where the Giants had been organized mainly on the strength of his reputation.

In December 1932, the Portsmouth Spartans played the Chicago Bears indoors for the championship in Chicago. George Halas owned the Bears. Eleven-thousand fans came to see the game.

In 1936 several teams organized the new American Football League (AFL). This league was in no way related to the earlier league by the same name. The new league included the Boston Shamrocks, the New York Yankees, the Cleveland Rams, the Pittsburgh Americans, the Syracuse-Rochester Braves, and the Brooklyn Tigers. The AFL never succeeded very well. In fact, in the late 1930s there were three AFLs. Meanwhile, the NFL attracted more and more spectators after national radio broadcasts popularized their games in the 1940s. Numerous sportswriters also attended these games. However, during World War II it became increasingly difficult to find football players who were not in the armed services. It was only after that war that attendance at such games reached a total of over 1 million for all teams playing in the country on any specific weekend.

The AFL had now been renamed the All-America Football Conference (AAFC) but encountered little success. There was also then a Pacific Coast Football Conference, but it too was regarded as "minor league." The last season in which the subsequent American Football League played was 1969, three years after the National Football League commissioner announced the merger of the AFL and the NFL. Combined scheduling began in 1970, allowing the league to become one of the most profitable enterprises in the United States.[3]

Because of the phenomenal success the NFL has enjoyed through the television medium, Vince McMahon, a wrestling promoter, founded the Extreme Football League (XFL) in February 2001. That league consisted of eight teams, including the New York/New Jersey Hitmen, the Los Angeles Xtremes, the Memphis Maniax, the Birmingham Thunderbolts, the San Francisco Demons, the Orlando Rage, the Chicago Enforcers, and the Las Vegas Outlaws. The first game of the XFL drew astoundingly high ratings on NBC, garnering nearly 10 percent of the viewing audience. Yet by the second week viewership had fallen to 50 percent of the previous week, and by the third week it fell another twenty-five percent. Thereafter the ratings declined so much that the XFL lasted only one season. Despite their belligerent names, these teams were unable to sustain an audience. It may well be that the crass jokes, silly announcements, loud and lurid scenes, and extra-sexy cheerleaders all contributed to the failure of the XFL. All told, the XFL achieved only twelve telecasts then failed to sustain an audience in its second year and was dropped from all telecasts when the audience became too small for the advertisers.[4] Now, only the National Football League survives as an outdoor league.[5]

In view of the failure of all other football leagues to compete successfully with the NFL, it is indeed surprising that two other leagues are now attracting an audience. One is the Women's Professional Football League (WPFL), and the other is the Arena Football League (AFL), which seems to have succeeded.

The Women's Professional Football League was organized in 1999, although women have played tackle football since the 1960s. The league formed when two teams of women met in Minneapolis, Minnesota. The teams were called the Minnesota Vixens and the Lake Michigan Minx. Their coach was John Turner, former Minnesota Vikings coach. The teams toured the country and concluded their travels with an all-star game in Miami. In addition, the women played an exhibition game prior to Super Bowl XXXIV in Atlanta and prior to Superbowl XXXV in Tampa.

Since then, six teams have joined the WPFL. The league has played two World Women's Professional Football Champion title games, won by Houston in 2000 and in 2001, before approximately 2,000 fans.[6]

Arena football, as the name suggests, is played indoors. The Arena Football League begins play in April and finishes in August so that football fans can see football on TV even in the summer months when the NFL does not play. There are, of course, a number of differences between arena football and outdoor professional football. These include the size of the field. The field in NCAA football and in the NFL is 120 yards long including the two end zones and is $53\frac{1}{3}$ yards wide. The AFL indoor field is only 66 yards long including two eight-yard end zones and is $28\frac{1}{3}$ yards wide. There are numerous other differences in the manner in which AFL and NFL games are carried out, scored, and played. These differences are in part the product of the indoor limitations faced by the AFL but not the NFL. Salaries in arena football are far less than in NFL football. In AFL football a quarterback can expect only $40,000 to $150,000, while typical salaries for all players range from $30,000 to $50,000.[7]

Other differences in rules are designed to make indoor football faster and more exciting and, above all, entertaining to the television audience.

THE COMING OF TELEVISION

On October 22, 1939, NBC (the National Broadcasting Company) televised a professional football game from Ebbets Field between the Brooklyn Dodgers and Philadelphia Eagles. The Dodgers won 23-14. This game was attended by a crowd of 13,050 and seen by about 500 New York viewers who had a television set at that time. The entire game lasted only two hours and thirty-three minutes. There were only two cameras and no lighting, so the picture depended on the amount of sunlight available. Whenever a cloud covered the sun, there was no picture.[8]

Since 1939, television has caused the greatest revolution in sports history, as football and other sports increased their followings by millions. The New England Patriots beat the Carolina Panthers 32-29 in Super Bowl XXXVIII, played on February 2, 2004. This win had been expected by the media and the gambling establishment, although few thought the margin of victory would be so small. Because more than 100 million viewers watched that game, CBS charged $2.3 million for each thirty-second spot, up from $2.2 million the previous year.[9]

Fox Television also signed an $8 billion, eight-year contract with the NFL to broadcast these games. More than thirty companies will each pay more than $1.8 million for each thirty-second commercial, or more than $53,000 per second. Nevertheless, advertising on NFL games on broadcast and cable TV declined 23 percent in 2002 in one of the worst markets since World War II. The reason for this was undoubtedly the glut of sports-content television programs as well as the recession that began in January of that year.[10]

The value of a professional football team has become phenomenal. When the Washington Redskins were sold to a conglomerate of investors in 1999, they paid $800 million for the team. The owners are only too willing to pay such prices because they demand lavish new stadiums from the cities in which they operate. These stadiums are financed by the taxpayers so that the owners gain the profits at the expense of the public. It was in that spirit that Hartford, Connecticut, offered the New England Patriots a new stadium worth $280 million in order to lure that football team from Foxboro, Massachusetts. An additional $70 million was guaranteed by the city to acquire the site and provide 26,000 parking spaces. A $15 million practice site was also included in this deal, another $10 million was to be spent on environmental cleanup, and another $170 million was to be set aside for future improvements. When the city and the owner of the Patriots, Robert Kraft, failed to agree on these provisions, the Kraft family built its own stadium with private funds next to the old Foxboro, Massachusetts, stadium. The old stadium was torn down. This makes the New England Patriots one of only a few teams in the United States playing on a privately financed field.

The owner of the Patriots, Robert Kraft, is to receive all stadium revenues from food, parking, and surcharges on each ticket sold. Although Kraft financed his own stadium, most of the others are taxpayer funded.

When the Rams and Raiders left Los Angeles for St. Louis and Oakland, respectively, the Cleveland Browns went to Baltimore and changed their name to the Baltimore Ravens, despite the offer by Cleveland to spend $175 million on a new stadium in a year that saw the closing of eleven Cleveland schools for lack of money.[11]

In 1999 a new expansion team brought professional football back to Cleveland. The new team was once more called the Cleveland

Browns in honor of coach Paul Brown, who coached the team from 1946-1962. Numerous other moves occurred by football teams whose owners gained immense profits from such moves or by threatening to move. For example, Denver, Colorado, spent $260 million on a new stadium after the owners threatened to leave the city after the Denver Broncos had just won the Superbowl by beating the Green Bay Packers in January 1998. The Packers, who had won the previous year, did not leave, nor did they threaten to do so. The Packers are community owned, while the Broncos are owned by one or a group of investors.

The Packers, then, are the objects of community pride. Moreover, football in Green Bay, Wisconsin, or elsewhere has always brought people of different backgrounds together. The rich and the not-so-rich, blacks and whites, women and men, old and young, all root for the home team, which they own. It is of course true that fans in other cities also display civic pride and a sense of gemeinschaft around the achievements of their football team. However, that civic pride can be suddenly destroyed when owners demand that taxpayers spend billions to satisfy their demands. In the 1990s, and until 2006, $7 billion have been spent or will be spent by taxpayers to meet the demands of owners who want new stadiums or renovations of old ones.[12]

Stadiums have an anticipated life span of twenty to thirty years. Therefore, most owners prefer to build a new stadium at the end of such a period rather than renovate the old facility. Since the expense of such a new stadium is usually borne by the taxpayer, it is evident why renovation is not popular among owners. The owners are obliged to share their radio and television revenues with the NFL. That, however, does not apply to money earned in the stadium.[13]

Even more money is made by the owners by selling fans a so-called Personal Seat License. The "license" allows the licensee to pay a second time for a ticket. This means that the average taxpayers who funded the stadium will not be able to afford attending a game in the stadium as the price for a poor seat at an NFL game is now $40 to $50. This means that two people attending an NFL game pay approximately $100 for the seats and also pay for parking and food. More expensive seats went for $200 and even $360 each to see the Miami Dolphins play the Detroit Lions on September 8, 2002.

More money is made by selling upward of 15,000 seats for $2,000 to $3,000 a year; in addition, luxury boxes in each stadium increase revenues even more.

Some claim that the states and cities gain from these football investments because the usual 10 percent tax on all purchases related to football games gives the state a return on the taxpayers' money. That, however, is highly unlikely and is generally no more than an unrealizable excuse used by politicians who need to entertain the voters before the next election.[14]

In June 1999, Professor Andrew Zimbalist of Smith College testified before the U.S. Senate Committee on the Judiciary. Zimbalist is the author of a number of books concerning the economics of sports. His testimony held that "all academic studies have found that there is no statistically significant positive effect from having a new team or stadium in an area's economy."[15]

The income from televised football also includes the revenues gained from advertisers. It contains the salaries paid football players and the money paid sportscasters. "Top" sportscasters earn $1 million a year or more. Even football analysts and play-by-play announcers earn between $300,000 and $600,000. Examples are Bonnie Bernstein, a CBS-NFL reporter who receives $175,000 to $200,000 a year, Joe Gibbs, a football analyst who earns $300,000 a year, the famous Pat Summerall who receives $1.5 million a year, and former NFL quarterback Norman J. "Boomer" Esiason who receives $1.6 million from ABC as a football analyst. CBS sportscaster Jim Nantz receives $2.5 million from CBS, and John Madden received between $6.5 million and $8.5 million a year as a football analyst for Fox TV. This contrasts sharply with the mean annual earnings of sports announcers throughout the country, dealing with all sports, whose annual wage was only $27,320 in 2000.[16]

Beginning with the 2002-2003 season, the team of Summerall and Madden ended when Madden was appointed to comment on Monday Night Football. Madden was replaced by Brian Baldinger, who retired from thirteen years as an NFL offensive lineman in 1995.[17]

Television is not the only medium broadcasting football games. Sports are also broadcast on the radio. The NFL used Westwood One/CBS Sports as the exclusive network for all eighty-seven games broadcast in the 2002-2003 season. Westwood One serves more than 7,700 radio stations.[18]

In view of all the money derived from football, the players too have achieved considerable salaries. Examples include some of the players among the Kansas City Chiefs: Marc Boerigter, a wide receiver, received $2,955,000 over seven years; Lew Bush, a linebacker, signed for $11 million over four years; Duance Clemens, a defensive end, will earn $16 million over five years; Todd Collins, the backup quarterback, receives $1,200,000 per year; and Trent Green, quarterback, will earn $17,650,000 in five years.

It is noteworthy that the median and mean salaries paid by various teams to football players vary a good deal among them. For example, the median salary paid by the Buffalo Bills in 2001 was $396,847. In that same year, the Miami Dolphins paid a median salary of $695,000. Other teams paid median salaries between these extremes.[19]

These salaries may seem large, yet baseball player Alex Rodriguez signed a $252 million contract over ten years with the Texas Rangers, which the New York Yankees continued when he joined that team in 2004. Huge salaries are also paid to basketball players. Baseball players can earn salaries far higher than those paid to any football player because baseball does not involve a salary cap, as is required in football. The NFL shares its income from television with all teams equally, no matter how much or how little each team collected from TV broadcasts. This permitted each team to spend $71 million for players' salaries in 2002 and $73.9 million in 2003. Evidently, such a salary cap makes it imperative that not too much is spent on any one player, since the certainty of injuries requires that good backup players are available to each team. The average roster of NFL teams is fifty-three players. In 2003, the total league players' salaries amounted to $2,387 billion.

Owners receive additional income from the sale of seats, from corporate sponsors, from the sale of food during the game, and from parking fees. Players may earn extra income from endorsements as do other entertainers. For example, in April 2002, the Adolph Coors brewery paid $15 million in annual rights fees, $25 million in guaranteed promotion, and additional millions in advertisement spending to the NFL for the privilege of becoming the official beer sponsor of the National Football League.[20]

Entertainment of all kinds is extremely profitable for those who achieve the highest salaries in their field. Similar to some superstars in the sports entertainment industry some actors collect equally high incomes. Harrison Ford, one of the biggest moneymakers in movie history, receives $25 million for acting in one movie for twenty days. This salary is justified by the movie industry because Ford has made twenty-eight films which earned the industry $5.4 billion. In addition to these salaries, the best known entertainers and athletes also collect considerable compensation for endorsing numerous products, particularly athletic equipment.[21]

In 1993, Coca-Cola USA signed twenty-eight NFL football players to a series of ads called "Monsters of the Gridiron," including former New York Jets defensive back Ronnie Lott, Los Angeles Raiders former defensive lineman Howie Long, former New York Giants linebacker Lawrence Taylor, former Minnesota Vikings defensive end Tim Doleman, and former Detroit Lions linebacker Pat Swilling.[22]

Since then, Dallas Cowboy Emmitt Smith has endorsed Visa and the long distance service 10-10-220. Texas Ranger Rafael Palmeiro was featured in ads for Viagra, and Alex Rodriguez promoted Radio Shack. All three of these athletes received six-figure incomes from these advertisements.[23]

Likewise, three members of the Indianapolis Colts football team succeeded in gaining large incomes for endorsing a variety of products in 2001. Quarterback Peyton Manning has endorsed Adidas shoes, First Tennessee Bank, Tennessee Beef, Tops grocery chain, Sprint, Gatorade, and others for between $3 million and $5 million. His success is no doubt due to his status as Heisman Trophy runner-up, but also because his father Archie Manning was already known as former quarterback with the New Orleans Saints a generation ago. Colts running back Edgerrin James and wide receiver Marvin Harrison profited from endorsements of Nike shoes and Degree antiperspirant, respectively. Neither earned as much from these endorsements as Manning. Nevertheless, both men made deals in the mid-five or low six figures. Of course, the greater the exposure of a football player, the greater his chances of gaining lucrative endorsements. This would be true of those who are included in Monday-night football as well as those whose performance gains national attention.

Maximum marketing opportunities are of course available to those who win the Superbowl, as did John Elway, former quarterback of the Denver Broncos.[24]

Former Buffalo Bills quarterback Doug Flutie has endorsed Fleet Bank, Quality Inn, Wegman's, Coca-Cola, Puma, and others. Flutie seeks to increase the assets of his "Doug Flutie Jr. Foundation," a charitable organization devoted to the cure of autism and established for his son.[25]

Eric Moulds, also a Buffalo Bill and a wide receiver, has endorsed NITRO-TECH, a natural protein supplement. Although that supplement contains no ingredients on the NFL's banned substance list, Moulds has ceased all connection with the manufacturer, who also produces other products that are banned by the league.[26]

Football heroes who have turned their fame into moneymaking business careers can be exemplified by Roger Staubach, the chief executive officer of the Staubach Co. of Dallas, Texas. Staubach won the Heisman Trophy while playing college football in 1963 and was a two-time Superbowl winner with the Dallas Cowboys. He retired in 1979 and continued his off-season career in real estate to become the head of a company earning $250 million in 2001.

Such business success is largely the product of the ex-football player's fame. To quote one of Staubach's competitors in the real estate business: "The difference is, I go into a customer's office and make a presentation, and I say, 'I hope the chairman liked me.' Roger goes in, and the chairman says, 'I hope Roger liked me.' "[27]

Amid all these financial successes are the majority of "average" NFL players. The average player plays only 3.2 years in professional football. Furthermore, all but the most successful face the continuous threat of being dropped from the roster because the NFL has a strict limit on the number of players a team may employ. The most senior players are at greatest risk of losing their jobs because a continuous stream of younger men is constantly entering the football arena. At the same time, these young men may be dropped from the roster because they have not been able to establish their value to the team. In short, football is a risky occupation.[28]

Professors Hadley, Poitras, Ruggiero, and Knowles found that winning teams had an average of four yards per rush, while losing teams had an average of 3.9 yards per rush—a small, yet important

difference. The difference is, of course, related to player performance. Yet the evidence indicates that coaches also make a difference. According to the study by Hadley and colleagues, "an efficient
head coach can gain three to four additional victories for his team"—
a very significant number since professional football teams play sixteen games per season. It is also certain that the most experienced
coaches are generally more efficient than those who have little experience. Therein lies another dilemma for football coaches who are unlikely to retain their jobs if they lose. How does a beginning coach
gain experience if he cannot stay on the job unless he wins at once
like someone with years of experience behind him?[29]

RACE AND THE NFL

Football coaches and football team owners are also confronted
with the race issue. From 1933 to 1946, blacks were entirely excluded
from the National Football League. It was not until the end of World
War II that this racial barrier was eliminated.

During the early years of the NFL some blacks were on the rosters
of several teams. Robert Marshall, the first black to play professional
football, played for Rock Island. Fred Slater played for Chicago, and
Paul Robeson, Fritz Pollard, Jay Williams, Joe Lillard, and Ray
Kemp constituted the rest of the black contingent in professional
football. All these men played for the NFL before 1933.[30]

Thereafter, no more blacks were hired by the NFL until 1946.
Those who, like Kemp, had played in earlier years faced constant harassment. Black players were unable to stay in the same hotels as
white players, and had to rent rooms in hotels catering only to blacks
in black neighborhoods. Blacks could not eat in the same restaurants
as white players, and therefore coaches who had black players on
their team faced logistic problems. In addition, white players and fans
insulted black players as well as the mostly white team on which a
black was playing. Such harassment was also directed at Jewish players such as Sid Luckman in football and Hank Greenberg in baseball.

Although blacks were not hired and had disappeared from the
game entirely by 1934, owners and coaches insisted that there was no
racial bias in professional football. It is important to recall that before

World War II and even before the 1960s blacks were treated atrociously in all facets of American life. Segregation was almost total before 1960. There were separate schools, separate churches, separate restaurants, even separate drinking fountains. Therefore, the unjust treatment black football players endured was consistent with the injustices to which blacks were subject all over America.

Before the Civil Rights Movement of the 1960s, Southern colleges refused to play any sport against desegregated teams. Therefore, blacks were benched when such games were played. Outstanding black players were denied recognition and were excluded from captaincies, conference honors, or All-America recognition.[31]

During World War II, a few black players were recruited to play minor league professional football on the West Coast. In 1944 the Pacific Coast Professional League and the American Professional League had several desegregated teams. As the war progressed and many black servicemen and -women served their country, the exclusion of blacks from employment became more and more obnoxious to white Americans as well as blacks. Prodded by black labor leaders, President Franklin D. Roosevelt established the Committee on Fair Employment Practices. This committee became a catalyst in increasing employment opportunities for blacks, including employment in sports.

The end of segregation in professional football came when coach Paul Brown of the Cleveland Browns invited Bill Willis and Marion Motley to play for the Cleveland franchise. Both men encountered racial taunts and both were barred from playing against Miami because Florida law forbade integration. After Cleveland, Baltimore, Los Angeles, and San Francisco signed black players, racial exclusion for professional football players came to an end entirely in the early 1950s.[32]

Nevertheless, according to a report released by lawyers Johnnie Cochran Jr. and Cyrus Mehri, the National Football League continues to discriminate against black coaches. That report shows that the NFL hired more than 400 head coaches since 1920. Only six (1.5 percent) were black. Only two of the most recent twenty-two head coach hires have been of African descent. In addition to coaches, NFL coordinators are 72 percent white even though 70 percent of all players are black. Only two of the thirty-two NFL teams have African-American coaches. They are Tony Dungy of Indianapolis and Herman Edwards of the New York Jets. This discrepancy may come to an end soon because the NFL does now have 154 black assistant coaches.[33]

Race may also have an effect on the opportunities and compensation of football players. It has been argued that racial discrimination in professional football uses "racial stacking" as a means of denying black players equal opportunities to access the central positions. The consequence of that denial is that African-American players must compete for peripheral positions. If that is true, then it can be readily understood that blacks will have less opportunity to exhibit leadership in football than is true of whites, solely because they are prevented from occupying positions that allow leadership to be exhibited. Most important is the position of quarterback. Traditionally, all quarterbacks in the NFL have been white. This has now changed. In January 2001 four of the eight teams remaining in the National Football League play-offs had black quarterbacks. These included Minnesota Vikings Daunte Culpepper, Donovan McNabb of the Philadelphia Eagles, Shaun King of the Tampa Bay Buccaneers, and Aaron Brooks of the New Orleans Saints. The evidence that blacks can do well in the position of quarterback is best illustrated by keeping in mind that in 2002, six of the top eight rushing quarterbacks in the NFL were black.[34]

FOOTBALL FANATICS

Those who are totally wedded to the excitement and entertainment offered by football are usually called "fans" or fanatics. The need to identify with a sports team has a number of features which have been observed for many years. For example, season ticket holders will view every college and professional football game they can attend for thirty or forty years or more.

A good deal has been written about the motivation of such fans. There are those who say that watching violent games serves as a catharsis for the fans and allows them to relieve themselves of the aggression they would otherwise visit upon others. Dr. William Beausay, president of the Academy for the Psychology of Sports, interviewed 800 football fans and concluded that watching football games was "far more therapeutic than six months of therapy for a lot of neurotic people."[35]

Because sports appeals to so many people, neurotic or not, it appears fairly certain that football provides many viewers with an opportunity to escape the difficulties of daily life for a brief time each week or more. Sports are an escape valve allowing the viewers to forget their troubles and to identify with success, power, and aggression. In the South, football takes on an additional meaning. There it is a statewide religion. Football, like religion, is performed in a place specifically designated for that purpose. Like a house of worship, a synagogue, church, mosque, or temple, a football field is used only on specified occasions. Sports and religion celebrate an activity in a "consecrated" culturally significant place. It has been said that in "The Boston Garden of the Celtics" or "The Forum of the Lakers," which are "cathedrals of sport," we find "a moment of peace and of aspirations." Football, nevertheless, promotes a great deal of excitement because it is time-bound. The fans know that the game lasts only one hour, so that a great deal of emotion is attached to the pressure that expiration of the game engenders.[36]

Sports, also like religion, creates a community of worshipers. Sports allow the spectators to feel a sense of belonging by creating in-groups and out-groups.[37]

This is visible in the creation in 1963 of the Football Hall of Fame, which was organized in Canton, Ohio. In January 2004 it included 225 players. Among them are Roger Staubach, Harold "Red" Grange, and such renowned players as Elroy Hirsch, Mike Ditka, Terry Bradshaw, Walter Payton, Johnny Unitas, and the Bills quarterback Jim Kelly and his coach, Marv Levy. The 2004 inductees in the Pro-Football Hall of Fame were Bob Brown who had played with the Philadelphia Eagles, the Oakland Raiders, and the Los Angeles Rams. Carl Eller of the Minnesota Vikings, Barry Saunders who played ten years with the Detroit Lions, and the great quarterback John Elway of the Denver Broncos were also selected. Such a "hall of fame" takes on a quasi-religious coloring as the "saints" of the profession are "worshipped" in a sacred place where their reward is certain.[38]

One of the greatest football "saints" is Jim Thorpe, whose statue is the first a visitor sees on entry to the Football Hall of Fame. Exhibits include "The First Century of Pro Football." A "Pro Football Adventure Room" includes exhibits concerning the "Other Leagues," that is, other than the NFL; an "Enshrinee Mementos Room" displays mementos concerning the teams of each Hall of Fame honoree; and several interactive theaters allow visitors to be quarterbacks and participate in a Super Bowl game.

This quasi-religious atmosphere may be also seen and heard at any football game when the fans shriek and scream in the manner of a revival meeting. Football is a performance that has predictable experiences, including the opportunity to escape isolation and become part of the greater human society. Football is very predictable because it has so many rules. These rules restrict, but they also determine that actions will not be done at random. The fans know that these rules make for controlled violence, which differs from uncontrolled violence in that the former is not really dangerous but the latter can be deadly. In addition, fans enjoy the identification with the achievements of the football players. This has the danger of leading some fans to actually live in the world of football (or other sport) to the exclusion of anything else. Such overidentification of some fans with football suggests a form of emotionally retarded behavior which makes the superfan appear like someone who has never left childhood.[39]

Such retardation is most visible in fans who seek to maintain a positive social identity by identifying with aggression. Students of aggression have generally approached spectator aggression from one of three theories. Beginning with Sigmund Freud and continuing with Konrad Lorenz, the "instinctual" view was continued by Otto Fenichel. That view as well as the second theory, the "frustration-aggression" hypothesis, has had its critics and proponents. Third is social learning theory, which holds that aggression is learned, as is everything else we do.

The psychologist Daniel Wann has used the definition of spectator identification with football aggression, which he developed in 1992. Spectator identification is described as "the extent to which individuals perceive themselves as fans of the team, are involved with the team, are concerned with the team's performance, and view the team as representatives of themselves." The principal contention here is that the degree of identification with the team is a major element in predicting spectator behavior. Wann argues that "spectator aggression is more likely to occur in persons high in identification with the team, relative to those low in identification." This then can lead to aggression against members of the opposing team and their supporters.[40]

Such aggression permits the spectators to maintain their social identity in the same fashion as is generally done by everyone. Three such tactics are used by football fans and others. The first may be called "basking in reflected glory." This tactic can be used to enhance one's self-esteem by associating with successful groups. Research has shown that the number of students wearing university insignia increases with the number of victories achieved by the university football team. A second tactic is for students and others to use the word "we" more often when describing a victory while attributing defeats to "they" or "them." Evidently, defeat led to a decrease in the wearing of identifying badges and insignia. Finally, there are those who "blast" others when they feel their identity is threatened by defeat. The target of such aggression may even be someone not at all responsible for the defeat.[41]

Sachs and Chu studied the association between professional football games and domestic violence. They found that the number of police dispatches concerning domestic violence in Los Angeles County increased 100 percent per week during football season and 264 percent during the Super Bowl week. Such domestic violence increases were also found during the entire football season compared to the months when professional football was not played.[42]

Domestic violence induced by football becomes most visible when conducted by football players. Football is a collision and combative sport legitimating violence. Some have called football "controlled violence" because the game includes numerous rules as to how violence may be carried out.

THE DOMESTIC LIVES OF FOOTBALL PLAYERS

It is no secret that sports and masculinity are regarded as synonymous in American culture. This is the outcome of the gradual abrogation of male superiority in American life. As the American frontier disappeared, as the need for two-fisted laborers in such industries as steel and coal declined precipitously, as women's rights and female ascendancy gained more and more power in the United States, men retreated to sports, and particularly football, as the last refuge of those who could no longer ascertain their dominance in the marketplace or the home.[43]

This need to dominate in the domestic sphere and not only on the playing fields is accentuated by the position occupied by wives of football players in the lives of their husbands and in their families. Ortiz has summarized this attitude in the phrase: "You are like a kid; you are seen but not heard."

Because most wives of football players have children, it is not possible for them to travel with the football club more than on a few occasions. Many football clubs discourage the presence of wives because many managers view their presence as disruptive, believing that wives belong at home and not "on the road."[44]

This makes wives strangers if they travel on the road trips with their football player husbands, so that they have nonperson status which forces them to adopt a code of conduct that is unwritten, but nevertheless enforced. Ortiz explains that a variety of rituals are used in the all-male world of the football club which are designed to keep wives under control.

Ortiz interviewed numerous wives of football players and found that those who travel with their husbands are often lonely or do not trust their husbands on the road because adultery is quite common among professional athletes. Ortiz calls this the "adultery culture," which exists in all major sports as the players travel from city to city during the season. Ortiz shows that team players stay in hotels which usually have a bar where so-called "groupies" gather in order to score with the athletes. Here, married men meet other women, so that wives traveling with athlete husbands are forced by public opinion to stay away from these bars so that they do not become witnesses to the meetings between married men and women who seek them out in these bars. Wives, then, must stay out of hotel bars. Ortiz reports that "in the world of the professional football player the hotel may also be off-limits for the wives on away games." This is also necessary because many of the athletes make little effort to conceal their sexual activities with other women in bars. Wives are afraid of getting caught watching the adultery of married team members who regard wives as a threat. This is also true of husbands who bring their wives along and who need to support the "code" which allows adultery to go "unseen" and "unmentioned."[45]

Adultery is not the only form of deviance conducted by professional football players. The other form is violence against women. This behavior becomes acute when the controlled violence of the football field spills over into the larger society or the private sphere of the football players. Evidently a few football players employ hypermasculinity together with aggression and elevated status as a means of sanctioning violence off the field. Sexual aggression is particularly identified with football, as the language used to describe sexual aggression indicates. Thus, attaining sexual intercourse is called a "score." To score sexually is viewed as a victory and the female objects of such scores are called "trophies" or "conquests." The word "beating" is used to indicate defeating the football opponent as are other words which have a double meaning, one for football and the other for sexual aggression.[46]

Because athletes, and in particular football players, have elevated hero status, prestige, and privileges, they are more likely than athletes in other sports to contribute to sexual aggression. Football players also run the risk of false accusations. Sexual aggression against women by football players is so common that examples of such conduct are easily obtained and include the following. In August 2002, Georgia football player Brandon Williams went on trial in that state for rape, aggravated sexual battery, and aggravated assault.[47] In September 1996 Lawrence Phillips, a St. Louis Rams running back, pleaded no contest on charges of battery and sexual assault on a female student at the University of Nebraska, which he had attended. Phillips was accused of beating the woman and holding her against her will.[48] Shortly thereafter, Phillips was arrested for driving intoxicated and speeding at eighty miles an hour with a flat tire.[49]

In January 2001, Rae Carruth, former NFL player, was sentenced to eighteen years in prison for plotting the shooting death of his pregnant fiancée. That same month, New York Giants defensive lineman Christian Peter was dropped from the roster because of his extensive history of violence against women. In one case Peter pleaded guilty to third-degree sexual assault.[50] Likewise, in 1996, NFL player Warren Moon was convicted of choking his wife. Moon had assaulted her in

1995 as well as on several other occasions. Moon was acquitted of these charges because his wife refused to testify against him. Later that year Moon extended his contract with the Vikings for another three years, earning $15 million.[51]

No doubt the most spectacular case of wife abuse by a professional football player was the accusation and indictment of O. J. Simpson, former running back for the Buffalo Bills, of murdering his wife, Nicole Brown Simpson, and a waiter, Ronald Goldman, in June 1994. Simpson was found not guilty of these killings in October 1995 but was found liable for murdering both victims in a civil trial in 1997. The civil jury awarded the victims' relatives $8.5 million.

Professor Michael Welch of the Criminal Justice Department at Rutgers University has analyzed the positions played by 100 football players convicted of assaulting women and found that running backs, receivers, cornerbacks, and safeties, i.e., scorers and defensive backs, made up 59 percent of his sample. Welch attributes this excess of offensive backfield players among the assaulters of women to the need for these players to dominate their opponents. It may be reasonably added that many football players, beginning with high school, believe that they are entitled to dominate and violate women.

PROFESSIONAL FOOTBALL PLAYERS AS VICTIMS

In June 2002, 260 NFL rookies were assembled at a golf course in Carlsbad, California, to hear the warnings of veteran players, financial experts, and others concerning the dangers they face in playing for the NFL. The dangers discussed at the symposium had nothing to do with the physical violence they all face on the football field. Instead, the dangers discussed had everything to do with financial swindles, sex and its offshoot paternity, lawsuits of all kinds, and the danger of cosigning for other people's debts.

Because so many of the young football players have no financial experience, they are easily divorced from their money. Because they suddenly earn millions of dollars these young men are led to spend huge amounts on family and friends until they have nothing left. Some football players buy cars for their girlfriends, pay off mortgages for relatives, or invest in restaurants and other enterprises which fail.[52]

Most dangerous for the young, sudden millionaires of the NFL are criminal investment counselors. An example is the career of Donald Lukens, who was convicted in 2001 of defrauding investors in four mortgage-backed "security" offerings. Lukens operated a business he called Global Sports and Entertainment. He claimed to be of help to professional athletes, particularly football players. With the money football players and others entrusted to him, Lukens secretly enriched himself through undisclosed commissions and fees. He also claimed that he would invest millions of dollars entrusted to him by investors in stocks and other securities. Instead he used the money to pay off his personal debts. All told, he diverted between $12.5 and $18 million, mostly derived from football players who trusted him and did not understand finances.[53]

Lukens is by no means the only one who swindles NFL players out of millions. The FBI investigated Von C. Cummings, an Ohio man, for defrauding Minnesota Vikings all-pro running back Robert Smith. In January 2001, a federal grand jury indicted Darnell Jones and James E. Brown on fifty-six counts of fraud and money launder-ing. At least three NFL players, including Washington Redskins run-ning back Stephen Davis, were defrauded. Davis alone lost $200,000 in Jones's and Brown's schemes. Likewise, Luigi DiFonzo induced a number of NFL players to invest in his firm called DFJItalia. Then, in March 2000, DFJ collapsed under a mountain of debt and the inves-tors lost everything they had given DiFonzo. Even former teammates have defrauded NFL players. In August 2001 former tight end Terry Orr was sentenced to fourteen months in prison for defrauding three former Redskins team members and "friends" of $50,000 each when he used their money to pay personal debts instead of investing their funds in a shoe company he claimed to own.

The NFL Players Association announced in 2002 that in the three preceding years seventy-eight players had been defrauded of $42 mil-lion. Because many players are too embarrassed to report the fraud, the $42 million are probably just the tip of the iceberg.

Women as well as men are involved in schemes designed to de-fraud football players. For example, a former teacher, Linda Fryk-holm, invented the United Nations Trade Honduras Project. This false name allowed her to raise nearly $15 million, mostly from NFL players. She used the money to travel to Switzerland, enroll her children in private schools, and buy a $2 million home. Last year she began a twelve-year prison term for fraud.

Then there is the story of Antoine Winfield. He received a $3.5 million signing bonus from the Buffalo Bills, which he invested with the aid of his closest friend, Duanyasha Mon Yetts. Yetts promptly cheated Winfield out of $1.35 million by putting Winfield's money in his own personal account while lying to Winfield about profits in the stock market, which never existed because none of the money was ever invested there.[54]

The lure of power, money, and sex which accompanies the success of professional football players has been well described by Deion Sanders, the only man to score an NFL touchdown and a home run in the National League in one week. The book describes the destructive influence of so many advantages gained so soon for those who have little experience in resisting every temptation. Sanders may be the only athlete to have succeeded so well in two sports. He is, however, not the only one to have wasted his money, ruined his emotional life, and fallen victim to sexual escapades which yielded only misery.[55]

Finally, football players are victims of the danger inherent in the sport. Head trauma from football injuries often leads to neurological problems in later life. This finding was presented to the American Academy of Neurology at their fifty-second annual meeting in San Diego in May 2000, by Dr. Barry Jordan, director of the brain injury program at Burke Rehabilitation Hospital in White Plains, New York. This study supported earlier findings by other researchers showing cumulative and long-term neurological effects from repeated blows to the head, leading to the "punch drunk" syndrome of speech and movement impairments as seen in some boxers.[56]

PROFESSIONAL FOOTBALL AND SOCIAL CLASS

When football was first played as a college sport it was limited to the so-called upper class, who could afford to send their sons to Harvard, Yale, or Princeton Universities. This limitation of football to the upper strata of American society was also true at the outset of professional football, when only white men played. Before 1889, the All-American Football Team had only English names on its roster. Then, in 1889, one German name, Heffelfinger, was added. Thereafter, some Irish names also appeared on the rosters of football teams. By 1904 a number of Jewish players were included.

Sociologists David Riesman and Reuel Denney wrote that "there is an element of class identification running through American football since its earliest days."[57] The earliest days are the days when football was played only in elite colleges, particularly Yale University. The participants were therefore wealthy college boys of "Anglo" descent. However, when Notre Dame took up the game and became a football powerhouse, men of Irish, Polish, and other ethnic groups entered the football arena and became professional players as well. Prior to 1915 and even some years later, few poor boys could enter college, and therefore only those wealthy enough to do so were ever even near a football game. Furthermore, as the game evolved into the two-platoon system and the T formation, talent was more and more important. Coaching also changed as the game evolved. Coaches became "group-dynamic leaders." In professional football in particular, ability and talent are important while ethnicity is of no concern. This became very visible as the newspapers, radio, and finally television made football into a huge moneymaking enterprise. Those who own football teams demand that their teams win at least some of the time lest they forfeit their audience and their income. Therefore, men of every ethnicity and race are now welcome to play college and professional football.[58]

SUMMARY

Professional football began in the United States in the 1920s, although a few college players had already been paid for playing a game here and there for a local football club. The National Football League was founded in 1922. It was an outgrowth of the American Football League, a name attached to a number of leagues founded and dissolved over time. Radio began to broadcast professional football games in 1940 and together with newspapers made it into a fairly popular sport. Television, beginning in 1939, increased the interest in football immensely. Both the reborn AFL and the NFL prospered, leading to a merger of the two leagues in 1966 and explosion of money and fame for football players, coaches and owners. The Super Bowl, advertisements, and the media created a huge football industry. Taxpayers' money was now spent on stadiums. Enormous salaries are paid to players as the game has acquired numerous followers, some of whom are indeed football fanatics or fans.

Football players are frequently men who cannot handle their sudden wealth and fame and are often led to commit violence in public and against their own families. Their inexperience also permits swindlers to deprive them of their money.

Although football was at one time the province of wealthy Ivy League college boys, football is now played by men from all social classes and ethnic groups of America.

Chapter 4

Football and Social Stratification

THE STATUS OF FOOTBALL PLAYERS

"Social stratification refers to a system by which a society ranks categories of people in a hierarchy." Four basic principles underlie social stratification. First, social stratification is a trait of society. It is much more than differences among individuals. For example, children born into wealthy families are more likely to enjoy good health than children born into poor families.

Social stratification persists over generations. In almost all societies, parents pass their social position on to their children, so that few ever live in a social stratum different from that of their families for untold generations. In American society, however, and in some other industrial and postindustrial societies, some people are able to change their social standing and move up or down on the stratification ladder, a phenomenon known as "social mobility."[1]

Social stratification is universal. In some societies social stratification is related only to inherited wealth. In others, competence and political manipulation are alternatives that allow a few to change their social position. The latter is true of the United States.

Social stratification involves beliefs. Members of some societies believe that social mobility is important and that individuals have a right to advance their own interests if they can do so. Here the Western industrial nations and the United States are the prime examples. In other societies members believe that the status quo must be maintained at all cost.[2]

Social stratification results in status differences. *Status* is any social position that person occupies. Sociologists divide status types into "ascribed" and "achieved." An ascribed status is attained at birth and is beyond the individual's control. Male and female are ascribed statuses because biological differences have social implications. The life cycle of a female is not the same as that of a male in any society. Likewise, race is an ascribed status imposed by social conventions in every society. This is also true of place of birth or sexual orientation. In contrast, occupation is an achieved status, as are education, income, and membership in the Hall of Fame. Every status is part of our social identity. In the United States and in other industrialized countries that identity is usually focused on occupation. The most important feature of status has been labeled as "master status" by sociologists. A football player may have the status of son, husband, father, or club member, yet he will be known for his identity as football player.

Status includes wealth and income, race, religion, place of origin, gender and sexual orientation, and, because it is our master status, active or retired occupational standing. These facts concerning social stratification certainly apply to football and its participants.

WEALTH, INCOME, AND THE FOOTBALL BUSINESS

In the United States the influence of wealth and income on the social standing of Americans is readily apparent. That influence is so great because upward mobility has been a feature of American life since the country's beginnings. In fact, through most of U.S. history we can observe economic expansion, a rise in the standard of living, and the accumulation of immense wealth in the hands of a few. Today about 5 million millionaires live in the United States, and a number of these millionaires are current or former football players. However, the opportunity to earn millions is quite restricted and instead there has been a downward slide in the number and proportion of those who are able to escape poverty or middle class stagnation. Among those who have the opportunity to escape both of these economic dead ends have been professional athletes, particularly football players. For many players athletic ability has been an elevator out of the most abject poverty.

These are, then, the reasons why football as a business and a profession is highly valued in the United States giving its participants an aura of prestige not associated with any occupation not requiring extensive education (as is demanded of professors, doctors, lawyers, and accountants).

This prestige is enhanced by the work football players do, not only because it is part of the entertainment industry but also because it represents power, masculinity, aggression, endurance, and teamwork, attributes highly prized in American culture.

The evidence that football is a very good business is abundant. The National Football League is a $4 billion annual industry. It earns about $1.4 billion in profits every year, which is five times that of the National Basketball Association and far ahead of major league baseball. The NFL is by far the most popular target of sports investors. In 2002 the average salary of football players was $1.4 million, with major stars earning a great deal more. The combined salaries paid in 2003 to all players topped $2.38 billion.

The National Football League has completed twenty-two stadium building projects since 1993 at a cost of over $5 billion, and its investment bonds are rated higher on Wall Street than those of any other major sport.

The franchise values of some NFL teams are also very large. For example, *Forbes* magazine has rated the Redskins at $845 million, the Cowboys at $784 million, and the Browns at $618 million.[3] These financial considerations alone make football a high prestige occupation.

RACE AND FOOTBALL: A "MIXED MARRIAGE"

In the early years of college football the game was played almost exclusively by white, upper-class boys attending Ivy League universities. These universities were closed to racial and religious minorities and to the "ethnics" who were pouring into the United States after 1880 from Southern and Eastern Europe. Therefore, football did not become the universal sport of Americans until after World War II, when African-American and lower class young men first came to college through assistance from the Servicemen's Readjustment Act, also known as the "G.I. Bill of Rights."

For some of these newcomers to American higher education, sports became a social elevator, allowing a few to rise from poverty and contempt to wealth and admiration. However, for the vast majority of those who then and now dream of a sports career, that social elevator does not exist. Instead, most of those who place all their efforts into basketball or football in the vain hope of becoming rich and famous find that they achieve little if anything in college and also fail to achieve a sports career.

This danger is particularly visible in the black community, which places more emphasis on sports than is true of whites. According to a study by sociologist William J. Rudman, blacks are more likely than whites to incorporate sports into their daily lives and to be affected by the outcome of sporting events. This difference between whites and blacks is not racially determined but is the product of differences in social class. Rudman found just that when he included education, age, and social class into his factor analysis. The results clearly showed that the affinity for sports in the black community is related to living in lower income groups.[4] The high value placed on sports has produced unrealistic hopes for millions of youths in the black community. The chances of becoming a professional athlete are very small, and even at the beginning of the twenty-first century many barriers to racial equality in professional sports still exist.

These barriers exist in both college and professional football, where "stacking" is still practiced. This game plan consists of locating African-American football players in mostly defensive positions while giving offensive positions disproportionately to whites. Today, at least 65 percent of all American football players are black. However, almost all quarterbacks, most centers, and a disproportionate number of guards are white. On the defensive side, nearly all cornerbacks are black, which also holds true for most linebackers, defensive tackles, and ends.[5]

Even more pronounced than the "stacking" of black players in some positions is the failure of owners or administrators to appoint black football coaches. In 2003 only five, or 4 percent, of 115 Division 1A college football coaches were black, although 65 percent of players were black.[6] According to Richard E. Lapchick of Northeastern University, about fifteen head football coaching jobs are available each year. Yet few if any of the colleges with openings bother to even interview a black coach. As a result, in Division I only 2.9 percent of football coaches are black, and in Divisions II and III black coaches account for only 1.4 percent of all coaches.

Because black football players seldom occupy such central positions as quarterback, offensive line, and inside linebackers during their college years, black assistant coaches are generally assigned to noncentral positions. Blacks face the additional obstacle that influential alumni and fans prevent the hiring of black coaches to central positions. When black coaches are hired it is often for the sake of monitoring black athletes and not because of their strategic understanding of the game.[7]

Despite the fact that racism continues to create obstacles, both latent and overt, for black football players, the sport attracts black students from their earliest childhood into maturity. The reasons for this great interest in football and other sports among blacks may be found in the "four wishes" outlined by sociologist William Thomas. Thomas wrote that American culture leads Americans to feel strongly about security, response, recognition, and new experiences. These four wishes are culture bound and learned but are nevertheless so strong that they are sometimes mistaken for inborn drives.[8] Because many poor young men are born into unstable families, they discover that sports may give them an "instant family." Sports give those who play together a kind of closeness or response that many may have never felt previously. Therefore, adopting Thomas's scheme, we can understand that sports fulfills the wish for security and response as well as the wish for recognition and new experience. Certainly, achievements in football meet all of these conditions and can go a long way toward fulfilling the needs the "four wishes" represent.

Organized sports are hierarchical, which means that a pyramid of recognition and approval exists which adults confer on youngsters who participate in football, basketball, and other sports in school. As the better football players and other athletes receive more and more recognition from their sports achievements, they pour more and more energy and time into sports activities and less and less into academics. Children therefore learn that being a winner at football is more important than achieving high grades. Performance and winning become very important and may create so much pressure on athletes in school that even the "fun" of playing the game is negated by the need to win and please the audience of adults and other children.[9]

During the high school years, successful athletes will be faced with the choice of making athletics their "master status" or backing away from sports as their only interest.

As mentioned earlier, the chance to fulfill a boyhood dream of becoming a professional athlete, such as an NFL player, is rarely achieved. The hierarchy of sports increasingly narrows as students move from high school to college and then to the professional level. The chances of attaining professional status in football or any other highly paid competitive sport is only four in 100,000 for a white man and two in 100,000 for a black man. Therefore, the majority of would-be football players are informed by coaches that they are not suitable to continue as football players. Others recognize this themselves and weed out the weakest and least talented as they climb up the ladder of the football hierarchy.[10]

Despite the small chance of ever attaining a professional football career, a number of rewards are available to those involved in playing football in high school and college; football opens doors for some and is used as a survival strategy by others. Both in job opportunities and in community affairs, ex-football players are accorded opportunities that might not otherwise be available to them. Ex-football players bring with them an aura of prestige which allows them to make sales, enter board rooms, and bond with other men to a far greater degree than is true of nonathletes.[11]

For a good number of athletes success at football or some other sport is a survival strategy because nothing else is available to elevate themselves from a lower-class life to a higher status. In large American high schools, class and ethnic inequality is very obvious. Clothing, transportation methods, and social activities all serve to differentiate students along class lines. In short, the poor are given little respect unless they achieve in athletics or academically. Poor young women are more likely to follow the academic route because the most popular sports, football and male basketball, are not available to them. Women's basketball does not gain much public attention, although it has some followers. Poor young men usually live in neighborhoods where schools are inadequately equipped and where anti-educational and anti-intellectual attitudes are pervasive. Masculinity in such communities is therefore best attained through athletic achievements and particularly by football, the most aggressive of all team sports. We may say, then, that athletic achievement, and particularly football achievement, represents a survival technique for those who do not have money and therefore face an occupational dead end.

THE JEWISH FOOTBALL EXPERIENCE

Prior to 1948, when Israel became an independent country, Jews everywhere were stereotyped as having no fighting ability, no physical courage, and no sports competence whatsoever. The reasons for these negative beliefs can be found in European Jewish history, which is aptly described by saying that the "Jews of Europe were treated in the same fashion as the blacks in Mississippi before the civil rights movement."[12]

It is not necessary here to refute these bigotries. Suffice it to say that behavior is learned and that the anti-Jewish beliefs and attitudes of American college administrators, faculty members, and students allowed Jewish students to enter American institutions of higher learning in very limited numbers until after World War II. Therefore, Jewish students were seldom represented among the elite football playing colleges, such as Harvard, Yale, or Princeton, at a time when college football, and not professional football, received most of the attention of the American public.

On the eve of World War II, the U.S. Ivy League colleges were almost totally closed to Jewish students. During the 1920s and 1930s, these colleges selected their freshman classes by giving applicants an examination, offering admission to only those who scored high. However, by the middle of the 1920s the examination system had been abolished because "too many" Jews and other ethnic minorities had passed the examination with high marks. Therefore, the three Ivy League colleges, Harvard, Yale, and Princeton, and other colleges, decided to abandon academics as the center of attention for their students and to substitute athletics. "Indeed, scholarship was looked down upon."[13]

As scholarship declined, only those who lacked the financial resources and cultural values that marked the "gentlemen" now achieved high grades and engaged in scholarship. These were the Jews, who looked upon college as the path to upward social mobility. Christians, overwhemingly Protestants of English ancestry, opted for "a gentle-man's C."

As the Jewish students entered Harvard, Yale, and Princeton in ever greater numbers in the 1920s, white, Anglo-Saxon Protestants feared that their dominance of the "Big Three" colleges was threatened. They decided to impose a quota system restricting the number of Jews accepted each year.[14] That quota system was enforced until World War II produced so many veterans whose tuition was paid by the U.S. Veteran's Administration that these prejudices could no longer be supported, as every "Tom, Dick, and Harry" came to the Ivy League colleges and other schools at the expense of the government.

Nevertheless, the inclusion of Jews into the so-called elite colleges of the United States was not fully achieved until the revolutionary 1960s. In the 1950s anti-Jewish discrimination continued in many schools, as depicted in the movie *School Ties* (1992), which deals with the rejection of a Jewish student by his classmates when it became known that he, the star quarterback on the school team, was Jewish.

Inspection of a list of Jewish football players reveals that both before and after the imposition of the anti-Jewish quota system, Jewish football players were members of the teams of Harvard, Yale, and Princeton. For example, Phil King was an All-American in the 1890s at Princeton. Israel Levine played for Pennsylvania in 1905-1906, and Ralph Horween played for Harvard in 1916. Thereafter, only the great Sid Luckman played for an Ivy League school before 1945. Luckman played for Columbia University, a college that had also tried to keep Jews out or at a minimum. However, the presence of a large Jewish population in New York City made it more difficult for Columbia to impose a Jewish quota on admissions than was true in other localities. Luckman is now a member of the Columbia University Football Hall of Fame and of the Pro Football Hall of Fame. After playing halfback at Columbia, Luckman joined the Chicago Bears in 1939 and played quarterback.

Ron Mix, also Jewish, began his career in 1960. Ron Mix has been called "the greatest tackle who ever lived." He was born in Los Angeles in 1938 and attended the University of Southern California on a football scholarship. He played for twelve years with the San Diego Chargers and then the Oakland Raiders. His career as a lineman was so impressive that the Chargers retired his number, 74. In 1969 Mix was named to the all-star AFL team, and in 1979 he was inducted into the Pro Football Hall of Fame.

Mix studied law at night during the football season and became known as "the intellectual assassin." He practices law in San Diego and represents retired players in workmen's compensation claims for athletic-related injuries. After Luckman and Mix, Jewish football players became commonplace in the NFL and in colleges throughout the country, including Jay Fiedler, an engineering graduate of Dartmouth College and starting quarterback for the Miami Dolphins.[15]

PENNSYLVANIA, OHIO, AND TEXAS: MOTHERS OF AMERICAN FOOTBALL

An unusual number of football players, both in higher education and in the profession, were born and raised in Pennsylvania. That this is "unusual" may be seen at once when we consider that as of 2002, twenty-five of the 216 members of the Pro Football Hall of Fame were born in that state, which had only 6 percent of the country's population in 1960. I use the year 1960 as a benchmark because so many of those who are now in the Hall of Fame started their football careers then or shortly before or after that year.

Beginning with Johnny Lujack who was born in Connellsville, Pennsylvania, in 1925, a whole array of famous and not-so-famous football players have come from that state. The coal mining industry offered young men little economic opportunity other than following their fathers and grandfathers into the mines. Therefore, football became an elevator out of the misery of living in the mining country.

Connellsville was typical of many other towns in southwestern Pennsylvania in the 1920s. A town of only 9,250 people, it had at one time been "the king of coal and coke" with a population of 22,000. However, when coal heating gave way to electric and gas heating the town and the county went bust. Coming from such a background, Lujack starred in high school football and earned a scholarship to Notre Dame University. There he won the Heisman Trophy in 1947 after serving three years in the U.S. Navy. In 1960 Lujack was elected to the College Football Hall of Fame.

George Blanda was born in 1927. He too, came from the coal mining country in Western Pennsylvania. His hometown was Youngwood, Pennsylvania, in Westmoreland County, a small railroad town of 3,372 inhabitants. Here too, football was a means out of poverty and lack of opportunity, as Blanda became one of the great football stars of the 1950s and 1960s. Blanda was pro football's all-time leading scorer with 335 field goals. As late as 1967, when he was forty years old, Blanda played for Oakland and kicked 201 consecutive extra points. At age 43, he led Oakland to four wins as the replacement quarterback for Daryle Lamonica. Blanda finally retired one month before his forty-ninth birthday in August 1976.

Joe Namath may well be the most famous football player of all time. He was born in Beaver Falls, Pennsylvania, in 1943. In 1985 he was inducted into the Pro Football Hall of Fame after a thirteen-year career. Namath played for Coach "Bear" Bryant at the University of Alabama and then went to the New York Jets in 1965. That year he was named Rookie of the Year and Most Valuable Player in the AFL All-Star game. Named Player of the Year several times thereafter, Namath received a number of AFL awards as well. He led the Jets to victory in Super Bowl III and ended his career while with the Los Angeles Rams. Namath then appeared in several movies and became the owner of a restaurant that used his nickname, "Broadway Joe."

Fred Biletnikoff was born in Erie, Pennsylvania, in 1943. In 1988 he was inducted into the Pro Football Hall of Fame. Biletnikoff started his football career in high school, where he also starred in basketball and baseball. Biletnikoff had an inborn athletic ability, allowing him to also excel in track and field. He played for Florida State University and was then drafted by the Oakland Raiders as wide receiver. He played in three AFL championship games, six AFC title games, and two Super Bowls, including the 1977 Super Bowl XI, in which he earned MVP honors as the Oakland Raiders beat the Minnesota Vikings 32-14.

Joe Montana is a native of New Eagle, Pennsylvania, where he was born in 1956. He too, came from the coal mining area of his state. As a young boy Montana showed a great deal of talent in basketball and baseball. However, he became an All-American quarterback in his senior year of high school. From there he went to Notre Dame University as a quarterback. In 1979 he was drafted by the San Francisco

49ers where he became the starter in his second season. He remained with the 49ers until a ruptured disk forced him to undergo surgery in 1986. He returned to playing and earned the Most Valuable Player award three times in 1982, 1985, and 1990, and went to the Super Bowl in 1982, 1985, 1989, and 1990. He retired at age thirty-eight in 1994.

Dan Marino, the long-term ex-quarterback of the Miami Dolphins, was also born in Pennsylvania. A native of Pittsburgh, he came from the Oakland neighborhood, which was an ethnically diverse, working-class section of the city when Marino was born in 1961. Educated in the Catholic school system, Marino played quarterback in high school and went from there to the University of Pittsburgh. In 1983 he was drafted by Miami, where he literally became a South Florida icon. No doubt he was the most prolific quarterback in the history of Miami when he retired after the 1999 season. He was the leading passer in the AFC in 1983, 1984, 1986, and 1988. He set an NFL single-season record for touchdown passes in 1984, passing 5,084 yards for forty-eight touchdowns, and was all-time leader in career touchdown passes, passing yards, attempts, and completions.

Jim Kelly, who played quarterback for the Buffalo Bills for eleven seasons, was born in East Brady, Pennsylvania, in 1960. A master of the "no-huddle" offense, he captained the Bills in four Super Bowl appearances, an unprecedented achievement. Kelly first moved to Buffalo in 1993 and joined Hall of Fame coach Marv Levy. He led the Bills in seventeen playoff games and retired with an 84.4 passer rating. In 2002 he was elected to the Pro Football Hall of Fame.

Many other football players also came from Pennsylvania, but all of them cannot be listed here. It is significant, however, that football serves now and in the past as a social ladder for poor boys from mainly "ethnic" families. Since 1960, 23 percent of all Americans live in poverty, defined here as a family of four living at or below the official poverty line established by the U.S. government. A large number of football players came from families who met that criterion.[16]

Pennsylvania is not the only state that has sent an unusual number of football players to the colleges and the NFL. Ohio, which had 5.3 percent of the total American population in 1960, has furnished nineteen, or 9 percent, of the 216 members of the Hall of Fame. The nineteen members include several coaches. No Ohio player born after 1952 has been inducted into the Hall of Fame. The majority of the Hall of Fame members were born in small towns. Large cities such as Cleveland, Columbus, and Cincinnati are all under represented.

For example, Larry Csonka was born in Stow, Ohio, in 1946. Stow has a population of 32,000 and is located in Summit County, about thirty miles from Cleveland. Csonka played eleven seasons in the AFL and the NFL, gaining 8,081 yards. In 1973 and 1974 he won two Super Bowls with the Miami Dolphins. He was named Most Valuable Player in the 1974 Super Bowl, rushing for 145 yards and two touchdowns. He was elected to the College and Pro Football Halls of Fame.

Jack Lambert was born in the village of Mantua, Ohio, in 1952. The village has a population of 1,178 and is located in the Akron area. Lambert attended Kent State University, where he played as a linebacker. He then played eleven seasons with the Pittsburgh Steelers from 1974-1984. In both 1976 and 1981 he was named the club's Most Valuable Player. He was selected as Defensive Player of the Year in two years and All-Pro seven times. He played in nine Pro Bowls from 1975 to 1983 and participated in four Super Bowls.

Likewise, Paul Warfield is a native of the small town of Warren, Ohio, with a population of 42,000. Warfield was drafted by both the Buffalo Bills and Cleveland Browns, for whom he played until he went to Miami. He is credited with catching 427 passes, gaining 8,565 yards, and achieving eighty-five touchdowns.

A number of other natives of small Ohio towns are members of the Pro Football Hall of Fame. Among them are Cliff Battles, born in Akron in 1910; Len Dawson, born in Alliance in 1935; Wilbur Henry, born in Mansfield in 1897; and Alan Page, born in Canton in 1945.

A third state closely associated with football is Texas. The great interest in football there has lured numerous sportswriters to the state. A few of these sportswriters have published books about football. Best known among these books is H. G. Bissinger's *Friday Night Lights,* which deals with football in Odessa, Texas.[17] Bissinger shows how football became the "secular religion" of Odessa. Bissinger used the subtitle *A Town, a Team, and a Dream* to illustrate the energy with which football is pursued in that state. Bissinger, a Philadelphia journalist, spent over a year in Odessa and shows the attachment of the townspeople to their high school football team. High school football teams in Odessa and other Texas towns create a sense of community.

Texas has produced a number of outstanding football players, among whom is Joe Don Looney Jr., whose biography, *Third Down and Forever,* was published in 1993. Looney had been an outstanding football player at Fort Worth High School. He then went to the University of Oklahoma, where he was dismissed from the team for "gross insubordination," or refusing to take orders from coaches. Thereafter he played for several professional teams but wore out his welcome at all of them in just a few months. Looney demonstrated how all the dangers associated with football can ruin those who cannot resist them. He partied, drank too much, used drugs and steroids, and was repeatedly arrested. He died in a motorcycle accident in Texas in 1988.[18]

Several novels depict Texas football. Among these is *The Last Picture Show* by Larry McMurtry. The story is set in a small Texas town and depicts the feelings of a former high school football player who returns to his high school one more time.[19] In addition, many nonfiction books about Texas football have been published, such as Gary Shaw's *Meat on the Hoof,* which sought to expose the unethical tactics of a so-called legendary football coach.[20]

Then there is *End Zone* by Don DeLillo, who is a New York novelist. This novel is largely about nuclear annihilation and about the language needed to comprehend that horror and football. Language is the focus here, as DeLillo shows that each play in a football game must have a name which must be used before that play can be used. DeLillo views football as a battle similar to military battles. Football demands teamwork, as does any military effort.[21]

The Last Texas Hero, a novel by Terry Douglas, shows the ugly side of the college football hierarchy, the money-grubbing coach, the bullying of the players who demean the freshmen and others, and the assistant coaches who treat the team like a drill sergeant treats the recruits. The book also depicts how an ambitious freshman becomes the very type of psychopathic "hero" he despised when he was only a beginner. It also shows how all of heroism is financed and supported by the business establishment.[22]

GENDER AND SEXUAL ORIENTATION

Today, among all college athletics, football is afforded with more interest and importance than any other sport. This is true of both students and alumni. This can be interpreted to mean that both students and alumni feel that their masculinity is at stake when rival teams meet on the gridiron. College fund-raisers know this and appeal to alumni on the grounds that the contributor is investing in male dominance and masculine prestige.

Further evidence of the need to express masculine power are the celebrations of the Rose Bowl for college football heroes and the Super Bowl for professionals. Other "bowl" games serve the same purpose. Evidently, something in the American psyche favors football and its aggressive, risky, domineering, all-male display. The evidence for this is the number of Americans who attend or watch football games as compared to other sports. Moreover, many football fans are motivated to watch the game because they seek to identify with power, control, and dominance. This is so because few of us have any power. On the contrary, most of us are bossed on the job, are obliged to pay taxes, and are subject to police and other controlling people all the time. Therefore, identifying with the controlled violence of football gives many fans a chance to at least pretend to have some power on Saturday or Sunday afternoon.

A telephone survey called *Portrait of America,* conducted by the CBS broadcasting system, found that "football is king" to American sports fans. The results of the survey reveal that 48 percent of Americans watch football on television, 35 percent attend football games, that 44 percent say that football is the most popular American sport. This may be compared to baseball, which is second in attendance and TV interest. Only 12 percent of Americans say that they watch baseball on TV, only 16 percent attend baseball games, and 20 percent ranked baseball is the favorite American sport. Basketball comes in third, with 12 percent watching games on TV, 16 percent attending, and 20 percent considering it the most popular sport.

It is therefore no surprise that the Super Bowl is the highlight of all sporting events each year. Of all Americans, 41 percent watch that game, while only 19 percent watch the baseball World Series; the NBA championship games are seen by only 15 percent.[23]

The reasons for this fascination with both the American and British version of football have been explained in various ways. Many years ago, Johnson argued that football was originally a solar ritual and therefore a fertility ritual in which the disclike ball represented the sun, the source of all life on earth. This view is supported by the finding that in England and France married men played football against single men after a newly married woman threw out the ball, over which the bachelors fought with the married men. The distinction between the married and the unmarried suggests to some anthropologists that the game represented a test of socially sanctioned fertility.[24]

Some view football as a male initiation ritual. The anthropologist William Arens argues that "football is a male preserve that manifests both the physical and cultural values of masculinity." Arens further notes that the equipment worn accents the male physique through the enlarged head and shoulders and narrowing of the waist, with "the lower torso poured into skintight pants accented only by a metal codpiece." Arens notes further that football players dressed in this manner can hold hands, pat each other on the bottom, and hug one another. Such behavior would be strongly disapproved if conducted by men in any other situation.[25]

Some psychoanalysts seek to interpret football in terms of its possible sexual symbolism. Such analysts see the ball and the goal or the end zone as symbolic of the male ejaculation and its reception in the female uterus. Others seek psychoanalytic meaning in the language used in American football. The word "penetration" of the opponent's territory is often used by sports announcers and writers. The word "screw" is often used to indicate that one team seeks to "screw" or defeat the other team. Even the term "end zone" is interpreted by the psychoanalytic minded to represent the human anatomy. The so-called three-point stance in which the center presents to the quarterback could be interpreted as indicating a homosexual interest. Even the word "touch" as in "touchdown" is interpreted by some to indicate a sexual meaning. "Score" in common parlance refers to sexual intercourse. "Sacking" the quarterback can be interpreted as an allusion to rape.

David Kopay, an admitted homosexual football player, had a ten-year career in the NFL as a running back; he played for San Francisco, Detroit, Washington, New Orleans, and Green Bay. He describes the words used by coaches in injecting a winning attitude into his players as being full of allusions to homosexual performances. According to Kopay, the language used is not only pornographic but particularly full of aggressive homosexual implications.[26]

RETIRED FOOTBALL PLAYERS

The concept of retirement usually refers to the termination of a career in any occupation. Ordinarily this means that retirement must be considered together with aging, since many retire on or after reaching age sixty-five. By definition, then, retirement implies withdrawal from the social scene, diminution of one's abilities, and the end of one's usefulness to society. This in turn leads to a devalued status and the assignment of a stigma, which we define as a label of disapproval.[27]

Retirement can be voluntary or involuntary. Some workers such as police, airplane pilots, and firemen are forced to retire at a given age. Others retire or are forced to retire because of physical difficulties caused by old age. Among these are athletes, who are generally quite young in comparison to all other retirees.

All retirement leads to stress regarding those aspects of an athlete's life which had given him recognition, a large income, and entry into a profession. On retirement, the athlete can no longer rely on his sport to give him the satisfaction he had so far enjoyed. Those who retire at the usual ages of sixty-five or more also face these problems. Some make the adjustment from active work to retirement with ease and truly enjoy the retired state. Many more find retirement dreadful and view themselves as useless. This is principally an American problem, because the Protestant work ethic dictates that a positive value is attached to gainful employment and that those not working are somehow unworthy and dishonorable.[28]

Working people maintain many social contacts while employed. Working people also feel that they are making a contribution to society and that their status in the community is dependent on that work.

Football players, unlike typical retirees, are far younger on retirement than is usually expected. Furthermore, football is a seasonal occupation, so that those retired from that work have always spent a good part of the year independent of the football work schedule. This affords those who recognize that football is only a short-term career an opportunity to ready themselves for life without football. Unfortunately, many football players do not plan for this change and face a truly unfortunate retirement status.

Football players and other athletes generally reach the peak of their performance in their late twenties or early thirties so that the football player needs to plan for his life career after football at a young age.

The reasons for retirement from football and other sports have been listed by the sociologist M. A. Milhovilovic. Accordingly, approximately 32 percent of athletes retire because of injuries. This is particularly the case with football players. More than 27 percent retire because of their age, family reasons lead to 23 percent of retirements, about 7 percent retire because of bad relations with coaches and other players. Another 7 percent are forced out by younger players and 4 percent retire for a multiplicity of other reasons.[29]

After retirement from football, retired players must find some work. A good number of these former football players continue employment in football as coaches, trainers, announcers, and/or analysts. It appears that 99 percent of all football coaches are former football players. This is also true of most announcers and analysts who regularly appear on television. These, however, are only a few of the retired football players, most of whom do not attain the profitable coaching or broadcasting appointments that are usually offered only to the most famous retirees.

Carl Banks retired from professional football after the 1995 season. At that time he concluded a twelve-year career with the NFL, playing linebacker for the New York Giants and thereafter Washington and Cleveland for a career total of 173 games. Today he designs clothing for the G-III apparel group company, located in New York City. He also serves as the company's vice president. He began designing while still playing football because he could not find clothes that would fit him. Banks has also co-authored a health and conditioning book for young athletes.

A remarkable talent permits Mike Hamby, formerly of the Buffalo Bills, to engage in an unusual occupation among football players and, for that matter, anyone else. Hamby is a sculptor who has only recently sculpted the bust of Joe DeLamielleure for the NFL Hall of Fame in Canton, Ohio. DeLamielleure played a number of years for the Bills where he ended his football career as did Mike Hamby. Hamby played for the Buffalo Bills from 1985-1989 when an injury ended his football days.

Instead of permitting this permanent injury to make him an invalid, Hamby turned to his great talent and entered the highly competitive field of sculpture. He has created some remarkable works of art including a statue called "Meet the Challenge" which is located at his alma mater Utah State University. Hamby's eight-ton, twenty-six-foot-tall sculpture of two grizzly bears tower over the headquarters of Cabela's sports outfitters in Dundee, Michigan. He has also enhanced his adopted hometown, Buffalo, with a number of beautiful and exciting sculptures.

Mike Hamby is also blessed with a musical talent allowing him to play the guitar and compose music, contradicting the prejudice that football players are stupid and incompetent.

Mike Hamby was born and raised in Lehi, Utah, where he played Pop Warner football and then went on to play in high school. He played at Utah State and was then drafted to the Buffalo Bills where he was coached by Hank Bullough and Marv Levy. He still lives in the Buffalo area.[30]

Kermit Alexander was sixty-three years old in 2004 and lives in Southern California. He is a former defensive back who played with the San Francisco 49ers for seven seasons. Alexander now works as a business consultant. He allies companies with one another and consults for political candidates.

Besides playing defensive back, Alexander was also a special teams player. Traded to the Los Angeles Rams in 1970, Alexander led his team in interceptions six times.

Don Beebe retired after the 1997 season. He played wide receiver for the Buffalo Bills and two seasons for the Green Bay Packers. He is today best remembered for his role in Super Bowl XXVII, in which his speed allowed him to catch up with Dallas defensive tackle Leon Lett, as Lett was about to reach the end zone. Beebe ran from twenty-five yards back and tackled him almost at the end zone. Beebe now runs a chain of clinics called the House of Speed. The training sessions at the House of Speed are designed for any athlete in any sport.

Terry Bradshaw, without doubt one of the most talented quarterbacks to ever play the game, was born in Shreveport, Louisiana, in 1948. His thirteen-year career included leading the Pittsburgh Steelers to eight play-off appearances from 1972-1979, six AFC championships, and four Super Bowl wins. Retired since 1984, he was inducted into the Pro Football Hall of Fame in 1989 and then took up a broadcasting career. He has also appeared in several feature films and television shows. In addition, he has written three books.

Dave Chappel spent five years as a punter for the Los Angeles Rams. In 1972 he led the league in punting and set an all-time record for the longest punt and was named All-Pro for that performance. Chappel left professional football at a young age and then devoted himself to wildlife art. His work is so good that it was selected for a postage stamp and earned numerous other honors at various art shows.

Mike Ditka was born in Carnegie, Pennsylvania, in 1939. He was the first tight end elected to the Pro Football Hall of Fame. He was rookie of the year in 1961 and represented the Chicago Bears in five straight Pro Bowls. He was all NFL for four years and ended his career with forty-three touchdowns and 427 receptions. After retirement from football he coached, most recently with the New Orleans Saints, until 1999. Today he owns the successful Mike Ditka's Restaurant in Chicago.

Bob Griese was born in Evansville, Indiana, in 1945. He has been a broadcaster for twenty-one years and has been an analyst for ABC's College Football for sixteen years. For fourteen years, from 1967 to 1980, he was quarterback for the Miami Dolphins. He was inducted into the Pro Football Hall of Fame in 1990.

A more ordinary retirement from a football career would be the postfootball employment of George Izo, who made a name for himself while playing for Notre Dame from 1957 to 1959. During those years he threw for 2,095 yards and eighteen touchdowns, leading to his drafting by the St. Louis Cardinals in 1960. His promising career did not materialize because a knee injury forced him to play no more than six games in any season, as he bounced from St. Louis to Washington, Detroit, and Pittsburgh. He left professional football in 1967 and entered the business community. First he invested in a construction business, then in a food company, leading to his involvement in

California Sunshine Milk. He also arranges to fly football stars to military bases in Guam, South Korea, and Japan.

Mel Renfro was inducted into the Professional Football Hall of Fame in 1996. He was born in Texas but raised in Oregon where he lives now. Drafted by the Dallas Cowboys in 1963, he played for them for fourteen years, including four Super Bowl appearances. He is currently working for the Bridge Center in Portland, Oregon. The Bridge Center works to help inner-city youths. In recognition of his football career and his current efforts he was cited by the Oregon legislature on his induction into the Hall of Fame. The legislature passed a resolution congratulating him not only on his induction but also on his contributions to the Oregon community.

I have presented a limited number of retired football players who were able to make some adjustment to their new status by entering the world of business or continuing in some other capacity in the football world. Numerous other former athletes and football players have had great difficulty in retirement. Such difficulties are not limited to football players. Some retirees have difficulty adjusting to retirement because identity, status, and occupation are so closely linked in the United States. Therefore, those who are retired can lose both status and identity, although some are quite comfortable in retirement and do not miss the work world at all. For football players who retire at a far younger age than Americans normally retire, the problem is not so much finding something else to do, but to live without media attention and to relinquish the fame that usually accrues to their profession. The retired football player must adjust to the change in status from being known to being unknown. This can mean that the former celebrity needs to maintain a level of self-respect not dependent on being in the public eye.

"Many retired football players who leave the game cite feelings of abandonment, loneliness, paranoia, despair and loss of self-esteem. . . . Many players are forced into psychiatric counseling."[31]

Retiring football players need to be prepared for the unspectacular life that awaits them unless they succeed in becoming professional coaches or TV announcers. The first of these preparations refers to the need to enter a new occupation. Unlike ordinary retirees who are at the end of their careers, retired football players are usually quite young and therefore need to consider how they can earn a livelihood if they have no skill other than playing football. Some, like the Miami Dolphin quarterback Jay Fiedler, have useful degrees. Fiedler has a degree in engineering from Dartmouth College.

Usually, the skills and requirements that the football player possesses cannot be utilized in a nonfootball environment. Although some outstanding players may be employed for ten to twelve years, the average career for a professional football player is only five years.[32]

Retirement from football is not only caused by advancing age but also by the cumulative damage inflicted on most football players over the years. Head trauma from football injuries often leads to lifelong neurological problems, as reported to the American Academy of Neurology at their 52nd annual meeting in San Diego in 2003. That report revealed that 60 percent of all professional football players had experienced at least one concussion during their playing careers and that 25 percent had suffered three or more concussions. Players who have had concussions were more likely than anyone else to suffer neurological complaints such as speech impairment, memory loss, hearing impairment, and numbness in their extremities. Some retired football players also exhibit the "punch drunk" syndrome evident in some retired boxers.[33]

Many ex-football players fear an early death because they notice the deaths of many of their former colleagues at a young age. For example, Richard McCabe, a former Denver defensive back, died at age forty-four, former San Francisco linebacker Matt Haseltine died of Lou Gehrig's disease at age fifty-five, and Bobby Lane, former Pittsburgh and Detroit quarterback, died of a heart attack at age fifty-nine. Hall of Fame linebacker Norm van Brocklin died of a heart attack at age fifty-seven, and Bob Waterfield, also a Hall of Fame linebacker, died of a heart attack at age sixty-two. Those who died even younger from heart failure were linebacker Larry Gordon, age twenty-eight, defensive end Wilson Faumuina, age thirty-two, kicker John Leypoldt, age forty, and defensive tackle Dudley Meredith, who died at age fifty-two.

A number of former football players have died young due to cancer. These include Steve Chomyssak, defensive lineman, age forty-four; defensive back Clancy Williams, forty-three years; fullback James Braxton, thirty-seven; Kirk Collins, twenty-five; and Ricky

Bell, who died at age twenty-nine. Then there are David Croudip, former Falcon, Cleveland Brown Don Rogers, and David Waymer, former Oakland Raiders safety, all of whom died of a cocaine overdose between the ages of twenty-six and thirty-four.[34]

Yet a study conducted by the National Institute of Occupational Safety and Health and the NFL Players Association concluded that retired football players do not die younger than other men. The study included 7,000 former NFL players who attained a life expectancy of seventy-two, which is normal for American men. The study also found that defensive linemen are more likely to suffer heart disease than is normally expected due to the bulk of these ex-players.[35]

Old age is a relative term. Some people have lived seventy-eight years or more and are still very productive. Some write books, paint, serve in Congress, conduct symphonies, or teach. For football players and other athletes, old age sets in when their physical skills decline. Stamina, speed, and power leave most athletes beginning with age thirty. This is particularly true of football players, whose profession demands more from their bodies than any other career. Football players drive their bodies and their psyche to the limit so that ordinary, minor consequences of aging assume great importance in their lives and careers. All humans must accept the physical decline old age demands. Football players and other athletes must accept this at a much younger age, so that it may be justifiably said that football players grow old before their time. Even the stigma of old age targets the relatively young retired football player in the eyes of yet younger players.[36] The stigma which "old age" confers on ex-football players may well be responsible for a good deal of alcoholism among retired football players. The number of examples is considerable, but two such well-known alcoholic football "greats" will illustrate this situation.

Thurman Thomas, former star running back for Oklahoma State and the Buffalo Bills, spent twenty-eight days in a Minnesota Alcoholics Anonymous rehabilitation program. In 2002 Thomas told an audience gathered to honor him that he became an alcoholic *after* he retired from football.[37] Likewise, Pat Summerall retired from football broadcasting at the age of seventy. Summerall played for the NFL in his younger years and then turned to broadcasting for a long and extremely successful career. Yet alcoholism led him to "living from drink to drink" until he turned to religion to save himself from the destructive consequences of his drinking.[38]

The need to work after a football career ends raises the issue of opportunities for employment for retired football players. In many instances, the retired football players depend on the organization to which they belonged to help them find postretirement employment. Others use their family or friends to link up to new work experiences. Many of the retired football players find work in scouting, coaching, broadcasting, management, or other sports-related activities. Those who want to coach football will find that the number of coaching positions is far too small to permit the entry of most retired football players. There are 117 Division IA college football teams active in the country today, and a few hundred more college teams in other divisions. Hundreds of high school coaching jobs are available and some can coach professional football after retirement. Of course, only a small percentage of coaching positions are vacant at any one time, leaving a retired football player with limited opportunities in that preferred area of work. This is also true of broadcasting positions.

Some football players have taken advantage of pension payments worked out by the player's union. Recently, the NFL has increased pension payments to players who played before 1977 by $110 million to 1,400 retired players. This raises pensions to $200 a month for each season played. This also means that 800 retired players who played before 1959 are receiving double the pension paid heretofore, i.e., they will now receive $200 per month for each season played. To qualify for a pension, a retired player must have played at least four seasons. Heretofore, five seasons were required.[39]

Recently, football players have hired legal and financial advisers who are expected to help players make good financial decisions and secure them postfootball financial security. We have already seen that some of these "advisers" are either incompetent or fraudulent. The NFL Players Association has in fact concluded that at least seventy-eight players have been defrauded of $42 million in only three years by some of these advisers. Yet legitimate financial planners claim that they can insure players against sudden retirement caused by career ending injuries.

SUMMARY

Social stratification is universal and appears in American society in several dimensions including wealth, race, religion, place of origin, and occupation. Therefore the income of football players and the great wealth of the NFL contribute to the high esteem earned by the football community in this country. Black football players have had to deal with racism in the football community even now. Jews had been victimized by religious bigotry in the past although such bigotry is no longer a factor in the employment of Jewish football players.

Three states have had an extraordinary impact on football over the years. These states are Pennsylvania, Ohio, and Texas.

Retired football players have exhibited some of the same strain that other retirees have shown, although football players retire much earlier than other retirees and therefore need to find new employment in the many years they live past retirement.

I have now explored the role of football players themselves and will now discuss those who participate in the football arena without actually playing the game themselves. That is the topic of the next chapter.

Chapter 5

They Also Serve

COACHES

Because "winning isn't everything, it is the only thing," the coach's role in producing a winning team cannot be exaggerated. This does not mean that coaches can create winners out of nothing; coaches whose teams have the best players and the most support from fans and management have better chances of winning than those who can rely only on their own skills. But it is the fate of coaches to be blamed for losses and praised for wins. This is by no means unjustified, because the central decision maker at any football game is the head coach.

Coaches are responsible for allowing young players to gain experience; however, this can only be done at the risk of inexperienced players accumulating a large number of mistakes during a game. This is only one of many dilemmas that face coaches at all levels of football, but in particular in the NFL. We can nevertheless assume that no one becomes an NFL player unless he has displayed considerable talent as a football player in college or elsewhere. Because all NFL players are talented and all teams are highly selective in employing football players, it is not surprising that economics are extremely influential in producing a winning team.

The coach's salary is a feature of football that can hardly be overestimated, as is true of coaching in other sports. The belief that coaching is important is best illustrated by the income of college and professional football coaches. For example, in 2002 Steve Spurrier became the head coach of the Washington Redskins at a salary of $5 million per year, thereby becoming the highest-paid coach in the NFL. In 1999 Mike Holmgren, the head coach of the Seattle Seahawks, was paid $4 million. George Seifert, head coach of the Carolina Panthers, was paid $2.5 million that year, and Jimmy Johnson of the Miami Dolphins earned $2 million. Other salaries for head coaches of professional football teams during the 1990s were $2 million for Steve Mariucci of the San Francisco 49ers and $1.5 million for Bill Parcells of the New England Patriots, Mike Ditka of the New Orleans Saints, and Dennis Green of the Minnesota Vikings.[1] In addition to these salaries, head coaches and assistant coaches can earn more money by speaking at conventions, dinners, and other gatherings and by endorsing products.

Professional football coaches are usually recruited from the ranks of college coaches. This is true of Steve Spurrier, who was head football coach at the University of Florida (1990-2001), where he succeeded in coaching the team to the championship of the Southeastern Conference, which the university had never previously won in its fifty-plus years of conference play. He achieved many additional successes as coach at Miami, his alma mater.

Spurrier is an ex-football player himself. He won the Heisman Trophy in 1966, served as Florida's quarterback coach in 1978, and then became offensive coordinator and QB coach at Georgia Tech in 1979. He then held a similar position at Duke University before becoming head coach with the Tampa Bay Bandits of the United States Football League (USFL) in 1983. He returned to Duke as head coach in 1987, where in 1989 he produced that school's first ACC championship since 1962. This led to his appointment at Florida and his great success since then.

Likewise, Marv Levy of the Buffalo Bills became a Hall of Fame member in 2001 because of his tremendous achievement as a professional football coach. Although a man with academic interests who earned an MA degree in British history at Harvard University, Levy found success coaching football. He began at the Country Day School of St. Louis after graduating from Coe College, where he played football as a running back. He returned to Coe College as an assistant coach. After coaching at several other universities, he moved to the Philadelphia Eagles as kicking coach and then became assistant to the highly successful coach George Allen in both Los Angeles and Washington, DC. After two seasons with the Redskins, Levy moved to Montreal for five seasons. In 1978 he took over as coach in Kansas City and finally ended up in Buffalo in 1986, where he led the Bills to four consecutive Super Bowl appearances. His other achievements are legendary.

These two examples and many others that could be cited here support the contention of sociologists that some people have "moral density," as Durkheim called it, or "charisma." This gift makes some leaders outstanding because they can motivate groups to play football or fight a war or play in an orchestra or succeed in business. The reasons for the possession of "moral density" by some but not others can be found in the annals of social psychology. Suffice it to say here that some football coaches have the ability to succeed where everyone else has failed and to be an inspiration to their team and their fans.[2]

Coaching football can create great emotional tension and pressure, and some coaches cannot tolerate this anxiety. Particularly when the coach's team is losing or has lost the game, these intense feelings can lead to violent outbursts among some coaches. An example of such violent conduct was the attack on Charlie Bauman, a Clemson University football player, by the head coach of the Ohio State University football team. Wayne "Woody" Hayes (1913-1987), who had won 205 football games at Ohio State, became incensed when Bauman intercepted an Ohio State pass two seconds before the game ended, resulting in an Ohio State loss to Clemson. Bauman was forced out of bounds on the play, where Hayes punched him. Hayes was fired the next day.

Hayes had a long history of assaulting people who were within his reach during his frequent temper tantrums. He hit a photographer during the 1975 Rose Bowl game and a TV cameraperson during the 1977 Michigan game. In 1977 he beat a student reporter during the Oklahoma game and in that same year punched his own fullback. In January 1978 he even hit a goalpost.

At one game he tore the official sideline markers to pieces and later stormed off the set of a TV show because a majority of respondents thought he should retire. Of course, Hayes always lashed out when he was losing or thought he was in danger of having his omnipotence questioned. He used invectives such as "you can go straight to hell," and he often threatened physical assault against anyone who questioned him.[3]

Likewise, in November 2002, two assistant football coaches at Miami University of Ohio were suspended for violent behavior after their team was defeated by West Virginia's Marshall University. Miami defensive coordinator Jon Wauford was led off the field in handcuffs after he punched a Marshall fan who ran onto the field after the game was over. Meanwhile, enraged linebacker coach Taver Johnson of Miami damaged the visiting coaches box. Some have argued that such conduct illustrates a form of arrested emotional development shared by a few coaches.

SCOUTS

Football coaches make their own lives easier by employing scouts who watch games played by their teams' opponents and report their observations to the head coach for whom they work. Some scouts are retired football players and others are assistant coaches. A football scout may spy on opposing teams that will be faced during the season, or the scout can seek and recruit outstanding players for his or her own team. Their scouting reports are often quite detailed, with some scouts using computers and films.[4] Magazines such as *Sports Illustrated* also include scouting reports on a number of players, giving in-depth details and pictures concerning several NFL players of interest in each issue.[5]

Scouts travel incessantly, visiting college campuses day after day. All thirty-two NFL teams send out scouts who tour the same schools and attend college "pro" days to test players who have not been at the NFL "Scouting Combine." The combine is a four-day meeting at which the best college players are invited to exhibit their football talent in front of coaches, managers, and owners, who have the opportunity to see all the talent at once and make the best draft decisions possible for their teams. Since teams spend as much as $160 million on signing bonuses for first-round picks, it is vital that they make sound judgments.

Scouts study tapes of players who could be prospects for their team. They size the players, measuring their height, weight, arm length, and width of hands. They watch the prospective players lift weights to test upper body strength, and they measure the players' speed, endurance, and agility.

Once a scout has recommended players, the team's coach and the director of player personnel must decide how much they can spend on each player because football has a salary cap, which in 2004 was $80.5 million. Therefore, every team is faced with the dilemma of either appointing several extremely expensive superstars while paying little for everyone else, or fixing a salary for a position in advance and then finding a player willing to take that salary.

Players who are not under contract are called "free agents." These free agents must decide what is in their best interest, depending on available openings. For example, Chad Eaton, a Patriot defensive tackle, was offered a $10.7 million deal by the Seattle Seahawks in 2001, including a $3.5 million signing bonus. Despite Eaton's being one of Coach Bill Belichick's favorite players, the Patriots did not match that offer and let Eaton go. The Patriots operate under the motto "We are building a team, not collecting talent." This attitude led to championships for the Patriots, as they won the Super Bowl in 2002 and 2004.

The Patriots's attitude regarding free agents is becoming popular. Increased numbers of teams are letting extremely expensive players go, rather than weaken the team overall for the sake of a single superstar.

Another example of how to manage the salary cap is the experience of the Pittsburgh Steelers. At the beginning of the 2002 season they had spent the least "dead money" on nonroster players. That season they achieved a .656 win average and were division champions. Likewise, the Philadelphia Eagles appointed a winning team without spending vast amounts on any one player and reached a .750 average, as did the Green Bay Packers.

There can be no doubt that the NFL has moved from a stage for the display of supertalent to a team approach with far better results than stardom could ever attain.[6]

TRAINERS

Every professional football team, every college team, and some high school teams have professional trainers whose duties are extensive. They attend to injuries on the playing field and bring water to the players during the game. Trainers order supplies, make dental and medical appointments for players, schedule players for the training room, and pack supplies for road games.

The trainers' most important duties concern the physical development of the players. Such training consists of aerobic and anaerobic exercises such as long-distance running, high-intensity workouts such as 20-, 30-, or 40-yard dashes with only fifteen seconds' rest, as well as initial jogs of five to ten minutes. Trainers may also recommend the best nutrition to players.

Trainers are responsible for managing the potentially dangerous effects of heat during training camps at the end of the summer season. This is particularly true in the South. They make water and high-carbohydrate drinks available to players, who must often work out in considerable heat. Trainers also focus on safety by maintaining equipment designed to protect players and reduce injuries.

Trainers are usually members of the 25,000-member-strong National Athletics Trainers' Association, which certifies trainers as professionals. This education is important, because each trainer on the staff of any NFL team administers more than 5,000 medical treatments during a single season. Trainers are dedicated to their profession, and it is not unusual for trainers to work with athletes up to ninety hours per week during training camp.

In 2002 the Pittsburgh Steelers appointed Ariko Iso, a native of Japan, as the first full-time female trainer in the NFL. It is likely that even more women will want to enter this profession, thereby breaking one more barrier in the all-male world of football.[7]

OFFICIALS

Football is a culture complex that includes numerous culture traits. A culture trait is one small aspect of any culture that has little importance in itself but becomes significant in conjunction with numerous other culture traits called a culture complex.[8]

Innumerable culture traits are involved in football games. Furthermore, many roles must be played by various participants to make a school or professional football game possible. Absent any of these roles, the game as it is now played in the United States could not proceed. Therefore, the role of referee is crucial in making a football game possible.

The National Football League calls its referees "officials." Not all officials are referees, however. The label "referee" specifically refers to the crew chief, who can be recognized because he wears a white hat. These officials are usually recruited from among those who have officiated at college or high school games and who not only gathered a good deal of experience but also exhibit some characteristics believed to be necessary to working in such a high pressure environment.

The National Football League has issued a list of steps potential referees should take if they seek to work for the NFL. The first of these is to be physically fit. In addition, it is necessary to keep calm under pressure, to be a people person, and to enjoy football.

Normally, sports officials are high school graduates who are at least eighteen years old. A novice will join a local football-officiating association. The local associations start a beginner at small games, generally involving children. As the referee gains experience he of she will be allowed to work in more advanced games, reaching high school and then small college games. Working college games is very important, because college is as much a minor league training ground for referees as it is for players. There are many colleges, so an ambitious official can probably work a great deal on the college circuit. Those who have worked ten years in high school games and five years in college varsity games may then be eligible to officiate for the National Football League. The NFL employs scouts who watch referees at college games to find those who may be eligible to referee at the professional level. About 110 college referees are selected each year for possible consideration by the NFL, and of these, four to six are hired. Until recently, a first-year official earned $1,431 for each game. Second-year officials earned $4,330, third-year officials earned $9,800, and a referee at the Super Bowl earned $11,900 for that game.[9]

In 2002 a new contract between the NFL and the 119 NFL officials went into effect. That contract calls for a 50 percent increase in salaries in 2002 with subsequent increases reaching 150 percent in 2006. Similar increases were agreed upon for play-off games and the Super Bowl.[10]

It is commonly assumed that football referees work only weekends, spending three hours on the field on a Sunday afternoon, and are then relieved of their football duties until the following Sunday.

This is far from the truth. In fact, every NFL official spends at least fifteen to twenty hours or more studying videos of games played the previous week. In addition, the entire officiating crew discusses various calls, game situations, and rule interpretations. Because NFL football has nearly 1,000 rules, all officials are required to take a weekly written rules examination during the season, although exams are not "scored" by anyone since the only purpose of the examination is to keep the rules fresh in the officials' minds.

Because physical condition is so important, officials work out at least two hours every day. The referee must submit game reports to the head office every week. Officials keep in touch every week concerning travel arrangements and game tapes. The crew members usually leave home on Friday night or Saturday morning to go to the city where their next assignment will take place. Once there, they meet and again review game videotape.

In total, officials spend thirty to forty hours on each game each week. They are also given random drug and alcohol tests.[11]

Although the job of an NFL official is highly stressful, some humor is permitted. Here are three one-liners that officials have frequently enjoyed:

- After shooting the blank gun to end the half, the Dallas Cowboy players came shooting back with live ammunition.
- Anyone who makes a call against the Detroit Lions risks the anger of the remaining fan.
- Just when we thought it was safe to be an NFL referee, we have to go back to Cleveland.

NFL officials come from all occupations and all ethnic groups. Some are lawyers, others factory workers; some are businesspeople, others short-order cooks. The one quality they have in common is that they are willing to make great sacrifices of time and effort to be part of the game.

CHEERLEADERS

Lifestyle Media of New York City publishes a magazine titled *American Cheerleader.* That publication and similar ones reveal a good deal about the interests of cheerleaders, whose purpose it is to incite their team's fans to cheer the team to victory.

Cheerleading has advanced quite far from its beginnings in the 1880s when a few male students cheered on the Princeton football team by shouting in unison, "Ray, Ray, Ray! Tiger, Tiger, Tiger! Sis, Sis, Sis! Boom, Boom, Boom! Aaaaah! Princeton, Princeton, Princeton!" This chant and others like it were subsequently performed at college football arenas. In the mid-1890s, University of Minnesota fans decided that something needed to be done to improve their football team's poor performance. They elected "yelling captains" charged with conducting the cheering in a systematic manner. The yelling captains brought megaphones to the game and eventually included drums and other noisemakers.[12]

In the 1920s, cheerleaders at many colleges began to incorporate gymnastics and tumbling into their cheers. At Oregon State College, flashcards were introduced to encourage crowd participation in the noisemaking. All of this was done by men. In fact, Franklin D. Roosevelt led cheers at Harvard during a football game against Brown in 1903.[13]

In the 1920s more women arrived on the campuses of American colleges and entered into some of the activities formerly available only to men. By then, mandatory public education had become universal in the United States, and many secondary schools imitated colleges by instituting cheerleading before and during football games.[14]

It wasn't until World War II that women came to constitute a majority of cheerleaders; most men had been drafted and almost all colleges were ipso facto nearly all-female schools. Even when the men came home, women remained in cheerleading positions, not only because they had proven themselves competent to do so but also because sex appeal evidently enhanced the cheering.

In 1948, Lawrence Herkimer, a former cheerleader at Southern Methodist University in Dallas, Texas, formed the National Cheerleaders Association (NCA). He invented the "Herkie" jump as well as the cheerleader pom-pom. He then founded a corporation, Cheerleader Supply Company, which manufactures pom-poms as well as sweaters, skirts, emblems, and other cheerleading accessories. In addition, Herkimer founded several summer camps that have taught thousands of young people the sport of cheerleading.[15]

In 1978 CBS broadcast the Collegiate Cheerleading Championships, leading to greater interest in the sport than ever before. Subsequently, men and women participated in co-ed cheerleading as stunts and pyramids grew in size and difficulty. Men are still encouraged to participate in cheerleading, and those who do so are generally gymnasts who compete in regional and national championships. Competition grew as well, and by the 1990s saw the sport spread to Europe and Japan, giving rise to the "dance squad," an offshoot of cheerleading.

Today competition has reached such heights that numerous titles and championships are awarded. There is an American Open Partner Stunt title and there are choreographers who rely on videos to work on the routines. Cheerleaders who want to reach the national championships in April begin practice in September. There are twenty-one regional tournaments, ten "open" championship series, and six invitationals. The performances of these cheerleaders are danced to music and become a form of entertainment in themselves, divorced from any football game.

Cheerleading has also become its own industry. The entire cheerleading scene is accompanied by an immense amount of advertising for shoes, clothes, cosmetics, physical fitness equipment, food, tampons, hair products, travel, skin treatments, and a host of other products. Inspection of cheerleading magazines devoted to cheerleading reveals that 85 percent of all pages in such magazines are devoted to advertisements.

There are about 3 million cheerleaders in the United States today. Their needs are met by a number of corporations such as Varsity Spirit, which has yearly revenues of nearly $150 million, while the magazine *American Cheerleader* has a circulation of 250,000 and a readership of 1 million. The articles featured in *American Cheerleader* discuss the experiences of cheerleaders, including pictures of a number of teenagers associated with the sport. Varsity.com awards a "Cheerleader of the Month" title to a young person deserving of the accolade.[16]

An estimated 500,000 cheerleaders attend cheer camps each summer. Ninety-five percent of these cheerleaders are women. The sport has become so competitive that children only six years old are enrolled in such camps, which usually emphasize gymnastics. In addition, 1,500 All-Star programs are operating in 613 gyms.

Cheerleading's importance has grown so much that others outside the sport have given it both attention and respect. The University of Kentucky now awards full in-state scholarships for cheerleading. In addition, 225 colleges and junior colleges offer full and partial scholarships for cheerleading. Cheerleading is now also a televised sport, as the competitions organized by the National Cheerleaders Association are broadcast on Saturday afternoon.

Cheerleading has definitely become a sport in itself. The competitions and practice for them involve no additional sport (i.e., no football team) and no fans other than those who want to see the cheerleaders' acrobatics themselves. These stunts are often practiced for as long as three hours per day. Such activities, however, also introduce physical risks. It has been estimated that each year twenty-five women suffer catastrophic injuries as a result of cheerleading activities.[17]

Professional football teams employ paid cheerleaders who earn no more than fifteen to fifty dollars per game and possibly two free tickets to the game. Nevertheless, many women are willing to work for these low wages; some cheer professionally because they want the glamour and publicity associated with cheerleading, as well as a possible introduction to a modeling career. Professional cheerleading was invented by Tex Schramm in 1971, when he was owner of the Dallas Cowboys. He wanted beautiful models as cheerleaders who could perform Broadway-style dances. The result were entire teams of cheerleading dancers, such as the Dallas Tex Anns, the Apache Belles, the Kilgore Rangers, and later the Dallas Cowboy Cheerleaders and the Buffalo Jills.

FOOTBALL DOCTORS, INJURIES, AND DRUGS

In 2000, the National Football League Players Association asked its members to rate the medical staff caring for them. Of the thirty-one teams involved, 1,152 players participated in this survey. Six teams considered their medical staff to be 100 percent effective. On one team, Cincinnati, only 19 percent of players rated their doctors as good or better. The majority of NFL players gave their doctors ratings of 83 to 97 percent.

Team doctors are appointed by management, thus some observers have questioned whether the doctors are responsible to the players or to the owners who pay them. Some players fear that the team doctors care little for them in comparison to the team owners; but some protections for players do exist. For example, players are entitled to seek a second opinion if they do not trust the team doctors and the owners must pay such for examinations.

Team owners may not have many options available in appointing doctors for their teams because many doctors are reluctant to accept such positions in view of the enormous insurance costs and the threats of lawsuits which can ruin a doctor and his or her insurance company. For example, some players earn so much money that hardly any doctors could afford to defend themselves against allegations of malpractice.[18]

Such allegations can easily be made considering the dangers football players face and the consequences of such a dangerous sport. Players at all levels, from high school to professionals, have died in the course of a game. Other players suffer hip injuries, broken fingers, knees, and shoulders, and concussions. Concussions have been compared to an auto accident, with the brain the passenger and the skull the vehicle. In a concussion, the delicate brain slams against the bony skull, ripping nerve fibers and blood vessels, leading to memory loss, confusion, headaches, and nausea. Multiple concussions received during a short time are called "second impact syndrome," leading to brain swelling which can result in nervous system damage and death.[19]

Death came to Korey Stringer, an offensive lineman for the Minnesota Vikings in July 2001, during morning practice in Mankato, Minnesota. On that day the heat reached 90 degrees during a midsummer heat wave. Stinger had vomited during practice with full gear on that day in July. The next day, in similar heat and again wearing full gear, Stringer died after practice. Hospitalized, Stringer's temperature had reached 108.8 degrees, which did not allow him to sweat. The heat was trapped in the body, causing organ failure. His blood would not clot, his kidneys failed, his heart failed, and he died.

It may well be, as the NFL doctors claim, that safety precautions in the NFL are sufficient. No doubt the "macho" culture of football may have contributed to Stringer's failure to remove himself from further practice after his experience on July 30. No doubt, that culture also contributed to the deaths from heat strokes of eighteen high school and college football players between 1995 and 2002.[20]

Wear and tear on the body are not the only physical dangers faced by high performance football players. An additional danger is performance-enhancing drugs. Amphetamine use appeared in the NFL immediately after World War II, in 1946. According to Dr. Arnold Mandell, team physician to the San Diego Chargers from 1972 to 1974, football players at that time believed they had no choice but to use amphetamines because they faced opposing players who were using them.[21]

Mandell conducted in-depth interviews with eighty-seven football players from eleven NFL teams in 1981. He found in that study that two thirds of the players were using amphetamines. He also found that the use of drugs was position related. Defensive linemen used the highest doses so as to become fearless and became enraged. Quarterbacks and wide receivers used little or no drug enhancement since their performance is much more skill related than that of linemen.[22]

Beginning in the 1970s an escalation occurred in the use of anabolic steroids, which were then very much accepted in the NFL. Some players estimated that steroids were used by 90 percent of all players while others indicated the number was closer to 75 percent.[23]

Former NFL players suffer a great deal in retirement. Pierce Scranton, MD, former team physician for the Seattle Seahawks, believes that if 200 former NFL players were asked about injuries, all of them would, at a minimum, report "crippling" arthritis. He said that even if the constant tackling is discounted, "the simple wear and tear of the game ruins the players' joints." A survey of 1,090 former NFL players revealed that 60 percent of them had suffered at least one concussion.[24]

Retired professional football players, and some former college players, have traditionally faced numerous health problems. Knee revisions are very common, as are back injuries and joint difficulties of every kind. The poor health record of previous football generations may now be changing. In 1993, the National Football League and the NFL Players Association formed a safety and welfare committee. This committee has kept abreast of new developments in sports medicine. That branch of medicine has improved considerably during the past twenty years so that a number of operations which were not possible in the 1980s are now used regularly. In addition, a great effort has been made to prevent smoking and drinking. Anabolic steroids have been banned from football although they are still used surreptitiously. Doctors complain, however, that not enough has been done to prevent injuries in the first place, although it is hard to imagine how that can be accomplished.[25]

GENERAL MANAGERS

General managers of professional football teams can earn $1 million a year or more, although some earn much less. The task of a general manager is considerable and can be grouped into six major areas: labor relations, marketing, financial management, administration, personnel evaluation, and public relations. Labor relations refers to the negotiation of personnel contracts and negotiations of contracts with the media. Marketing refers to the need to present a product for public acceptance through advertising by using general marketing techniques. In this case the product is football. General managers are also responsible for the financial management of the team. Financial management refers to the need to solicit funds, to organize fund-raising events and programs, and to be able to predict economic developments having an impact on football consumption. Financial management also involves the construction of a budget. General managers must also handle day-to-day administration which can be as complex as reading the architectural blueprints for stadium construction. General managers must also attend required social events. Personnel evaluation refers to the duty of the general manager to recognize athletic skill, to understand the psychological factors influencing athletes, to use and understand the physical training program, and to identify new recruits.

General managers are often retired football players. It is therefore somewhat astounding that only one African American has been appointed general manager. He is Ozzie Newsome, a Hall of Fame player, credited with giving the Baltimore Ravens the Super Bowl XXXV championship in 2001.[26,27]

OWNERS

The owners of football teams, with the exception of the Green Bay Packers, are wealthy women or men who have invested in a business that is better supported by the taxpayer than any other except farming.

The AFC East teams are the Miami Dolphins, the Buffalo Bills, the New York Jets, and the New England Patriots.

The owner of the Miami Dolphins of the American Football Conference East is H. Wayne Huizenga. Beginning his working life as a garbage truck driver, Huizenga created Waste Management, Inc. This led to further business ventures including Blockbuster Entertainment Corporation, which reached sales of $2 billion in 1993. Huizenga bought 15 percent of the Dolphins for $30 million in 1990 and then succeeded in becoming the sole owner by a variety of business manipulations. Huizenga is the only individual who owns three professional sports teams: the Dolphins, the Florida Marlins baseball team, and the Florida Panthers hockey team.

Robert Kraft is owner of the New England Patriots. Kraft became sole owner of the team in 1994. Kraft also owns the New England soccer team called the Revolution. He was born in Brookline, Massachusetts, where he attended public school. He then attended Columbia University where he also played football. Thereafter he earned an MBA from the Harvard University School of Business. Founder of International Forest Products, Kraft also presides over several other enterprises. He has been active in numerous charities and donated a new football stadium in Jerusalem, Israel, where he also contributed to the Ethiopian community in that country. He is the owner of Israel's largest packaging plant. In the United States he contributed $11.5 million to Columbia University to establish the Robert K. Kraft Center of Jewish Student Life.[28]

The New York Jets had been owned by Leon Hess, founder of Amerada Hess Oil Company, since 1963. After the death of Hess at age eighty-five in 1999, his son sold the Jets to Robert Wood Johnson IV for $635 million. Johnson, the heir of one of America's greatest fortunes, is the president and CEO of Johnson & Johnson, a medical supply corporation. The family, one of the oldest in the United States, has contributed enormously to hospitals, medical foundations, universities, research, and a host of other charities and scientific groups.[29]

Ralph Wilson is the founding owner of the Buffalo Bills. Starting out in his father's insurance business, this native of Columbus, Ohio, built a business empire including radio and television stations, construction, and contract drilling operations. Wilson owned the Buffalo Bills before the merger of the AFL and the NFL in 1966.

The teams of the AFL North are the Pittsburgh Steelers, the Cleveland Browns, the Baltimore Ravens, and the Cincinnati Bengals.

The Pittsburgh Steelers are owned by Dan Rooney. Rooney inherited the Steelers from his father, Art Rooney, and has been president of the Steelers since 1975. Because of his exceptional contributions to football management he was inducted into the Football Hall of Fame in July 2000. His skill as a labor negotiator has earned him considerable admiration in the sports world.

Arthur Modell was born in Brooklyn in 1925. Owner of the Baltimore Ravens, he owned the Cleveland Browns from 1961 until 1995 when he moved the team to Maryland. In 1964 the Browns won the NFL title. Modell served as president of the NFL from 1967 to 1969 and also served as chairman of the owner's labor committee. He was also instrumental in negotiating with ABC to start Monday night football. This and more led to his inclusion in the Pro Football Hall of Fame in 2002.

Despite this record of achievement Modell has been the target of some of the most vitriolic verbal assaults ever published. This came about when he moved the Cleveland Browns to Baltimore. He did so because in Baltimore he was promised the use of a new $200 million stadium rent-free for seven years. The city also paid the NFL's $29 million relocation fee, the $12 million in damages Modell owed the city of Cleveland, a new $15 million training facility, and all moving expenses for the team. The city of Baltimore financed all this by selling seat licensing agreements. A seat license gives the licensee the right to buy a season ticket. In 2000, the Baltimore Ravens were sold to Stephen J. Bisciotti for $600 million. Bisciotti, a Baltimore-area native, is the owner of Aerotek, described as "the world's largest provider of temporary employees for technical jobs such as computer engineering."

The Cleveland Browns were owned by Alfred Lerner until his death in 2002. The ownership has now passed to his family. Lerner paid $530 million in 1998 to revive the franchise of the Cleveland

Browns, who started playing in the NFL in 1999. He was a minority owner of the Browns when Art Modell moved the team to Baltimore. Lerner was born into a Jewish family in Brooklyn. He served as a Marine Corps pilot and thereafter entered the real estate and banking business. His wealth became so great that he gave $100 million to the Cleveland Clinic and created the World Trade Center Heroes Fund to help survivors of that attack. Lerner was also a member of President George W. Bush's Foreign Intelligence Advisory Board and also served on the board of the New York Presbyterian Hospital and the board of trustees of Western Reserve University.

Mike Brown is the owner of the Cincinnati Bengals, so named by his father, Paul Brown, who founded the team in 1968. Paul Brown was also the coach of the Cleveland team which bears his name. The team was named after an earlier Cincinnati team which held the franchise in the 1930s and 1940s.

The AFL South includes the Indianapolis Colts, the Tennessee Titans, the Jacksonville Jaguars, and the Houston Texans.

The Indianapolis Colts are owned by Jim Irsay. Robert Irsay acquired the Colts in 1972 in exchange for the Los Angeles Rams, then owned by Carroll Rosenbloom. At that time the Colts were located in Baltimore. In 1984, after a great deal of wrangling including numerous lawsuits, the Colts moved to Indianapolis where a new $77.5 million stadium called the Hoosier Dome had just been opened.

The Colts owner, Robert Irsay, died in 1997 and the team passed on to his son, Jim. The city of Indianapolis now pays the Colts $12 million per year generated from leases on luxury suites, naming rights, concession sales, and parking.

The Tennessee Titans, also part of the AFC South, are owned by K.S. Bud Adams, chief executive officer and owner of Adams Resources & Energy, a Houston-based oil exploration company with sales of $7 billion a year.

Adams paid only $25,000 in 1959 for the Houston Oilers, who became the Tennessee Titans in 1997. In view of inflation, $25,000 would be about $150,000 in 2003. It has been estimated that the Titans would sell for $700 million in 2003, so the owner could realize a profit of 4,666 percent on his $25,000 investment.

The Jacksonville (Florida) Jaguars began play as the NFL's thirtieth team in 1995. The principal owner of the team is Wayne Weaver, part owner of Shoe Carnival. Among other team owners are Jeb Bush, governor of Florida, and Tom Petway, Hamilton Jordan, Arthur Sherrer, and David Selden, who is also chief operating officer. Calling themselves "Touchdown Jacksonville," this group invested $68 million in the expansion team. In August 1995 the city of Jacksonville agreed to renovate the city stadium for $145 million.

Robert McNair, the owner of the thirty-second NFL team, the Houston Texans, is listed by *Forbes* as one of America's wealthiest people. Founder of Cogen Technologies, a natural gas company, he sold that company to Enron for $1.5 billion. He then became owner of the Texans in 1999 for $700 million.

The AFL West includes the Denver Broncos, the Oakland Raiders, the San Diego Chargers, and the Kansas City Chiefs.

The Denver Broncos have been owned by Pat Bowlen since 1985. Originally he paid $43 million for 60 percent of the team. Bowlen is a graduate of the University of Oklahoma law school. He owns natural resources in Alberta, Canada, and has real estate holdings in California, Colorado, and Arizona. An athlete, Bowlen competed in the Iron Man Triathlon and in other triathlon competitions as well as several marathons.

The San Diego Chargers are owned by Dean Spanos. Spanos inherited the team from his father, Alex, who bought it in 1984. He became president in 1994. He is also president of the ASG Financial Corporation. Spanos is a member of numerous business boards of directors and serves on the boards of numerous charities as well. An outstanding golfer, Spanos is considered a real estate tycoon.

The owner of the Oakland Raiders, Al Davis, has a long time football career. Inducted into the Football Hall of Fame in 1992, Davis started as assistant coach of the old Los Angeles, then San Diego, Chargers. Later he became head coach and then moved on to become commissioner of the American Football League. Thereafter he became principal owner of the Raiders. Davis is a graduate of Syracuse University in New York, where he played football, basketball, and baseball in the 1950s.

In recent years Davis has annoyed other owners because he revealed to the *Los Angeles Times* that the average operating profit of the NFL's football franchises is $11 million. The other owners claim that this figure does not include numerous expenses and that it is therefore inaccurate. Davis also lost a lawsuit against the NFL for $1 billion, claiming that the NFL forced the Raiders to leave Los Angeles.

Lamar Hunt, a wealthy Dallas businessman, formed the American Football League together with Ralph Wilson and Bud Adams. Each of these men contributed $25,000. Today the Kansas City Chiefs, owned by Hunt, are worth more than $500 million. The Chiefs had originally been called the Texans but were moved to Kansas City by Hunt in 1962. Hunt also owns several other sports teams.

The National Football Conference East includes the Philadelphia Eagles, the New York Giants, the Washington Redskins, and the Dallas Cowboys.

The owner of the Eagles is Jeff Lurie, who bought the team for $195 million in 1994. Lurie is a native of Boston. He is the grandson of the owner of General Cinema. His family has numerous other financial interests such as Neiman Marcus and Reed Elsevier.

Lurie holds a PhD in social policy. His early business efforts included a failed movie-producing company. Because of that failure he decided to enter the football business, with far more success.

The New York Giants of the NFC East were founded by Tim Mara in 1925, when he purchased a football franchise for $500. That same year Mara invested another $25,000 in the franchise. The Giants won the NFL championship in 1927. Tim's son, Wellington Mara, became president of the Giants in 1965 after the death of Wellington's older brother, Jack. Mara has spent his entire working career in the Giants organization.

Preston Robert Tisch is co-chairman and co-owner of the New York Giants. Tisch and his brother Laurence are co-chairmen of the Loews Corporation, which began with owning one hotel in New Jersey and has grown to a $21.3 billion conglomerate including hotels, the Lorillard Tobacco Company, CNA Financial Corporation, Bulova Corporation, and Diamond Offshore Drilling.

Dan Snyder owns the Washington Redskins, for which he paid $800 million in 2000 after selling his Snyder Communications newspaper empire for $2.1 billion. Snyder is a partner of publishing tycoon Mortimer Zuckerman.

After spending $40 million to renovate FedEx Field, Snyder fired numerous employees and began to charge $20 for admission to training camp practice. Because Snyder was only thirty-five years old when he bought the Redskins, many have viewed his detractors as envious. Nevertheless, Snyder has the reputation of being arrogant and aggressive and insensitive to the feelings of others.

The Dallas Cowboys are owned by Jerry Jones, who had amassed a fortune in the energy exploration business, as have so many other owners of professional football teams. In 1989 Jones paid $140 million for the team. He promptly fired coach Tom Landry, the only coach the team ever had. He then hired Jimmy Johnson as coach, who coached the team to a Super Bowl championship in 1993. Nevertheless, Jones fired Johnson in 1994. Jones acts as his own general manager. He has hired Troy Aikman, Emmitt Smith, Michael Irvin, and other superstars. The Cowboys won the Super Bowl championship in 1994 and 1996.

NFC North teams include the Green Bay Packers, the Detroit Lions, the Minnesota Vikings, and the Chicago Bears.

The Packers were named after the long defunct Acme Packing Company who sponsored the first jerseys and equipment for the team in 1919-1920. The Packers are owned by 110,000 citizens of Green Bay, Wisconsin, who paid $200 each for a share in the team. The Packers are considered one of the best teams in the NFL, having won the championship twelve times.

The great grandson of Henry Ford, William Clay Ford, is CEO of the Ford Motor Company and owner of the Detroit Lions. In 1964 his father, William Ford paid $4.5 million for the team. The Lions are one of the weaker teams in the NFL, having never won a Super Bowl. The Lions have traditionally hosted a Thanksgiving Day game for the NFL.

Billy Joe "Red" McCombs, the owner of the Minnesota Vikings, is a native of Spur, Texas, and co-founder of Clear Channel Communications. He owns interests in car dealerships, sports franchises, insurance, real estate, oil exploration, ranching, and communications. He has been involved in over 300 business ventures. He owned the Denver Nuggets, the San Antonio Spurs in earlier years, and began his interest in sports teams when at age twenty-five he bought a Texas "Big State" baseball league team. McCombs has shown some interest in selling the team.

The Chicago Bears have been owned by the same family since George Halas founded pro football and the Chicago "Staley's" with membership at $100 per club. The Bears were one of these clubs. In 1925 "Red" Grange signed with the Bears. In 1933 the National Football League began, and in that year the Bears won the NFL's first championship. When George Halas died in 1983 his son, George Halas Jr., became owner and president. Michael McCloskey, grandson of George Halas Sr. and son of Virginia Halas McCloskey and Ed McCloskey, became the third owner of the team. Michael McCloskey was a business school professor and also operated a consulting firm in Boston. Since McCloskey became president the team has had nine winning seasons, went to the NFC title game three times, and won Super Bowl XX.

The four NFC South teams are the Tampa Bay Buccaneers, the New Orleans Saints, the Atlanta Falcons, and the Carolina Panthers.

Malcom Glazer owns the Tampa Bay Buccaneers, which he bought in 1995 for $192 million. Glazer has had amazing success with his team. In 1999 Tampa Bay captured the first division title in eighteen years and continued with a play-off appearance in 2000 and a championship in 2003. Glazer promoted the construction of a new "state-of-the-art" stadium, which hosted Super Bowl XXXV in 2001. Thereafter a new training facility has also been constructed.

Malcolm Glazer was born in Rochester, New York. Glazer started working in his father's watch parts business at the age of eight. When he was fifteen his father died and he assumed responsibility for the family. Since then he has owned a food service equipment firm and has invested in food packaging, marine protein, broadcasting, health care, real estate, banking, natural gas, oil exploration stocks and bonds, and internet publications. The Glazer Family Foundation has distributed millions in assisting charitable and educational causes.

Tom Benson is the owner of the New Orleans Saints. Benson bought the team in 1985 for less than $71 million. The team is now worth approximately $600 million. The State of Louisiana has agreed to give the owner $12.5 million for two seasons, $15 million for the next two seasons, including an agreement that the Saints can leave the Superdome after 2003. Benson is a U.S. Navy veteran who has remained interested in the navy since leaving it as an enlisted man. He is the only enlisted man who ever served on the board of trustees of the U.S. Naval Museum in Pensacola, Florida. A major contributor to the National D-Day Museum in New Orleans, he also serves on that museum's board of directors. During Benson's ownership the Saints have hosted four Super Bowls, in 1916, 1990, 1997, and 2002. A generous donor, Benson has pledged to give $50 million to the Gulf South community and to a number of charities.

Arthur Blank bought the Atlanta Falcons franchise in February 2002 for $545 million. He founded Home Depot in 1978, a business that became one of the Fortune 500 companies. Blank retired from Home Depot in 2001, the year his company was ranked first in social responsibility. Home Depot has donated more than $113 million to charitable foundations. Blank is also a faculty member at Emory University in Atlanta and chairs the capital campaign of the Atlanta Symphony Orchestra.

In 1993, Jerry Richardson, former wide receiver for the Baltimore Colts, brought professional football to the Carolinas when he bought the Panthers franchise for $206 million.

Richardson had made his money by entering the fast food business. He bought his first Hardee's restaurant franchise in 1961 and then continued to buy franchises, so that by 1993 he owned Flagstar Company, which had revenues of $23.7 billion that year. He owned over 700 restaurants including Denny's.

As with many other owners, Richardson relied on the public to pay for a stadium. First he got the right to build a stadium on $60 million worth of real estate for which he pays $1 a year, and then he sold lifetime rights to buy season tickets to raise the bulk of the money for the stadium.

The NFC West teams include the San Francisco 49ers, the St. Louis Rams, the Arizona Cardinals, and the Seattle Seahawks.

The San Francisco 49ers are owned by Denise DeBartolo York, the sister of the previous owner Eddie DeBartolo Jr., who was forced to relinquish ownership in May 2000 after his conviction on several counts of bribery and extortion. DeBartolo was placed on probation and assessed $1 million in penalties.

DeBartolo is the owner of a $16 billion real estate investment trust with 111 shopping centers in thirty-two states. In 1977 he bought the 49ers for $17 million with backing from his father. By 1980 the team had won twelve division titles. The 49ers have won five Super Bowl championships. Forbes magazine estimated in 2002 that Eddie DeBartolo had a personal wealth of $830 million.

Denise DeBartolo York has had twenty-five years of experience in real estate and sports management. She learned business from her father, Ed DeBartolo Sr. When he died in 1994 she assumed the presidency of the family's real estate business and the presidency of the Pittsburgh Penguins hockey team. She and husband John York have made great contributions to numerous charities, educational foundations, scholarship funds, and particularly to the National Center for Missing and Exploited Children.

Georgia Frontiere is the principal owner of the St. Louis Rams. She is a former lounge singer who inherited the team from the sixth of her seven husbands, Carroll Rosenbloom. Rosenbloom, a wealthy textile manufacturer, acquired the team in 1972 when he traded the franchise of the Baltimore Colts for the Los Angeles Rams. Carroll Rosenbloom drowned in the ocean in 1979. Some call that drowning "mysterious." Upon the death of Rosenbloom, his widow fired Carroll's son, executive vice president Stephen Rosenbloom. Thereafter, Georgia married Dominic Frontiere, a professional musician, who was later indicted for ticket scalping. She divorced him in 1988.

The Arizona Cardinals have existed since 1898, when they were called the Morgan Athletic Club. Since then they have changed their name repeatedly until they moved to Phoenix, Arizona, in 1988 as the Phoenix Cardinals. In 1994, the owner, William Bidwell, changed the name to Arizona Cardinals. Bidwell had inherited the team from his mother, who died in 1962. She was the widow of Charles Bidwell, who had bought the franchise in 1933 for $50,000. The Cardinals are an average team, having achieved a .500 record several years in a row.

Paul G. Allen is the owner of the Seattle Seahawks. Allen was born in Seattle in 1953. In grade school he met Bill Gates and began programming in BASIC using a teletype machine. After graduating from high school, he entered Washington State University. Together with Gates he bought a $360 Intel chip and developed a computer to measure traffic. They then started a computer company called Traf-O-Data. Thereafter, he and Gates founded Microsoft in 1975. Struck by Hodgkin's disease, he left Microsoft in 1983 but continued in the computer business with such success that he became a billionaire. Allen established six charitable foundations and entered the movie and entertainment business.

This listing of the thirty-two owners of the NFL teams reveals that only the wealthiest Americans can own a football team in the twenty-first century.[30] Although professional football was at one time an obscure game played in out-of-the-way places, the media have helped make professional football America's favorite sports spectacle.

SUMMARY

Coaches are the principal decision makers at all levels of football. Professional coaches and some college coaches may have incomes exceeding a million dollars a year. Some of the most successful coaches have personality characteristics labeled "moral density" or "charisma." Such characteristics include the ability to withstand emotional pressure.

Scouts are of great aid to coaches in recruitment, leading to signing of competent players. The NFL spends upward of $160 million on signing bonuses each year. Trainers and referees are also important participants in the football culture. Referees in particular must be willing to travel and be acquainted with nearly 1,000 rules.

Cheerleaders are women who earn very little in order to appear at games. Cheerleading has become a sport of its own, including acrobatics. There are 3 million cheerleaders in the United States.

Team physicians are appointed by owners and may or may not work in the best interests of the players, many of whom have drug problems in addition to taking the risks of injuries on the playing field, as well as heat strokes, arthritis, and other physical consequences of this violent sport.

The daily operation of any professional football team lies in the hands of a general manager, who may have been a professional football player in earlier years. General managers can earn $1 million a year. Their work includes labor relations, public relations, and recruitment alongside the coaches and owners.

There are thirty-one individual owners in the NFL and one communal owner, i.e., Green Bay, Wisconsin. The owners are usually exceedingly wealthy men, although two women are also owners of professional football teams.

In addition to coaches, trainers, scouts, officials, cheerleaders, physicians, and owners, the media make a great contribution to football both on the college and professional level.

Chapter 6

Fanatics

THE FOOTBALL HALL OF FANS

The ancient Romans called a temple a *fanum,* thus someone inspired by a god was termed a *fanatic.* Some Americans might be described as religious fanatics, but they are few compared to those whose allegiance to a football team makes them true "fans" of America's favorite game.

In 1999, the Pro-Football Hall of Fame in Canton, Ohio, inaugurated the Visa Hall of Fans. This is the third hall of fame pertaining to football, since Notre Dame has supported the College Football Hall of Fame in South Bend, Indiana, for some years. The Visa Hall of Fans is a part of the Pro-Football Hall of Fame. It was inaugurated to honor the customers who make the football business possible and whose loyalty guarantees the league's existence.

Each year, thirty-two people are honored by inclusion in the Hall of Fans, with each fan representing one of the NFL teams. A contest promoted by each of the NFL teams asks contestants to write a fifty-word essay explaining "why I should represent my team's fans at the Pro-Football Hall of Fame."[1]

One inductee is Matt Andrews, who supports the Baltimore Ravens. Andrews travels in a customized van known as the "12 Man Fan Van," which includes painted Raven logos, players' and coaches' signatures, and external speakers that blast Ravens calls. Andrews is known as "Fan Man" and as "the Millennium 2000 Ultimate Raven Fan." Together with other fans, Andrews tailgates and attends all away games, in addition to being present at all charitable, social, and public events. One picture of Andrews shows him wearing a mask, a shirt covered with "Ravens" icons, and a bandanna around his baseball cap. His face is painted and his fist is raised.

Other Hall of Fans members include Jim "Torchman" Convery, who supports the Philadelphia Eagles, and Charles "Darth Raider" Ybarra, a supporter of the Oakland Raiders. Chris "The Texans Freak" was the first supporter of the Houston Texans to be included in the Hall of Fans. These winners usually wear bizarre clothing, including a barrel. They lead cheers and generally conduct themselves in a manner that most people would consider embarrassing and juvenile.[2]

FEMALE FOOTBALL FANS

Until recently, few women could be described as true "football fans." Prior to the 1980s, most American women were discouraged from showing interest in aggressive sports.

Now, in the twenty-first century, with women's participation in sports significantly expanded, more women are encouraged to show an interest in football. Fifty million women in the United States avidly follow professional sports, including professional football. Women who enjoy football also like the excitement of other sports. For example, female NFL fans are 48 percent more likely to attend NASCAR events than other women.

One factor in this shift has been Title IX of the Educational Amendments of 1972, which prohibits sex discrimination in the allocation of funds for government-sponsored sports programs. This legislation increased female inclusion in many high school and college sports and paved the way for more female sports fans than was possible heretofore.[3]

The NFL has also encouraged women to become football fans, sponsoring workshops that teach women the history and basics of the game. As a result, women now make up 43 percent of American football fans. More than 375,000 women attend football games each weekend.

In a survey of women's favorite sport, among women interested in sports

- 31 percent selected football as their first choice;
- 28 percent chose baseball;
- 19 percent chose basketball;
- 13 percent chose NASCAR;

- 13 percent chose golf; and
- 10 percent chose hockey.

Football can arguably be named the number one interest of sports fans of both sexes in America.[4]

The Super Bowl's half-time entertainment has proven to be a powerful lure for female fans. Likewise, the Super Bowl is now considered the best opportunity for advertisers to gain the attention of female viewers.[5]

THE FOOTBALL CULTURE

The huge American interest in football is of course not confined to the NFL. College football and high school football also have huge followings. It has been estimated that during the football season more than 200,000 fanatics watch Saturday football games. These fans follow college and high school teams for ten weeks every year. After each game they rehash the action and participate in postgame activities just as they participated in pregame activities such as tailgate parties.

One example is Deborah Joseph, a South Carolina social worker. She watches football three or four nights a week: the high school game on Friday night, the state university game on Saturday, professional football on Sunday, and Monday night football. Joseph also tailgates with her women friends before games. The tailgaters have a reserved parking spot at each game for three months where they serve food prepared by each member of the tailgating party. She and her friends try to attend all of the twelve games played by a college team in any one season.[6]

Fans bring expectations to a football season. Those expectations differ with each team and may have some bearing on the season's outcome. For example, a 7-4 season for Memphis would be a real triumph because Memphis won only two games in 2002. The same ending for Tennessee would be viewed as a disaster because Tennessee won conference honors that year. Likewise, Kentucky fans were happy when the team won four and lost two at the beginning of the 2002 season, while Alabama fans felt frustrated when the Crimson Tide posted the same results after six games. The winners and the losers therefore need to explain their results not only to themselves but also to their fans. This phenomenon was studied by social psychologist Charles Horton Cooley, who originated the phrase "the looking glass self." This refers to the view that our self-image is based largely on the way we think others see us.[7]

Fans are seldom guided by reason. Emotions of the moment dominate the reaction of sports fans, while logic is generally absent. For this reason the coaching profession is quite treacherous. A losing coach knows that every decision will be reviewed by the fans who are sure that they could have done better and produced a better outcome.

Similarly, many football fans like to second-guess referees. They are usually loud, screaming fans who are particularly vocal in favor of the home team. Referees need to have a stoic impartiality not to be swayed by 40,000 screaming fans. Nevertheless, a study by sociologist Alan Nevill revealed that referees judged 15 percent fewer plays as illegal against the home team than the visitors in a controlled experiment conducted in England, where the fans of a home team are almost entirely residents of the town in which the home team lives.[8]

The reason for the vehemence with which some fans denounce losers or praise winners is that many fans allow the football team to define their existence. Even winning teams find that the more they win the more the fans expect them to win and the greater the anger and disappointment expressed at even one loss.

Sociologists call this phenomenon "existential validation." This refers to the need to identify with a group or cause which gives the individual a sense of reality and worth. The Latin origin of "validation" is *valere*, which means "to be strong." That meaning is quite applicable here. Football fans seek strength in identifying not only with the power of the game but also with winning. Associating oneself with a team is not the only source of existential validation, which is also known as self-validation. Identification with symbols and groups has the effect of "restoring and reinforcing the sense of self-worth, meaning of life, and personal identity and competence through a variety of activities and interactions with the . . . social environment." This is exactly what motivates football fans.[9]

In addition to existential validation, "relative deprivation" is also at work here. Relative deprivation refers to the idea that some people feel deprived not because they are destitute but because others have more. This also explains why football fans will criticize a winning coach, because any loss, any mistake, any setback makes them feel that they took a loss, that they made a mistake or suffered a setback.[10]

"Basking in reflected glory" is another motive for the support football fans give their team. According to a study by Robert Caldini, students are more likely to wear their university-affiliated apparel after their school's team has won. Likewise, fans were more likely to use the pronoun *we* when describing a victory and *they* when describing a defeat. Sports fans' attachment to their team affects their self-esteem, promotes a sense of belonging, and even defends against depression.[11]

According to psychologists C. E. Kimble and B. P. Cooper, sports provide their fans with a form of pleasure; stress, tension, or sensation; gratification of aggressive tendencies; entertainment; and vicarious achievement. Kimble and Cooper also noticed the tendency of fans to associate with winning teams and to disassociate from losers; fans of winning teams are elated, while fans of the losing side appear dejected after a game. It has been suggested that fans who feel such emotions are those already seeking excitement and sensations. Moreover, those who seek to gain excitement through winning also risk experiencing negative emotions when losing.[12]

REGIONAL AND GENERATIONAL DIFFERENCES AMONG FOOTBALL FANS

In the United States supporters of a football team do not necessarily come only from the large city in which any particular football team is located. Televison and other media help to gather support for football teams from many areas of the country, so that support for all NFL teams is national. The salary cap has minimized major performance differences among NFL teams such as those frequently seen in hockey and baseball.[13]

Although football has many adherents in all parts of the country, there are regional differences in the amount of attention football receives. Unlike people in the South or the Midwest, most Westerners do not construct their lives around football. In the South many people fit their weekend schedules around football games, whether the team of interest is a high school team, a college team, a professional team, or some combination of these. In the West, the football game is only one part of what people do on the weekend; it is not the center of attention or the focus of everything done on Saturday and/or Sunday.

For that reason the University of Utah had a great deal of difficulty selling enough tickets to pay for their new stadium. In fact, some games are so poorly attended at Utah that only 15,000 of 33,000 ticket holders come to watch the game. Failure to regularly fill football stadiums is common in the West. This is particularly true of college football games and has been observed at the University of California, Stanford, Arizona State, and Colorado State University. One explanation for this is that the West is chiefly populated by people who have come from other states and who therefore do not have the same intensity of local pride as can be observed in the South and the Midwest. This is most significant for college teams who lack the advertising and entertainment resources available to the professionals.

In the Midwest and the South the stadiums fill up early. Many Southern and Midwestern tailgaters arrive as early as Thursday night. This is true of University of Tennessee games in Knoxville as well as for fans in Gainesville, Florida (home of the University of Florida), Ann Arbor, Michigan, and in Lincoln, Nebraska.[14]

It appears that the overall interest in watching football games may be fading with the rise of the first generation of the twenty-first century. According to a poll commissioned by the Sporting Goods Manufacturers of America, the number of youths age twelve to seventeen who describe themselves as ardent sports fans dropped 3.6 percent since 1999. A study by Nielsen Media Research found a 3 percent decline among the number of young NFL viewers. One reason for this decline may be found in the longer seasons most sports occupy, featuring many more games than played in the past. In addition, more sports are available to watch. Now golf and NASCAR compete with football, as do "extreme" sports. These other sports can be watched on almost any day at any time, in contrast to football games, which can be seen almost exclusively on weekends.

Video games, the Internet, DVDs, CDs, cable TV, and outdoor sports such as surfboarding, skateboarding, and lacrosse also have a role. Furthermore, some football players have received a good deal of negative attention in recent years. In part that negative attention is the consequence of crimes committed by prominent athletes. However, greed has also turned off many fans who view football salaries as outlandish and labor stoppages as inexcusable for the millionaires who play football. Free agency has also led many players to change teams so often that Jerry Seinfeld joked that the "fans cheer laundry," referring to supporting uniforms regardless of who is in them.[15]

THE TAILGATE PARTY AND THE FOOTBALL DIET

Many football fans drive to the game early and conduct tailgate parties in the parking lot outside the football stadium. Some tailgaters come a day early and sleep in their vehicles the night before the game. Perhaps the most unusual tailgate parties are held in northern California, where a special train is available to football fans who want to ride from the San Juaquin Valley and Sacramento to the football games in Oakland to see Raiders home games. These Raider trains are decorated in the Raiders' colors, silver and black, and carry the "Raiders Nation," as some fans like to call themselves. For the fans who ride that train, Oakland football is their religion. The "Raiders Nation" knows only football and lives in a football universe. Many of these fans have learned their devotion to the Raiders from their parents and their family. To them it is a family legacy. Some will even claim to have been Raiders fans before they were born.

Some residents of the Oakland area fear Raiders fans. This includes people who have witnessed the fans light a bonfire in the middle of a highway, torch an auto repair shop, and embarrass the Bay Area of California with conduct deliberately gross and aggressive. These fans object to being viewed as hoodlums, because they normally do not exhibit any of the behaviors they use to support their favorite football team.[16]

The conduct of violent football fans may be termed "militant enthusiasm." This has been explained by the Austrian biologist Konrad Lorenz in his book *On Aggression*. Lorenz argued that militant enthusiasm consists of the interaction of a phylogenetically evolved pattern of behavior with culturally ritualized social norms. He points out that the Greek word *enthousiasmos* refers to possession by a god and is translated into German as *begeistert,* meaning controlled by a spirit.

According to Lorenz:

> militant enthusiasms leads one to soar elated above all ties of everyday life. One is ready to abandon all for the call of what, in the moment of this specific emotion, seems to be a sacred duty.

Lorenz lists four conditions that lead to violent militant enthusiasm.

1. A group with which we identify seems threatened by an out-group.
2. The hated enemy is present and visible.
3. A leader or a group of leaders is available to arouse enthusiasm in the crowd.
4. Many other individuals are present and agitated by the same emotion.

All of these conditions are familiar among football enthusiasts and promote the militancy of so many fans around the country.[17]

Militant enthusiasm similar to that found in the Oakland area may also be seen in South Bend, Indiana, home of Notre Dame University and its football team. "It's not a sport; it's a religion" is what South Bend citizens like to say of Notre Dame football. The football stadium exhibits a mural called "Touchdown Jesus" and promotes its tradition and its legends even though Notre Dame is no longer the football powerhouse it once was. Notre Dame has a stadium seating 80,000 fans, and South Bend hosts the College Football Hall of Fame. Although the tradition at Notre Dame is Irish Catholic, the democracy of football is color blind and ethnicity blind. In reality, "the fighting Irish" come from a multiplicity of religious, ethnic, and racial groups with little more in common than a talent and interest in playing football.[18]

The preponderance of those who are closely associated with their favorite football team are members of the working class. Firefighters, construction workers, lumber mill hands, and others who do semiskilled and unskilled labor are overrepresented among football fans. Raiders tickets cost at least $57 per game, but the Raiders attract more than 57,000 fans to their games. Perhaps nothing proves the loyalty of the fans to their team more than the willingness of people earning rather low incomes to spend upwards of $114 for two to see their team play a game.[19] When Raiders fans are asked for their prime motive in supporting the team with such vehemence they generally agree with the view of one fan who said, "I have been an underdog all my life. That's why I am a Raiders fan."[20]

As described earlier, many fans drive to football games early and engage in tailgate parties. These parties include the consumption of fatty foods that can lead to hardening of the arteries for as long as three hours after the high-fat meal. The average football fan who watches two or three games a week may gain ten to twelve pounds during the season. Both at tailgate parties and in front of television, a great deal of eating and drinking of unhealthy foods is carried out. According to registered dietician Sherlyn Hogenson, such eating leads to restricted blood flow and can cause a heart attack if the person already has plaque buildup in his or her arteries.

Dr. Paul Pederson, team physician for Illinois Wesleyan University, reports that many fans eat early on Thanksgiving so that they can spend the day watching football, even eating more during the four- to five-hour stint in front of the TV. Such popular football foods as bratwurst and other sausages, chili, and hot wings are labeled as dangerous by the medical profession. One bratwurst has 290 calories, and 230 of these calories are from fat. Eaten on a bun, 500 calories are consumed by someone doing nothing more than sitting in front of the television. Those who typically eat six brats during two or three consecutive games are taking in 2,970 calories, although the average adult needs only 2,000 calories per day.

Furthermore, excessive consumption can cause people to fall asleep and miss the game they want to see. This is particularly true of drinking beer. One 12 oz. beer has 162 calories, so the average six-pack contains 972 empty calories. Added to that are six brats and a 16 oz. bag of snack chips for a total intake of 6,342 calories with no activity and almost no calories used during one football game.[21]

IN GROUPS AND OUT GROUPS

Raiders fans and fans of other football teams also like to draw a sharp distinction between themselves and the supporters of other teams. Supporters of one team often feel real hostility toward supporters of other football teams. Sociologists refer to this phenomenon as "in-group, out-group distinctions." The in group consists of one's peers; the out group are those who are outside the boundaries of intimacy. Such distinctions can develop around any quality or any cause, including those that some people would not even notice. For example, in a Chicago housing project boys made distinctions between those who lived in lighter or darker brick buildings. Usually, however, race, religion, income, ethnic association, or education are the distinctions that separate groups. In extreme situations the out group may even be hated. Some football fans express real anger and hatred for other teams and other fans. Football fans attached to one or another team may also be seen as reference groups, which individuals use as a frame for self-evaluation and attitude formation. Hence, reference groups serve as standards for comparison and also set standards for behavior and certain values. All of this is achieved by football fan clubs and even by crowds at football games and tailgate parties.[22]

The hostility some football fans feel toward teams other than the ones they support is sometimes also directed at their own coaches and players. Such hostility exists among college football supporters as well as those who support professional football. For example, Vince Dooley was hanged in effigy in 1967 when he coached the University of Georgia football team, even though the team had won an SEC championship the year before. In 1988 someone threw a brick through the window of coach Bill Curry of Alabama because the team had lost its homecoming game. These were isolated incidents in the past. Now, however, the Internet allows everyone to vent frustrations to anyone else. This is also true of talk radio, as both mediums allow the complainers to remain anonymous and thus unaccountable for what they say.[23]

Recently wide receiver Terrence Edwards of the Georgia Bulldogs dropped a ball in Jacksonville, Florida, in a loss to South Carolina. When he returned to Athens, Georgia, a number of nasty and threatening phone messages were waiting for him. Likewise, coaches receive voice mail and e-mail messages harassing them for decisions they have made or for losing games.

"Fans want blood. They want the opponents blood and if they don't get that, they want your blood," said David Housel, athletic director at Auburn University. That comment refers to the experience of a

Southern coach. Similar experiences have been reported by other Southern coaches and players. The degree of expected violence before, during, and after a football game frequently depends on the region of the country and the expectation of violence in each region. An inspection of violent crime reveals that year after year, the South exhibits higher rates of murder, aggravated assault, rape, and burglary than any other U.S. region.[24]

Some areas of the United States are battlegrounds for the loyalty of the football fans because more than one team has influence there. In areas where NFL markets overlap, loyalties to one team or another can lead to family arguments and some real fights as to who controls the TV remote. For example, some areas of Maryland are near both the Pennsylvania and Delaware lines. People who live there can read newspapers from both locations and can see televised football games from more than one area. This translates into loyalties toward some but not all advertisers and sales of sports paraphernalia. Advertisers vie for the fans of all teams through television ads, merchandising, youth clinics, and direct mail.

Some fans are not content with watching their favorite team but also need to express hatred for another team. Web sites by fans of various teams announce that the Web site owner hates the Steelers or the Redskins or the Ravens or some other franchise.[25]

Other fans hate one or another college team. Such hate may target well-known teams such as Notre Dame whose followers include some of the most devoted football fans. A Maryland woman was quoted as saying that she could hardly tolerate the sound of the Notre Dame football fight song and had to put her fingers in her ears to avoid hearing it. Some claim that Notre Dame is arrogant and therefore should be hated. Some fans love a team even if the team performs poorly.[26]

As previously mentioned, many Oakland fans view their interest in the Oakland Raiders as their religion. This may sound exaggerated to those not acquainted with the fervor with which some fans follow "their" team. Some fans have said that they will skip Sunday Mass and everything else other than their mother's funeral to see football games on television or in a stadium. Such fervor may be seen in the area of North Carolina known as the Triad: Greensboro, Winston-Salem, Burlington and several smaller communities. Here, and in many other parts of the country, football fans congregate in local bars and taverns on Sunday throughout the football season. Sports bars, as they are called, will induce large numbers of customers to visit by buying a dozen TV sets so that everyone can watch his or her favorite team all the time. Chicken wings and cold beer are served continuously. These bars pay between $1,000 and $2,600 for a program called NFL Sunday Ticket which allows the bar to show every game during a five-month season. The NFL Sunday Ticket program is also available at home at prices ranging from forty to seventy-five dollars based on the number of channels. Subscribers can see fourteen games each weekend. Most recently, a year-round NFL channel was initiated by the NFL and Hughes Electronics. Many football fans do not want to pay the fee for home Sunday Ticket and therefore see the games in a local bar. Such football viewing also extends to Monday night football.[27]

Some fans join "fan clubs" which follow their team in a bar who then turn on only one football game showing the efforts of the team whose fan club favors the bar. The fans usually make a great deal of noise. A number bet money on the games. On frequent occasions fans favoring opposing teams will sit next to each other in a sports bar. Such encounters are usually, but not always, friendly but nevertheless include the shouting of numerous obscenities.[28]

Sociologists refer to such conduct as a "moral holiday" because the behavior surrounding football viewing would not usually be accepted in other situations. Football fan crowds are usually joyful and fun loving.[29]

While sociologists call loud and boisterous fans an "expressive crowd," there are also "aggressive crowds" who produce violence and anger.

FAN VIOLENCE

Rioting after football games has become a tradition among some fans. This is notably true in Oakland, California, although it has occurred in other cities as well.

In January 2003, the Oakland Raiders were defeated 48-21 by the Tampa Bay Buccaneers. Thereupon football fans smashed windows and set cars afire, leading to the arrest of at least eighty people, mostly for public drunkenness. Others were arrested for throwing rocks and bottles at police and obstructing the police. A television news van was attacked and rioters broke its windows. Furthermore, nine fire department vehicles and twelve police cars were damaged in the riot. Someone threw a cement garbage can through a restaurant window. Thereupon the inside of that restaurant was ransacked and set afire, costing $30,000 in damages.[30]

In December 2001 Cleveland football fans threw bottles and other objects onto the field after officials overturned a call that helped Jacksonville win a game 15-10. The fans threw thousands of bottles, some filled with beer, on the field. The Jacksonville players literally feared for their lives as the game was stopped for about half an hour. Enraged about the loss, some fans tried to run onto the field. In 1995 Cleveland fans tore out rows of seats and started fires following the announcement that the team was moving to Baltimore.

The fans of the Philadelphia Eagles may have been the worst-behaved of all fans, at least in the past. For example, on December 15, 1968, Eagles fans threw snowballs at a man dressed in a Santa suit riding in a flatbed truck around Franklin Field. On December 9, 1989, Veterans Stadium fans pelted Cowboys coach Jimmy Johnson and Dallas players with snowballs as they left the field. On November 10, 1997, violence broke out during the final minutes of the 49ers victory over the Eagles. One fan was beaten by a crowd of drunks and suffered a broken ankle, while another fan shot a flare across the field and into the stands and was charged with arson. On October 10, 1999, Cowboys receiver Michael Irvin was badly injured after being tackled during an Eagles game. While he lay motionless on the field for twenty minutes, Eagles fans cheered when they realized that Irvin was hurt seriously. They then cheered again when paramedics wheeled a stretcher onto the field. These incidents and numerous others led the mayor of Philadelphia to appoint a judge to be present at every game. That judge is ready to hold "Eagles Court" on the spot to deal with as many as 650 fistfights during one game.[31]

College football has also been involved in violence by fans. In November 2002, Ohio State University fans celebrated a victory by rushing the field in an effort to tear down the goalposts. When that failed the fans set about thirty fires. Similar violence occurred in Pullman, Washington, after the University of Washington beat Washington State University 29-26 in 2002. Glass bottles and plastics of all kinds were hurled on the field, and the athletic director said she feared for her life. In Clemson, South Carolina, Tigers fans celebrated their victory over South Carolina by tearing down the goalposts and injuring one woman and a police officer. In Berkeley, California, a fight broke out between fans after California beat Stanford, and in Raleigh, North Carolina, twenty-one fans were arrested for fighting after North Carolina beat Florida. In 2000 a Raider fan stabbed a Charger fan. This lead to the conviction of the assailant, who was then sentenced to five years in prison.[32]

Louisiana State University Chancellor Mark Emmert found it necessary to apologize to the president of Auburn University after a football game in December 2001. This came about because the LSU fans taunted Auburn players as they tried to board a bus leaving the stadium. During that game some fans stomped on the LSU emblem. An Auburn fan who led the team's walk into the stadium was struck by a football. Other LSU fans threw objects, including bottles, into the fans on the other side of the stadium while making crude comments and gestures. As a consequence the LSU coach sent a letter to season ticket holders threatening to eject fans who exhibit "boorish" behavior. Two cameras were installed for the purpose of identifying disruptive fans, and extra police were on hand to prevent violence.

One more example of football fan violence will serve to illustrate the kind of conduct that plagues the game on both the professional and college levels. In November 2002 the Marshall College football team of West Virginia defeated Miami University, 38-34. After the game a group of fans assaulted Miami freshman defensive back Sean McMonigle who escaped a severe beating only because some Marshall football players defended him after he was already beaten by some Marshall fans. That same game saw the Miami defensive coordinator handcuffed by police after he assaulted a Marshall fan who had to be taken from the field in an unconscious condition after the game.[33] These examples serve to illustrate some aspects of active crowd behavior.[34]

Sociologists distinguish *active* crowds from conventionalized crowds. Active crowds are also called mobs and are defined as highly emotional and ready to engage in violence against people or property.

These active crowds conduct riots which need not target a particular person but can be justified by deep-seated antagonisms and hatreds. For over a century, ever since Gustave LeBon published his work *The Crowd,* many have noted the way a crowd takes on a life of its own and that the conduct of people in a crowd is contagious and not the responsibility of any one person. LeBon argued that anonymity permits each individual in the crowd to abandon reason and to act as part of a single organism, the crowd. He thought that he had discovered "the collective mind."[35]

More recent discussions of aggressive crowd behavior focus on the tendency of crowds to define a situation depending on the circumstances of the moment. Violent crowds will erupt when situations are new and unusual. This was precisely the case when the Cleveland Browns fans learned that their team would be moved to Baltimore. This was again the case when the Browns fans concluded that a revised "call" by the referees was unfair and would cost the Browns the game. Both were unusual and unexpected events leading to rioting by the fans.[36]

FANTASY FOOTBALL

In the mid-1960s a group of football fans patronizing a California bar, discussed their favorite sport and concluded that they could manage teams better than the real coaches and owners. They decided to pretend to manage and/or own a football team and called these pretensions fantasy football. Since then fantasy football has expanded into a multimillion-dollar industry attracting more than 10 million fans. This phenomenal growth was fueled by the Internet where fantasy football has been played since 1995.

Fantasy football consists of any group of people who deem themselves coach, general manager, and/or owner of a computer-based football team. The "team" consists of players from football teams who are "drafted" by deciding which players are to be assigned to which team. During the season, which coincides with the regular football season, each "owner" participates in a "lineup." Then statistics from real games are used to calculate a pre-set amount of points based on yards, touchdowns, and other categories.

There is also a "draft" which consists of picking a draft order to see which team selects first, second, etc. Then player names from real football teams are called out and recorded on each team's fantasy roster. Using a variety of league rules, teams score by using touchdowns, yards, rushing yards, receiving yards, field goals, etc. Teams then submit a lineup each week to the National Fantasy Football Center who determine the number of points each team scored in a week and thereby arrive at a winner and a number of losers.[37]

Football fanatics play this game at all hours of the day or night. This game allows "armchair" quarterbacks or coaches to gain athletic supremacy in their office or at home. There are those who play fantasy football as if their life depended on it. Although the Web sites where this game can be played were once free, it now costs up to $249.95 per team to participate. These sites now offer prizes for high performers in this "sport."

There is also a commissioner of the National Fantasy Football Center in Sacramento, California. The commissioner is James Mesick who is now seeking to introduce fantasy football into the California school system in the hope of including fantasy football in the math curriculum.

Some people view fantasy football as nothing more than computer-driven gambling, while others complain that office workers will use their computers to play fantasy football instead of working. Fantasy football players are constantly bringing up the game on their computers, spending time and money. Real football fanatics can spend hours playing the game on their computer and televison sets. Those who play this game will watch one or more real football games on one or more television sets on any given Sunday afternoon. This allows the fantasy coach to monitor individual players and then make decisions concerning his or her fantasy team.

There are now around 376,000 Web sites concerned with fantasy football. These sites deliver data, advice, and strategies to those playing the game. Prizes ranging from $150 to $1,600 are awarded by Sportsline to the winners in this game. Sportsline is a Web site operated by CBS. Alta Vista, a media and commerce network, has also introduced the Small World Fantasy Professional Football League.

Some of those who play this game say they are motivated by the opportunity to beat their friends and to show superiority in playing the game.

Some of the fantasy football leagues now charge entrance fees. Participants brag about their football exploits, although these are limited to computers. ESPN, *Sports Illustrated,* Fox Sports, CBS Sports, and *The Sporting News* all have Web sites dedicated to fantasy football. Some sites now ask the visitor to make a contribution lest the site be shut down. There are also fantasy football magazines, newsletters, and "experts." One of these magazines is called *The Fantasy Football Guide*. The purpose of the guide is to prepare the players for the coming season. The magazine sells for $5.99 and is published every three weeks.[38]

Part of the enjoyment in fantasy football for some of its participants is drinking beer with friends and exhibiting adolescent conduct by means of loud, rude, and aggressive language and jokes. Such behavior is frequently linked to masculinity in American society and is therefore gender induced.

THE INFLUENCE OF GENDER ON HUMAN CONDUCT

Gender is a rationale for various social arrangements. Gender is not sex. Sex is a biological function. Gender is a social arrangement. This means that individuals in every society are held responsible for exhibiting behavior is in accord with the gender images prevalent and legitimate in that culture. Prevailing ideas about gender and gender differences determine how we act in any situation. Gender therefore legitimizes or discredits behavior of any kind. Behavior that is normative, i.e., expected, is legitimate and supported by the culture in which it occurs. Behavior that is not expected for either gender is criticized, ridiculed, or even prohibited altogether.

Gender therefore shapes social behavior. Prevailing social and cultural ideas about gender determine how we adhere to our gender role. We do that which we have been taught is required of us as women or men, and we avoid behavior that is subject to criticism as unmanly or not "ladylike." Because all of us are constantly presenting ourselves in front of an audience of others, the evaluation and assessment of that social audience determine much of what we do or do not do. In any situation, our performance as a man or woman will be subjected to evaluation by others. The response we receive from those who assess our performance will depend on the manner in which our performance fits expectations. This limits us to certain gender roles and excludes us from roles not approved for our gender.[39]

Violent behavior is part of the male role in American and other societies. Some have argued that violence or at least aggression is the result of biological, inborn conditions that make men aggressive. This view holds that male sexual aggression is a guarantee that the next generation will be born. Some sociobiologists who support this view say that the chances of reproduction, i.e., pregnancy and birth, are small in a state of nature which has no medical or nutritional support for pregnant women. It is argued that it takes a great deal of sexual intercourse to ensure the birth of the next generation, as most sperm is unable to reach and fertilize the human ovum (egg). Therefore, male sexual aggression is inborn and that explains male aggression. Consequently, one explanation of sports fanaticism and sports rioting is the inborn male proclivity toward aggression.[40]

Susan Brownmiller, in her book *Against Our Will,* argues that violent, male aggression is psychologically innate and is grounded in the male anatomy.[41] Whatever the merits of these biological arguments, it is certain that violent behavior and all behavior is located in a social context. This is true of football fanaticism as well as behavior of any kind and by anyone. The social context of football fanaticism and its companion, football violence, is not only a form of inborn male aggression but also an expression of social class differences.

While middle- and upper-class citizens believe that they can gain social power by success in the professions and in business, this is not as true of working-class citizens. The working class, sometimes called the lower class, seldom derives much satisfaction from their routine and insecure jobs. The chances of "mastering the world" by great business success or professional advancement are not available to lower-class men or women.

Therefore, power must be expressed in a more direct form by lower-class men than is true of the "diploma chasers" of the middle class. Manual labor in particular is the embodiment of masculine power. It therefore not surprising that so many football fanatics are those who work in lower-class jobs. For these Americans, association with a football team represents an opportunity to identify with power and with violence.

Masculine power is a social script. It does not really exist in a physical sense in the lives of American men in the twenty-first century. In patriarchal societies such as may be found around the world among Moslems, Hindus, and for that matter almost anywhere outside the United States and Western Europe, masculinity is expressed by violence against women and violence against other men. In American society such behavior is no longer approved. In America, rape is a crime. Testimony by rapists reveals that this crime is committed by men who feel that they have lost their masculinity and that they have no power. Here are some comments by convicted rapists: "I felt very inferior to others. . . ." "I felt rotten about myself. By committing rape I took this out on someone weaker than me." "I felt so rotten, so low and such a creep. . . ." "I feel a lot of what rape is is not sexual desire as a person's feelings about themselves and how that relates to sex. . . ."[42]

Rape and other violence against women is not the only violence experienced by American men. Violence against and by other men is a certain and universal male experience. All men have been bullied in school or played the bully. Many men had fathers who were rough and crude in their conduct toward their sons. All men were at some time beaten up or picked on by other boys when in school, and all men have had to learn to deal with these experiences.

Men and boys want to show friendship and affection to other men. This, however, is not tolerated in American culture because it is met with intimations of homosexuality. Therefore, schoolboys will express their affection for other boys by punching each other in the arm or otherwise using physical means of showing such friendliness. Among adult men arm punching is not used. Instead, adult men tell gross jokes or make crude comments about sex. This varies according to social class, so that such expressions as "that fucking, etc., etc." are used a great deal among working-class men and in the military but not among the diploma elite. Nevertheless, many men feel the need to join all-male groups in gyms, in gangs, teams, on hunting and fishing trips, card games, and fraternities. These groups not only exclude women but also serve as sources of safety and security among other men who lived men's lives in the past and in the present. Surely, one of these expressive male groups are football fans. In my view, current feminism dictates that women too play the role of football fanatic. These women do so because men have induced them to participate. Women frequently participate in activities which make them feel that they thereby have more control of "their" man. Men, however, lead. Football fanatics and certainly sports rioters are almost always men.

Although women will sometimes imitate men and thereby gain power, men will not imitate women for fear that this would cost them power. For example, American women will wear clothes traditionally worn only by men, such as trousers, jeans, even ties and dress shirts. Men will not wear skirts or high-heel shoes. Power is a major issue in American life.

American men are repressed. It is "unmanly" to cry or to show fear, pain, or sadness. Therefore, association with a football team permits at least some expression of emotion relating to the fortunes of the team. If the team wins, the fan can loudly rejoice. If the team loses, the fan can show anger. The fan can exhibit fear that the other team will score or that "his" team will lose. In the framework of football fanaticism these emotions are allowed because they are balanced by the aggression football represents. This replicates the "punch in the arm" syndrome of the schoolboy experience.

Many men are unsure of their male identity. This is in part the product of the overwhelming presence of women in the teaching profession, particularly in the early grades. Women who teach in elementary schools prefer children who are "neat, polite, obedient, and nice." That attitude leads to the feminization of young boys who become uncertain of their masculinity as a consequence of an almost entirely female upbringing. Therefore, some men, fearing they are not sufficiently exhibiting male characteristics, find compensation in football fanaticism, sports rioting, and other excessive "male-dominant" conduct.[43]

CATHARSIS

It is popular to claim that watching violence, including football games, together with the violence some fans engage in themselves acts as a "safety valve." Those who believe this say that aggression on the playing field reduces interpersonal aggression and hostility. Yet objective investigations of the effect of viewing aggression reveals that "aggressive displays . . . serve to enhance, rather than diminish hostility in the onlooker."[44]

Several studies involving different sports conducted over a number of years have shown that viewing violence increases hostility. Viewing a great deal of violence also leads to a deterioration in the quality of interpersonal relationships. Changes in the mood of spectators at violent sports events indicate that these changes are generally negative and dispute the popular assumption that football promotes warm interpersonal relations and/or goodwill.[45]

Football is a commodity sold by the owners of football teams and bought by the fans. The fans, having bought the right to be spectators at a game, are, however, more than just onlookers. The fans create noise. The fans are participants in the football drama. The crowd produces the "home-field advantage" for one team and therefore creates a handicap for the other team. In fact, some fans are so emotionally involved in football that they may rush onto the field or throw things and/or curse and scream epithets. Whether a fan at a football game is watching in a detached manner or becomes so involved that he or she sees the other team as an enemy will decide what fans see at each game. No two spectators at a game can ever see the same game because no two people sit in the same seat. In fact, many sit at different distances and view the game from different angles and therefore see a completely different game.

Television has of course changed all that. Because the TV camera "sees" the same thing for all who watch the screen without being physically present, there are two kinds of fans: Those who see what the TV camera lets them see and those who see what they can observe from the vantage point they have bought with their ticket.

It is therefore theoretically possible to abolish football stadiums and use only television as a means of promoting this spectator sport. This is already true for many fans who see the huge televison "replays" while in the stadium so that the image becomes superior to the reality.[46]

That may well become the future for football, as it is already the present for many Americans who have substituted the chatrooms on the Internet for dealing with real-life people.

SUMMARY

"Fans" or football fanatics are the customers of the NFL and therefore so important that the Pro-Football Hall of Fame has created a Football Hall of Fans. This includes female fans who are becoming more numerous each season. Both sexes live in a football culture including tailgate parties and numerous other entertainments. Football fans tend to view supporters of other teams as the "enemy," leading to group conflict including violence. Some fans play "fantasy football" on the Internet. This has become a multimillion-dollar business.

The meaning of aggressive football crowd behavior may be sought in the gender roles available to American men.

Chapter 7

Football and the Media

ANNOUNCERS AND ANALYSTS

The introduction of television into the football scene created a level of interest in professional football that was at one time reserved for college football. Television introduced football to millions of Americans who had never attended a college and for whom college games were as remote as a college education itself.

Although the first professional football game was televised in 1939, it was after World War II that television became a mass-produced feature of American life. Therefore, the use of sophisticated commentators and analysts developed only slowly, until by the beginning of the twenty-first century football broadcasting has become a highly paid profession. That profession is, however, limited to a few, because only a handful of television networks employ such commentators.

Some work for CBS, others broadcast for ABC, and still others comment for CNN, but all of these televised programs are rooted in radio, which began broadcasting sporting events in the early 1930s. At that time wire service reports were used to describe sporting events hundreds of miles away. The broadcasters would then "re-create" the games being broadcast by using special effects and imaginative language.

The football games being broadcast in the 1930s were all college games. These broadcasts were seen as a threat to college football at that time, because the Depression led many fans to stay home and listen to radio broadcasts of a game rather than pay to attend the game in person. Therefore, the Eastern Intercollegiate Association, which included the Ivy League institutions and some others, voted to disallow radio for the 1932 season. Likewise, the Southern conference, including twenty-three institutions, banned radio that year.

Only three years later, several universities reversed this trend and sold their radio rights to local radio stations for incomes that were then considerable. For example, the University of Michigan sold its football rights to a Detroit radio station for $20,000, and Ohio State University received $10,000 for its radio rights from the Ohio Oil Company.[1]

The most famous of the radio sportscasters of the 1930s and 1940s were Mel Allen, Red Barber, Jack Brickhouse, Clem McCarthy, Lindsay Nelson, and Bill Stern. Bill Stern was the earliest football announcer. He was hired by WHAM in Rochester, New York, in 1925 for broadcast of football play-by-play. Another early football broadcaster was Ronald "Dutch" Reagan, who started football broadcasting in 1932 for WOC in Davenport, Iowa.

It has often been said that football and other sports reached their current popularity and success because television made that possible. The reverse is also true. Television became a mass medium after 1946 because sports broadcasting made it so. The vast majority of Americans discovered television because they watched a sports event. Thus, *Gillette's Cavalcade of Sports* remained on the air for fourteen years, from 1970 to 1984.

Television led sports owners and managers to use several devices to make these broadcasts more attractive to a large audience. One of these devices was the use of sex appeal involving female cheerleaders. The Dallas Cowboys Cheerleaders are an excellent example of that effort. "The Cowboys Cheerleaders flaunted heaving, skimpily covered breasts and short shorts which exposed some of the curvature of their posteriors."[2]

Another device used to increase attention and entertainment for football fans is the mascot (from the Latin word *masca* or witch). Mascots dress in a variety of clownish uniforms such as a chicken or other animal and conduct themselves in a gross and uncouth fashion, which evidently amuses large numbers of attending fans. Some other devices used to lure television audiences to games in which they were not initially interested are "exploding" scoreboards, artificial grass, tight-fitting uniforms, and, most important, new schedules and new rules. The rule changes were designed to produce more touchdowns and more excitement. For example, the sudden-death overtime rule relied mainly on winning a coin flip, because the team that gained possession of the ball first had a far better chance of winning than the loser, who seldom gained a chance to score.

The play-offs are another device designed to increase interest in televised football. Prior to 1970 only four teams competed in the play-offs. Excitement was increased by using the "wild card" device. This method allowed, at that time, one team from each conference to join the play-offs. The wild card team had the best record apart from the divisional champions.

"Position scheduling" is another device that increased television viewing of football games. This scheduling allowed a majority of the teams an opportunity to compete for a spot on the play-offs and therefore increased excitement and income. This may be seen by looking at the major television rights fees paid to the NFL by the networks. While CBS holds an eight year contract beginning in 1999 for $4 billion, Fox, ABC, and ESPN each pay the NFL $4.4 billion for eight years.[3]

The USFL, which played football after the NFL season ended, was entirely a child of television. The league failed after only two seasons but demonstrated that there were enough football fanatics in the United States to keep interest in football for eleven months of the year. Today television continues to earn income from the National Indoor Football League and the Arena Football League. Both have extensive schedules, keeping football on TV eleven months of the year. These two leagues may be called "the TV leagues" of football. They depend on the TV medium entirely.[4]

Although football increased the television audience almost as soon as it was shown, it was instant replay that revolutionized sports broadcasting at the end of 1963 and led CBS to pay the unprecedented sum of $28 million to the NFL in 1964. That investment paid off at once as two sponsors, Ford Motors and Phillip Morris, paid $14 million each for television sponsorship of their products.

Then, in 1967, the first Super Bowl was played on television when the Green Bay Packers beat Kansas City 35-10. The game did not attract enough customers to fill the Los Angeles Coliseum. However, by Super Bowl VI, in 1972, a new record had been achieved, as the game was watched by more TV viewers than any event ever broadcast on that medium. That game was carried by both CBS and NBC. Ray Scott, Jack Whitaker, Frank Gifford, and Pat Summerall were the announcers/analysts for CBS, while NBC employed Curt Gowdy and Paul Christman.

Frank Gifford began his career as a football commentator in 1970. In 1995 he marked his twenty-fifth consecutive year as a football broadcaster as a member of ABC's *Monday Night Football* team. In addition to numerous other sports broadcasting assignments, Gifford broadcast seven Super Bowls. Gifford played halfback for the New York Giants when he started his broadcasting career in 1957. In 1961 he became a part-time CBS reporter and then moved to ABC in 1971 on a full-time basis. In 1976 Gifford was inducted into the NCAA College Football Hall of Fame, and in 1994 he became a member of the University of Southern California Athletic Hall of Fame, his alma mater. The NFL alumni gave Gifford their career achievement award in 1985, and the March of Dimes honored him with its career achievement award in 1989.

Gifford had an outstanding career as a football player and thereafter did a great deal for the Special Olympics. He is also the author of two books, *The Whole Ten Yards* and *Gifford on Courage*. Gifford is married to the actress Kathie Lee, with whom he has two children.[5]

Perhaps the best-known and most accomplished of football announcers is Pat Summerall, who was associated with the NFL for fifty-one years. Since receiving an education degree from the University of Arkansas in 1952 and a master's degree in Russian history, Summerall played football for the Detroit Lions, the Chicago Cardinals, and the New York Giants. In addition to his football achievements, Summerall also became state tennis champion in Florida in 1946.

Summerall began his broadcasting career with CBS in 1961, covering football, tennis, and golf. He earned the Lifetime Achievement Award from the National Academy of Television Arts and Sciences and a number of other awards for his contributions to professional football.[6]

When John Madden was appointed to host Monday Night Football in 2002 he had moved from CBS to FOX over two decades. Madden had worked with Pat Summerall at CBS from 1981 to 1994, when he moved to FOX. Sunday announcers have only a limited visibility in view of all the games played on Sunday, but Monday Night Football is the only game in town and therefore gives the announcers a far greater audience than any one of them can achieve on Sundays. Madden signed a four-year, $20 million contract to pair with Al Michaels in a two-man booth. Madden not only has twenty-two years of experience as a game analyst but also served as head coach of the Oakland Raiders, finishing with a .750 record, the best in NFL history. Madden holds a master's degree in science from California Polytechnic Institute and has written several books.

Al Michaels has been with Monday Night Football since 1986. Prior to that he was a television journalist with ABC for ten years. Michaels graduated from Arizona State University with a degree in broadcasting. His competence in that profession earned him numerous awards as he hosted golf, basketball, auto racing, and football games.

Dan Dierdorf began his career as a play-by-play announcer for NFL telecasts in 1985. Prior to that assignment, Dierdorf was a sportscaster for a St. Louis radio station for seventeen years and announced NFL games for the CBS radio network. Earlier, Dierdorf had a thirteen-year career with the NFL, playing for the St. Louis Cardinals. Named the NFL's top offensive lineman three times, he was also voted All-Pro six times, and was selected for the NFL Team of the Decade for the 1970s.

Dick Engberg holds a doctorate from Indiana University, and he became a professor at the Northridge campus of the University of California. He has won numerous awards for sportscasting for CBS.

In more recent years, Norman J. "Boomer" Esiason has joined CBS sports as a studio analyst. Esiason quarterbacked for the Cincinnati Bengals, New York Jets, and Arizona Cardinals during fourteen years as a player. In February 2002, he retired from active play and joined the CBS television network. Esiason has been a commentator for a number of years at stations not affiliated with CBS. Esiason ended his playing career in 1993. Active in many charities, Esiason established the Esiason Foundation after his son was diagnosed with cystic fibrosis. The foundation is devoted to finding a cure for that disease.

A number of other football announcer/analysts are involved in conveying the football action to television and radio listeners. Among these are Marcus Allen, Randy Cross, Greg Gumbel, Kevin Harlan, Brian Holloway, Armen Keteyian, Dan Marino, Jim Nantz, Deion Sanders, and Phil Simms.[7]

Dan Marino is a former Miami Dolphins quarterback. He holds twenty-five NFL regular season records, having played for the Dolphins for seventeen years. Upon retirement in 1999 Marino became a co-host of HBO's "Inside the NFL." Marino was a first-round draft pick by the Dolphins in 1983. He was named the NFL's Most Valuable Player in only his second season. He won the Dolphins' MVP award twelve times. He played in eighteen postseason play-off games and went to the Pro Bowl nine times. Marino is a graduate in communications from the University of Pittsburgh. He funded the Marino Foundation for Children with Autism and lives in South Florida with his wife and five children.

Deion Sanders is one more former football player who entered communications following retirement from the NFL. Sanders became an *NFL Today* reporter in 2001 and joined the team of Esiason and Nantz in 2002 as a studio analyst. Sanders has been considered the greatest cornerback of all time by some. He is the only professional athlete to play in both the football Super Bowl (1994 and 1995) and the baseball World Series (1992).

Sanders played baseball with the New York Yankees in 1989 and the Atlanta Braves from 1991 to 1994 and later played for the Cincinnati Reds. He also qualified in the Olympic trials as a sprinter in 1988. Sanders is so unusual an athlete that his eventual inclusion in the Football Hall of Fame is assured. In fact, Sanders's achievements make him unforgettable whether named in any Hall of Fame or any list constructed by the media or not.

Lesley Visser is also "Mrs. Dick Stockton." Both she and Stockton are sportscasters. Visser was the first woman to ever be a sideline reporter on Monday Night Football and the first woman to act as sideline reporter in a Super Bowl. After spending seven years with ABC Sports, she began her career in 1974 as member of the *Boston Globe* sports staff. From there she was assigned to cover the New England Patriots as the first female NFL beat writer.

Melissa Stark is the third member of the Monday Night Football broadcasting team. She began her career in sports broadcasting in

1996 as the host of "Scholastic Sports America," which deals with high school sports. She has worked a number of different sports for ESPN after graduating from the University of Virginia with a degree in foreign affairs and Spanish.

Stark is not the only woman employed in sports broadcasting. Bonnie Bernstein joined CBS Sports in 1998 as a correspondent for the NFL. She then became a sidelines reporter on the Dan Dierdorf/ Dick Engberg team, broadcasting for CBS, including Super Bowl games. Previously she held a number of broadcasting jobs in various parts of the country. She graduated magna cum laude from the University of Maryland with a degree in broadcast journalism.

Jill Arrington joined CBS in 2000 as a reporter for the network's coverage of college football. She then went on to report for *The NFL Today,* the NFL's pregame studio show. Arrington also reports on tennis and arena football. Earlier she worked for FOX sports, having begun her career as a production assistant at CNN in 1993. Arrington is a graduate of the University of Miami and is the daughter of football player Rick Arrington, who played quarterback for the NFL in the 1960s and 1970s.

I have mentioned here some of the most successful and best-known sports broadcasters. It should be understood, however, that these nationally famous announcers and analysts represent only 1 percent of all sports broadcasters. The vast majority of American sportscasters work in small towns for small newspapers or radio or TV stations. Whether in Twin Falls, Idaho, or Great Bend, Kansas, the majority of sports announcers, analysts, and writers earn small incomes and seldom achieve the national spotlight attained by those listed here.

FOOTBALL AND THE WRITTEN WORD— PRINT JOURNALISM SUPPORTS THE GAME

Despite radio and television, football and all other sports still depend largely on the printed word to keep interest in the sport before the public. Newspapers were of course the first medium to report on football, and newspapers as well as magazines continue to be powerful archives for America's favorite sport. Hardly a newspaper in the

United States does not report on football during the entire season and often beyond. Every newspaper in the country exhibits the current standings in the NFL (and other sports), and every newspaper has sportswriters who cover various teams throughout the week.

Language is undoubtedly the most important feature of any subculture. This means that the language used by sportswriters or any other occupation will "set apart that segment of society from the majority population."[8] Hence, sportswriters use a language reflecting their interests and designed to make their message understandable to those who read it. This is also true of sociologists, accountants, lawyers, or any profession.

Inspection of news stories concerning football demonstrates the use of a special "football language" at once. First, there are constant references to various football teams using only the name of the team without disclosing its location. The assumption made by the sportswriters must be that the readers know that the "Bills" are located in Buffalo, that the Redskins are at home in Washington, DC, the Raiders come from Oakland, California, and the Cowboys are at home in Dallas, Texas.

Analysis of sports stories reveals a considerable subcultural vocabulary. A "draft" may be a beer or a current of air or a load being pulled by a draft horse or even a money order. In football, however, a draft is the selection of some men for a football team. A new recruit to a football team is called a "rookie," a word also used in other sports. A "rookie" may have been hired to act as "wide receiver" or "offensive tackle" or "cornerback." There are also "placekickers." Those familiar with American football language may have no trouble understanding all of these terms. However, none of this language is understood in other English-speaking countries where American football is not well-known. England is a good example.

A good deal of football language resembles the language used for warfare. There is an offense and a defense. Football players are said to "overpower" people and are expected "to go into combat."[9]

Football language includes the "snap," which consists of tossing the ball backward through the legs of one player to the hands of the "quarterback" whose position is not only one-quarter removed from "the line of scrimmage" but who also acts as field commander of the team in offensive action. The "line of scrimmage" is an imaginary line on which the ball rests and at which both teams line up. The word "scrimmage" is an obsolete old English word referring to a "skirmish" or a fight.

There are numerous names for various strategies a coach may employ. There is the "blitz," a German word for lightning, which denotes an extra rusher. Football players "play coverage" and "tackle" the opponent. A quarterback who is tackled and falls has been "sacked," a word not used to indicate falling down for any other player. Only quarterbacks can be "sacked." There are other strategies. There is the "pass," in which the quarterback throws the ball to another player, and there is the "spike" which allows a player to violently toss the ball into the ground.[10]

Not only are there "touchdowns," but there are also "field goals," which are accomplished by kicking the ball through the "uprights."

Football involves "free agents," or players who are free to sign a contract wherever they can find one.

In sum, there is a whole football language and therefore there are in fact football dictionaries. These include Howard Liss's *Football Talk,* Joseph Olgin's *Illustrated Football Dictionary for Young People,* and David Porter's *Biographical Dictionaries of American Sports.*[11]

WOMEN ENTER THE LOCKER ROOM

It is possible that Mindy Morgan was the first female sports reporter when she covered horse racing for *The New York Times* in 1869. Since then the controversy concerning female sports reporters has become a dispute between the right to privacy and the sexual harassment argument of women reporters. All this became acute at the beginning in 1978 when women reporters first sought to enter the all-male locker rooms. Although the presence of female public relations personnel, reporters, and camera operators is now commonplace, the controversy concerning this aspect of the equal rights effort of women has continued for over twenty-five years.

The dispute concerning women in the locker rooms is centered on two rights that can be accommodated only by compromise. The first of these is the right to earn a livelihood in the field of sports reporting. Women in sports journalism must meet the usual four-hour deadline for any newspaper story concerning a recent game. This means that women who wish to write such stories need to interview players who are still naked in the locker room as they shower and change their clothes. The difficulty lies in the insistence of women reporters that they must have an opportunity to interview athletes even as the same women file lawsuits complaining of sexual harassment because the men they interview are naked and make lewd remarks in a locker room the women entered freely and voluntarily. It is customary and common for men to use profanities and "locker room jokes." This behavior is unknown to women, who do not normally enter male locker rooms.

This dilemma is best illustrated by the experience of Lisa Olson, a sports reporter for the *Boston Herald* who interviewed several athletes in the locker room of the New England Patriots. Olson sued on the grounds of "personal and professional injury" after entering the all-male locker room in an effort to interview the players. She claimed that the football players made lewd remarks and "unsavory" gestures. Olson won $250,000 and moved to Australia to escape criticism of her actions.

Likewise, Elizabeth Anderson of Christian TV sued basketball player Charles Barkley for exposing himself in a locker room which she had entered in order to gain an interview and to ask Barkley to donate money to her church.[12]

MAGAZINES

Although the Arabic word from which *magazine* is derived was first used to indicate a storehouse, it has come to mean a collection of written material as well. One such example is a sports publication called *The Magazine,* which devotes a good deal of space to football at the beginning of the season. In line with the assumption that football players are "tough" men, the cover of the September 16, 2002, issue depicted four members of the Miami Dolphins staring unsmiling at the reader.

The inside of *The Magazine* includes articles by Bill Simmons, who calls himself "The Sports Guy." *The Magazine* also features pictures of football players and other athletes both in action and posing for the camera. These pictures are accompanied by captions that include sports humor. Surveys of fan opinion on some sports issue are also included.

The Magazine features stories about individual football players (and other athletes). There is the story of Musa Smith, whose father Abdul Muhaimin, or Kelvin Smith, was accused of running a Pennsylvania farm used to train terrorists connected to the 9/11 attack on the World Trade Center, the Pentagon, and possibly the White House. Musa Smith is a graduate of the University of Georgia in Athens, Georgia. Rex Grossman, a quarterback for the University of Miami whose father and grandfather had played football and who followed in the footsteps of his family under the guidance of coaches Steve Spurrier and Ron Zook, is also featured.

The reader is next treated to a picture of Ricky Williams, a superstar who played with the New Orleans Saints and the Miami Dolphins. Williams is shown wearing trousers that are unbuckled and partially open. The purpose of such a pose may well be the editors' secret. There is an NFL preview as well as a number of pictures of chests and muscles labeled "full bodied" or "perfect fit," all designed to arouse interest in the physiques of the athletes. *The Magazine* evidently strives to display male "skin" in the same sense as magazines devoted to the female form seek to sell sexy bodies to the customers.

Coach Bill Belichick of the New England Patriots is also featured in *The Magazine,* which announces that Belichick is a great strategist, psychologist, and "brain." An article by former coach, now announcer, John Madden lists five successful coaches followed by a detailed analysis of every one of the thirty-two NFL teams and their chances of winning the Super Bowl. All of this and more is included in this 10- by 12-inch magazine topped by advertisements which make up more than half of its 157 pages.[13]

Another magazine, *The Sporting News,* also devotes a good deal of its space to football during the football season. An example is the issue of December 22, 2002, which is devoted to "Greatest Running Backs." Featured are fifty men from Jim Brown, number one, who played with the Cleveland Browns from 1957 to 1965, to Wilbert Montgomery, number fifty, who played with the Philadelphia Eagles from 1977 to 1984 (as well as for the Detroit Lions in 1985). Included in this lineup is the great Walter Payton, who played for the Chicago

Bears from 1975-1987 and Emmitt Smith, only 5-feet-9-inches tall, of the Dallas Cowboys, who is credited with defeating the Buffalo Bills in Super Bowl XXVIII in 1994 when the Bills made their fourth and last appearance at the Super Bowl in Atlanta.

Included among the all-time running backs featured in the *Sporting News* is Marion Motley, who died in 1999 at the age of 79. Motley had been a running back for the Cleveland Browns from 1946 to 1953 and for the Pittsburgh Steelers in 1955. Bronko Nagurski, a name hardly remembered by the football fans of the twenty-first century, is also included in the *Sporting News* list of great running backs. He too has died. Born in 1908, Nagurski played for the Chicago Bears from 1930 to 1937 and again in 1943. Like Emmitt Smith, Nagurski is a member of the Pro Football Hall of Fame. Such famous names as Herschel Walker and Harold "Red" Grange are also featured in this magazine.[14]

In the same issue of *Sporting News* is a discussion of several professional football coaches, including "Butch" Davis of the Cleveland Browns and Broncos coach Mike Shanahan. The pictures of these coaches look just as ferocious as those of the players. Such pictures support the popular notion concerning the facial expressions and posturing expected by football enthusiasts of those who play the game.[15]

A typical article in the magazine *Sports Illustrated* is a portrait of Willis McGahee by Kelley King which appeared in the December 16, 2002, issue. Using all the terminology that football writers have developed over the years, King creates a word picture of McGahee's abilities that can be described as a masterpiece of English usage in the service of sports reporting.[16]

FOOTBALL BOOKS

The range of books dealing with football is immense. This becomes immediately visible if we inspect the subject guide of *Books in Print*, which lists 2,284 football books now available.[17]

One example of such a book is *Fields of Honor: The Golden Age of College Football and the Men Who Created It*, written by Sally Pont, the daughter of Yale coach Richard Pont. This book deals with the World War II veterans who created modern football. Included are Sid

Gillman, a member of the Football Hall of Fame and football innovator who invented the West Coast Offense. There are portraits of Ara Parseghian and Paul Dietzel, Woody Hayes and Bo Schembechler, Carm Cozza and John Pont. The author of *Fields of Honor* is John Pont's niece and therefore in a good position to know a great deal about these men on a personal level. *Fields of Honor* has been called a history of the founding fathers of modern football.[18]

In 2001, Mark F. Bernstein published *Football: The Ivy League Origins of an American Obsession.* Bernstein discusses both sides of the coin in this book, addressing the downside of the sport as well as its evident advantages. Bernstein shows how college football led to professional football and how the sports writing professional was also created by that American obsession. He also talks about the influence of money, the physical violence, and the pressure to win, with its corrosive effect on scholarly ability. He describes the drunken conduct of football fans, which began as early as the 1920s.[19]

Numerous books concern the lives of great football players, coaches, and owners. One example is *Rockne of Notre Dame* by sportswriter Ray Robinson. According to Robinson, Rockne was a superhero with few if any faults. Rockne is depicted in this book as a tremendous salesman who knew how to build a football team even if he had to include men who were not enrolled at the university.

An immigrant from Norway, Rockne understood how to promote himself. This is best explained in a book by Murray Sperber called *Shake Down the Thunder.*[20] Here Sperber discusses Rockne's relationship to George Gipp, who was portrayed by Ronald Reagan in the movie *Knute Rockne—All American.* Evidently, Gipp was a gambler, womanizer, and drunk who was thrown out of Notre Dame for bad grades and was readmitted only because of Rockne's political influence.

Robinson shows that Rockne was a very good businessman. He made a great deal of money from personal appearances, automobile and clothing endorsements, and coaching clinics. Rockne was so good at self-promotion that he was offered a salary of $25,000 by Columbia University while earning only $10,000 at Notre Dame.[21]

Stagg's University tells the story of Amos Alonzo Stagg and the rise and fall of football at the University of Chicago. This is the story of three men: William Rainey Harper, the first president of the University of Chicago; Stagg, who was hired by Harper to develop the football program; and Robert Maynard Hutchins, who put an end to football at that smaller university. The author shows how football fits into the higher education system in the United States and how football fits into American society generally. The author, Robin Lester, explains the marriage of athletics to academics in America. This book contains numerous tables and statistics which give it a truly academic flavor.[22]

John M. Carroll has written a biography of Frederick "Fritz" Douglas Pollard, the first black quarterback and head coach in professional football. Pollard's football career began when he joined the Brown University football team in 1915, leading his team to a Rose Bowl appearance. After graduating from Brown, Pollard played football with the Akron Pros of the old American Professional Football Association. The association became the National Football League.

Excluded from hotels and restaurants, Pollard had to change his clothes outside the team's locker room. Despite these experiences, Pollard made money in business after his playing career ended in 1926 founding the first black securities investment banking firm in New York City. There he also coached an all-black semi-pro football team called the Brown Bombers. In 1935 he became the publisher of the *Independent News*, the first black-owned tabloid newspaper in New York City.[23]

Another book by John Carroll concerning an early football hero is *Red Grange and the Rise of Modern Football*. This book once more recalls the career of the one man who ignited public attention for football with his astonishing feat of scoring four touchdowns in twelve minutes in a 1924 game. In the 1920s Grange ranked with Babe Ruth and Jack Dempsey as a super hero, a fame that has lasted into the twenty-first century.

Grange performed at a time when colleges were beginning to make football the center of their activities, when the mass media were beginning to pay attention to the sport, and when money was made available by alumni to win football games. Grange became the first play-by-play announcer of football games at a time when, according to Carroll, pro football had the reputation of being run by cheap crooks.[24]

Among the many books about football, *Glory for Sale,* by Jon Morgan, is one of the few that reveals the inner workings of professional sports. The book deals with the economics and the politics concerning taxpayer-subsidized stadiums. The author discusses the role of Art Modell in moving the Cleveland football team to Baltimore and acquaints the reader with former Colts owner Bob Irsay, Cleveland Mayor Michael R. White, and other politicians. The book focuses on the business of football, giving the reader a chance to understand the franchise process. Greed, rivalries, and football as a religion are fully explored in this unusual book.[25]

In addition to the large number of football books dealing with the history of the game, tactics used to play the game, or biographies of famous coaches and players, there are also some novels by American authors in which football plays a part. Some of these novels are for children or adolescents, as, for example, *Running Loose* by Chris Crutcher. In this novel, Louie Banks is introduced as a teenager who "has it all." He has an academic career, athletic ability, good friends, two part-time jobs, parents who treat him well, and a good-looking girlfriend. His only problem is his football coach, who demands that he take out the opposing team's star player. Banks refuses to do this and even refuses to play for the immoral coach. This means that he is no longer a football hero but instead a nobody in the eyes of his football fanatic friends. The book deals with sexuality, death, and moral problems and has been listed as a "banned book" by those who seek to censure literature.[26]

Imitate the Tiger is also a football novel, although it deals primarily with the problems resulting from alcoholism. The protagonist, Christopher Serbo, is a football player who must deal with tremendous pressure from his coach even as his drinking leads to one disappointment after another. His girlfriend leaves him. His home life with his aunt is a constant battle. He is always angry and depressed. His drinking leads to embarrassing episodes in public.

His coach and another teacher induce Christopher to enter a full-time rehabilitation program after the football season. He participates in the twelve-step program of Alcoholics Anonymous. The author then explains the reasons for Christopher's conduct by depicting a deathbed scene and a terrible beating from which Christopher recovers quickly. Evidently, a successful football player finds that the rules do not apply to athletes as much as to other people.[27]

Robert Brancato wrote *Winning* in 1977. This book starts with a description of a football player named Gary Madden who lies in a hospital bed with a spinal cord injury. He has no hope of walking again, although his upper body appears to be healing. The story deals mainly with the manner in which his significant others deal with him. There is a good deal of "sick room" diplomacy and the unintended hurts which some visitors inflict on the injured boy. His English teacher, herself a recent widow, helps by introducing him to literature. The theme of this book is not only the danger of playing football but also the dilemma of caregiving.[28]

The most popular and perhaps best classic of football fiction is *North Dallas Forty,* written in 1973 by Peter Gent, who played wide receiver for the Dallas Cowboys for five years. This book is a record of eight days in the life of a professional football player. Here we learn about drugs, sex, and, above all, money. There is also a good deal of pain and violence. The book is really an exposé of life in the National Football League, including the behavior of psychopaths and other social misfits making up a professional team. This book was made into a movie in 1979.

George Plimpton, who briefly played quarterback for the purpose, wrote *Paper Lion* in 1966. This may well be the best book written about pro football. This book gives the reader an inside account of how it feels to be a quarterback. Events inside the huddle are described. The book shows the reader the courage, the nerve, and the concentration necessary to play quarterback and also explores the styles of different coaches and players. This book also discusses drinking, sex, and violence and the general off-hours carousing strongly associated with professional athletes.[29]

FOOTBALL IN FILM

North Dallas Forty was made into a movie in 1979. Like the book, the movie shows the fear and desperation of a marginal football player in the NFL. The film deals less with football plays than with the price paid to play the game. The football business is emphasized.

Jim Thorpe—All American is a 1951 movie about the life and career of this great Native American athlete. Portrayed by Burt Lancaster, the movie shows Thorpe's great football skills while at Carlisle College and his subsequent sink into alcoholism after being denied his Olympic medals for negligible reasons. Anyone supporting diversity in American life will want to see this powerful biography.

The Galloping Ghost is the story of Harold "Red" Grange. A 1931 movie, it is primitive compared to the standards of 2003. It involves the efforts of gamblers attempting to fix a college football game by keeping Grange from playing.

Black Sunday anticipates the September 11, 2001, terrorist attack. It concerns a demented Vietnam veteran who seeks to kill thousands of innocent Americans at the Super Bowl in Miami by releasing a specially designed dart gun from the Goodyear Blimp as it flies over the stadium. However, a tough Israeli anti-terrorist agent, portrayed by Robert Shaw, prevents the slaughter of thousands by hard-to-believe heroics.

School Ties depicts a poor Jewish boy who is recruited by a Catholic "prep" school to quarterback their football team. The boy is remarkably talented and leads the team to victory. He is feted and applauded by his fellow students, the administration, and the alumni. He becomes involved with a Christian girl and meets her family. However, when it is discovered that he is Jewish, his girlfriend dumps him and his classmates insult him. He is blamed for a cheating scandal which actually involves a wealthy Catholic boy whose family has been prominent among the alumni. The emphasis in this movie is on the cruelty of religious bigotry, using football as a vehicle to demonstrate this.

No football movie is more famous and more often cited than the 1940 film *Knute Rockne: All-American.* This film biography of the famous Notre Dame football coach was portrayed by Pat O'Brien. However, it was Ronald Reagan who kept the movie alive as he used the scene in which he plays the dying George Gipp for political purposes during his campaigns for governor of California and later for president of the United States. Gipp was a real-life football star who died at a young age of pneumonia and who may have said to his coach, "Some day, when things are tough, maybe you can ask the boys to go in there and win just one for the Gipper." This line became Reagan's slogan, with great success.

The movie is based on the private papers of Rockne as preserved by Mrs. Rockne and the University of Notre Dame and includes a number of newsreel clips as well as appearances by such football greats as Glenn "Pop" Warner, Alonzo Stagg, and William Spaulding.

Burt Reynolds starred in *The Longest Yard,* playing Paul Crewe, an ex-quarterback who assaults his girlfriend, steals her car, drinks heavily, and is arrested by the police. He lands in Palm Beach County Prison because the warden wants him in his prison in order to coach his semi-professional football team. This is prevented by a brutal captain of the prison guards; Crewe is badly beaten and is assigned to build a football team within the prison.

Any Given Sunday seeks to profit from the antics of such football playing offenders as Rae Carruth, a former wide receiver who was charged with seeking to arrange the murder of his pregnant girlfriend. This is the story of an aging coach, an arrogant young quarterback, and a stubborn female team owner. The movie is full of sports clichés, tough guys, drunk scenes, and a host of linebackers. The movie includes Johnny Unitas and other "great old players" who get the recognition they deserve.

O. J. Simpson, at one time a star player, became the subject of a movie titled *The O. J. Simpson Story* after his criminal trial for a double murder ended in a not guilty verdict in October 1995. Simpson had been accused of killing his wife, Nicole, and a restaurant waiter, Ronald Goldman, who happened to deliver a pair of glasses to Nicole Simpson which she had forgotten at the restaurant. The motive of the criminal jury, consisting mainly of African Americans, for acquitting Simpson was evidently "jury negation," a phrase used by lawyers to indicate the manner in which predominantly African-American juries will adjudicate black offenders "not guilty" on the grounds that there are too many blacks in prison already and that the criminal justice system is racist, no matter what the evidence against the defendant.

The Simpson case became of interest to television viewers and newspaper readers because Simpson had been a true football hero. Born in 1947, he became a star football player at San Francisco City College, then at the University of Southern California, where he won the Heisman Trophy in 1968. In 1969 he was drafted by the Buffalo

Bills, where he played as a running back until 1977 and then played one more year for the San Francisco 49ers. During his football years he shattered all previous records for yards gained and most rushing in a season. Simultaneously, Simpson established a movie acting career and acted in *The Towering Inferno* and eight other films. He also became a football commentator and was seen in several TV commercials. He had so much exposure and was so well known that his trial became "the trial of the century." *The O. J. Simpson Story* does not deal with all of these aspects of Simpson's life. Nevertheless it is of importance to those who have an interest in this 1985 inductee of the Pro-Football Hall of Fame.

In addition to movies shown in theaters, a number of videocassettes of football movies are available. Among these are *Knute Rockne—All American, Little Giants, The Longest Yard, Necessary Roughness, North Dallas Forty, The Program, Rudy, Semi-Tough, Varsity Blues, The Waterboy,* and others.

FOOTBALL SONGS AND LYRICS

From grade school to university, schools have adopted songs with lyrics displaying loyalty to the school and an adolescent manner of praising the power of the football team. There is a German saying, "bei den Haaren herbeigezogen," which means approximately, "dragged in by the hair." This saying may be applied to the lyrics of most college, university, and professional team songs. The following are some examples.[30]

"Husker Power" is sung by supporters of the Nebraska University football team. A part of the lyrics are

> Game on, Yo, ready for action;
> and the Big Red is the main attraction

A better-known song is "Mr. Touchdown USA" written in 1950 by W. Katz, G. Piller, and R. Roberts. The second verse of this song contains these lyrics.

> They call him Mr. Touchdown;
> they always call him Mr. Team

Then there is of course "The Rambling Wreck from Georgia Tech."

> I'm a Rambling Wreck from Georgia Tech
> and a hell of an engineer,

Dartmouth College sings a football song which even names the "enemy," Harvard.

> For naught avails the strength of Harvard;
> when they hear our mighty cheers.

Some lyrics of the second stanza of the "Notre Dame Victory March" are

> Cheer, cheer for old Notre Dame:
> wake up the echos cheering her name.

FOOTBALL JOKES

Jokes are an important medium, displaying both approval and disapproval of the target. Jokes serve several functions and are a form of reality construction. There is, first, conventional reality consisting of expectations of any situation in any culture. When these expectations are suddenly violated by means of unexpected, unconventional cultural pattern, we have a joke. A joke is a contradiction, an ambiguity, or a double meaning of a situation that may be defined in more than one way. For example, these newspaper headlines are considered humorous in the United States: "Stud Tires Out"; "Drunk Gets Nine Months in Violin Case"; "Iraqi Head Seeks Arms"; "Teacher Strikes Idle Kids."[31]

Therefore, it is necessary to know something about the American football culture in order to understand an American football joke. Here is an example:

> A teacher asks her students to tell the class what their fathers do for a living. One child says that her father is an electrician. Another says that his father is an accountant, and yet another child

volunteers that his father is a carpenter. Then little Suzy says that her father is a go-go dancer in a strip club. The whole class is appalled and embarrassed. After class the teacher asks the girl to come to her desk and says, "Your father isn't really a go-go dancer in a night club?" "Oh no," says the girl. "I just made that up because I am too embarrassed to tell what he really does for a living." "You can tell me," says the teacher. "Well," says the girl, "the truth is my father is a linebacker for the Buffalo Bills."

Obviously, only an American football fan can understand this joke. It would mean nothing in any country other than the United States except perhaps in Canada, since American football is far from popular anywhere else and the word "linebacker" would be as meaningless as the phrase Buffalo Bills.

Here is another joke reflecting a partial truth:

A football coach walked into a locker room before a big game and told the star player, "I'm not supposed to let you play because you failed math. So I have to ask you a math question and if you get it right, you can play." The coach then asks the star player, "How much is two plus two?" The player thinks for some time and then says, "Two plus two is four." Whereupon all the other players shout together, "Com'on coach. Give him another chance."

Then there are a few one-liners, such as:

The coach was marching alongside the band when the majorette dropped her baton. A fan yelled, "I see you coach the band, too."

Our quarterback knows everything to do with a football except autograph it.

The team employs the "doughnut" defense: the one with the hole in the middle.

The linebacker has rung so many bells he has a fan club consisting entirely of Avon ladies.

SUMMARY

Television created pro football and sports created television. The immense interest in American football came about because television brought the game into millions of homes even as television profited from the interest in sports already present before its entry into American life after World War II.

The television-sports linkage led to the employment of professional football commentators and analysts, many of whom are retired football players. This began in the 1930s with radio announcements of college football games. Bill Stern and Ronald Reagan were among the first announcers. Several methods have been used to build interest in the National Football League broadcasts.

The introduction of women into the sports announcing and writing profession has had some unexpected consequences.

Sportswriting involves a subcultural language visible in magazines, newspapers, and other written materials concerning football. This language may also be found in football books, which are published extensively in the United States. These books may be technical "how-to" books or they may be novels. There are also books including football songs and lyrics as well as football jokes.

All of these communications concerning football have a considerable audience who are usually called football "fans" or fanatics.

Chapter 8

The Football Business

MONEY, MONEY EVERYWHERE

Further evidence of the popularity of NFL football can be seen in its revenues, particularly in comparison to those of other major sports. For example, the National Basketball Association receives about $770 million from television, major league baseball receives about $416 million, and the National Hockey League earns only $120 million from television each year.[1] In contrast, the NFL's huge television contracts yield $2.2 billion each season, in addition to $18 billion in longer-term network and cable contracts. Furthermore, the credit rating of the NFL is superb, further distinguishing the sport from hockey, in which two franchises have filed for bankruptcy, and baseball, which may have to drop teams for lack of attendance.[2]

A Harris poll taken in October 2002 revealed that 100 million Americans are very much interested in the NFL and that another 25 million are occasionally interested. In 2002 the number of NFL television viewers increased by 5 percent over the 2001 season, adding 14.4 million new viewers. The ten most-watched basic cable shows are also NFL games. An average of 15.8 million viewers tuned in to any given NFL game during the 2002 season. The NFL intends to show classic football games on a new digital cable channel devoted only to football and will charge a fee to fans who want to watch games from the NFL archives.

Ticket sales to games have also increased. After the addition of the Houston Texans to the NFL, the attendance at football games rose to more than 16.8 million fans in stadiums that were filled to more than 90 percent capacity during 256 regular-season games, for an average attendance of more than 65,000 per game. Tickets are of course not the only NFL sales item. Fans bought $2.9 billion worth of NFL merchandise in 2002, and Web site sales increased by 30 percent in 2002 over 2001.[3]

The NFL divides 63 percent of its total revenue equally among its thirty-two teams, thereby leveling the playing field so that every team turns a profit. Despite these successes, it is not certain that television agreements can continue in the future. NBC has already stopped from televising NFL games because the cost is too high. It is also possible that the market has reached a saturation point and no additional viewers can be found.

At present, however, sponsors literally line up to get a part of the NFL brand. This in turn leads to sponsorships. For example, Coors beer has sponsored advertisements costing $300 million. The total income from sponsors doubled to $4.8 billion between 1997 and 2002. Paul Tagliabue, NFL commissioner, estimates that revenue will increase by 1 billion dollars per year over the next three years.[4]

A number of enterprises earn considerable incomes by associating themselves with the football culture. This chapter will describe several groups or professions that benefit from football. Among these are, first and foremost, the television corporations and their advertisers, as well as film producers. Contract advisers profit by representing potential football players, and lawyers earn a good deal from disputes arising within the football community and by winning compensation for injured football players. Stadium construction is also very profitable to the construction industry. Finally, gambling on football games furnishes professional gamblers, if not a host of amateurs, a considerable income.

FILM PRODUCTION

NFL Films has 100 million feet of film in its vaults. The company's $45 million headquarters in New Jersey is referred to as "Hollywood on the Delaware" by its president, Steve Sabol. The building has its own 60- by 80-foot sound stage and a music studio large enough for a seventy-two-piece orchestra. The NFL intends to start its own digital cable network when its current television contract expires, because NFL Films can provide its own programming. NFL Films already produces more than 120 pieces each week for the networks and for its five weekly shows: *NFL Films Presents; Edge NFL; Matchup; Under the Helmet;* and *NFL Blast.* The company has a Web site that permits viewers to request assorted highlights from the 2002-2003 season. A project called *The NFL's Greatest Games* is also in the works.[5]

ADVERTISING

College Bowl Games

In 1902, the Tournament of Roses, at that time located in Los Angeles, was augmented by a football game. This proved so popular that the Tournament of Roses Association built a large football stadium in nearby Pasadena. A local newspaper called the new stadium the "Rose Bowl" and the name was then attributed to all postseason college football games. In 1914 Yale University opened a new stadium thereafter called the Yale Bowl. It is 930 feet long, 750 feet wide, and covers 12.5 acres, seating more than 64,000 fans (before alterations the Yale Bowl seated 70,000 people on several occasions).[6]

Since the 1950s, the chance to earn money from television broadcasts has led to the proliferation of bowl games. Business support of bowl games during the past fifteen years has been so important that companies' names are now part of the bowls' names; for example, the Orange Bowl is now called the FedEx Orange Bowl.[7]

College teams participate in twenty-five different bowl games, known as the Bowl Championship series. This game series developed when the Bowl Coalition was formed in 1992. In 1995 this coalition was renamed the Bowl Alliance with the intent of promoting an annual championship game between the regular season's two top-ranked teams. The Bowl Alliance has four members: the Rose Bowl, the Sugar Bowl, the Fiesta Bowl, and the Orange Bowl. These games attract a good deal of advertising. Advertisers during the Fiesta Bowl game paid about $500,000 for thirty seconds of television advertising; advertisers during the Orange and Sugar Bowls have paid $300,000 to $400,000 for each thirty seconds of television time.[8]

The Super Bowl and NFL on Television

A good part of football advertising revenue is derived from the Super Bowl, which is the most successful money-making event in the United States. Because the Super Bowl is the most-watched event on

TV, it is also the most expensive for advertisers. For example, ABC received an average of $2 million per thirty-second announcement in 2002, compared to $1.9 million in 2001. The Anheuser-Busch beer distributors usually advertise for five minutes, distributed in ten thirty-second spots. Pepsi-Cola and Cadillac made an appearance on Super Bowl XXXVII in 2003, as did clothing manufacturer Levi's and tax accountants H & R Block. Other sponsors of Super Bowl advertisements included the investment brokers Charles Schwab and Co.[9]

About two-thirds of all TV viewers, or about 138 million viewers, watched Super Bowl XXXVII in January 2003. In 2002 the New England–St. Louis game drew an audience of 132 million viewers. The largest TV audience for any Super Bowl game so far were the 139 million fans who watched the 1996 Dallas–Pittsburgh game.

Some advertisers are not willing to pay upwards of $900,000 per half minute of television time. A few of these advertisers made a deal with NBC allowing them to run ads only if the game goes into overtime. Separate ads were also sold by Crane Media for those who received the Super Bowl via satellite from WXIA in Atlanta, Georgia. In addition, companies such as Coca-Cola run ads prior to the game or directly thereafter and take advantage of the huge audience still tuned in.[10]

Despite the huge viewing audiences that football and other sports generate, NBC decided in 2003 not to carry the NFL, NBA, or Major League Baseball. The factors primarily influencing this decision were the huge fees charged to networks to be allowed to broadcast and televise the National Football League. These fees have risen by 133 percent to more than $3.5 billion. The three major networks report that they have suffered losses of $5.5 billion. Forty percent of these losses came from Monday night football alone. Similar losses have been experienced by other sports leagues. Instead of broadcasting NFL games, NBC has therefore concluded a deal with the Arena Football League.[11] The contract between the Arena Football League and NBC provides that NBC gets the first $10 million in advertising revenue for production costs. Thereafter, the league gets the next $3 million and advertising revenue will be split 50-50.[12]

Because NBC is no longer associated with the NFL, the NFL will deal with ABC, CBS, FOX, and ESPN through 2006 at a cost of $17.6 billion. These networks will lose billions on this deal. Nevertheless, the networks are willing to lose so much money because sports events promote nonsports programs, which then creates the profit needed to stay in business.

Total TV advertising revenues from football games during the 2001-2002 season amounted to over 2.3 billion. More than 2 billion of this money came from NFL games and $252 million from college games. ABC collected $362 million from the NFL, ESPN earned $650 million, CBS $448 million, and Fox $627 million.[13]

Commercial Artistry

Advertising involves a good deal of artistic talent. This is important to advertisers, who spend millions to attract customers and therefore must be sure that their ads are viewed and remembered long enough so that their product gains at least some customers. The artists who make attractive ads possible have various backgrounds, but all have a good deal of experience and talent.

Stefan Sonnenfeld is a professional colorist who owns his own company. Sonnenfeld has contributed to commercials for Mountain Dew and other products because he became known as an artist "who makes film glow." Colorists such as Sonnenfeld participate in meetings with directors to create film that justifies the millions spent by their clients.

Chris Ryan, also a colorist, has done Super Bowl advertisements for years. Beginning his career in the mailroom at Manhattan Transfer, his interest in photography allowed him to enter the advertising profession. He works well under pressure, which comes about when editing of advertisements occur as late as the Friday before the Super Bowl.

Chris Gibson, a colorist at Post Perfect, has worked on commercials for Coca-Cola, McDonald's, Toyota, Volkswagen, Ford, and a number of other major advertisers. He worked on a Super Bowl ad called "e-Cowboy" for a travel agency, using a takeoff on the movie High Noon.

Chris Gennarelli was the colorist on "Fingerprints," a Superbowl spot. He gained a reputation for his work on music videos. His job is to interpret what the film directors want and what the advertisers need.

These and numerous other colorists and advertising professionals are a large part of the success of the Super Bowl each year. They and their employers represent yet another segment of the economic impact of the Super Bowl.[14]

An NFL football game is composed of four 15-minute quarters but usually requires approximately three hours of airtime. During these three hours more than 150 commercial "spots" are broadcast. Commercials dominate the program while the football game itself is incidental to the sales pitches. Therefore, the audience can easily lose the continuity of the game. This problem is addressed by the commentators who narrate the progress of the football game for those many viewers who are distracted by the constant recital of commercial messages.[15]

It is quite possible that advertising during football games has reached a saturation point and cannot be further expanded. Yet because advertisements bring in such large amounts of money, some TV stations have used "compression" to increase their income during football games. Such a practice during an NFL football game can yield an extra $8,000. Stations using that technique can squeeze more commercials into their prime-time programming by speeding up each spot of other advertisers minutely.

MERCHANDISE

Licensed Goods

The NFL generates about $3.7 billion in revenues each year. This income is derived from home game and road game ticket sales, luxury suite sales, concessions, advertising, parking, naming rights, national media rights, local broadcasting rights, NFL properties, and expansion payments. The NFL even sells a book providing comprehensive data in all these areas. The book costs $1,095.

The thirty-two teams in the NFL earn significant revenue from selling expensive licensed goods. For example, an NFL gold towel costs $11.95; a golf club head cover sells for $34.95; a golf mallet putter endorsed and engraved with NFL logos costs $68.95; a golf towel embroidered with NFL team insignia sells for $19.95; and a helmet cover that looks like a football helmet sells for $22.95. Then there are jackets, shirts, shorts, gift baskets, and innumerable other items.

The most successful merchandise marketing of any NFL team is being conducted by the Green Bay Packers. A 65,000 square foot Green Bay Packers Pro Shop opened in July 2002 at Lambeau Field, home of the Packers. The store has a mezzanine level and other physical features appealing to customers. The NFL hosted a three-day trade show at Lambeau Field for licensed vendors and buyers for all teams. As a result, the Packers sold more than $6 million worth of merchandise during one fiscal year. The entire league sells $100 million worth of merchandise in each season, with this total anticipated to increase to $250 million in the next few years. These sales figures are possible because loyal fans spend about $100 per game, not including tickets or food.[17]

How much revenue any team may derive from these sales depends in part on the success of that team on the football field. This can be seen by the reduction in licensed goods sales by the Dallas Cowboys during the 2002 season, which the Cowboys concluded with five wins and eleven losses for an average of only 0.313. Cowboys fans hope that the hiring of Bill Parcells as head coach for a four-year contract at $17.1 million will turn everything around, including merchandise sales.[18]

Endorsements

Popular and successful coaches are not only good salespeople for the merchandise offered by their team; they are a monopoly unto themselves and can earn a great deal of money because they are winners. This includes Jon Gruden, head coach at Tampa Bay, whose Buccaneers won the 2002 Super Bowl. Gruden, unlike so many NFL players, is a sober family man. This makes him most acceptable and trustworthy to such advertisers as financial services, technical services, and consultancies and, in addition, gets him numerous speaking engagements.

These speaking engagements and endorsement opportunities permit popular players and coaches to earn considerable fees for their services. Sponsors include General Motors, Coors Light Beer, Warner

Brothers, and Pepsi-Cola. These companies sponsor NFL greats such as Miami linebacker Junior Seau, former Giants quarterback Phil Simms, or retired Oakland defensive lineman Howie Long. A number of clothing manufacturers also sponsor these football superstars. In the lead among these companies is no doubt the shoe manufacturer Nike, who concentrates on ads geared toward college students.[19]

The Food Factor

Restaurants also participate in the chase after the dollar at football games and the Super Bowl. During the 2002 Super Bowl at San Diego, Volume Services America, the concessionaire at the Qualcomm Stadium in San Diego, hosted the menu served to Executive Suite holders. They claimed they planned the menu a year earlier. The suite holders were given a meal as soon as the gates opened. This preliminary meal consisted of snack items and cheeses, antipasto, and salads. Then, midway through the first quarter, each guest was given an opportunity to select two entrees from a list of six choices. Beef, pork, and chicken were available along with seafood and a vegetarian dinner. The executive suite and the food cost $145, although some guests paid $250 for an "upgrade" consisting of chilled shrimp and sushi platters.[20]

Likewise, A&P, in partnership with Anheuser-Busch and Sunkist, put together an ad campaign dubbed "Bud Bowl 2003." This featured six-packs of Michelob Ultra for $5.99, Budweiser eighteen packs for $9.99, and special gift sets containing 1.5-liter swing-top bottles of Grolsch beer with two glasses. In addition, the snack included a 36-ounce bag of California pistachios costing $4.99. A survey of snacking behavior during the Super Bowl revealed that the game's watchers preferred salty snacks over sweets because such snacks complement the beer so many viewers drink during the game.[21]

Active and Retired Players

A unique idea for making money from football merchandise is the recently launched association between a Miami cigar manufacturer and NFL Hall of Fame member Tony Dorsett. Dorsett was a University of Pittsburgh superstar and then played for Dallas and Denver. The cigars are endorsed by Dorsett for the Players Cigar Company. The boxes in which the cigars are sold and displayed bear the autographs of Tony Dorsett and other players and sell for $5.00 to $8.50. The endorsement evidently succeeded, as Players Cigar Company sells more than 500,000 cigars per year.[22]

John Elway, former quarterback with the Denver Broncos and a Super Bowl superstar, heads an online sporting goods store that opened in 2000. The store is called Mvp.com and sells apparel dealing with every sport. Included is, of course, a line of football-related gear: $70 for a New Orleans Saints jersey, $65 for a Green Bay Packers jersey, a Super Bowl locker room shirt for $11 and for only $1,199.99 a Tri-Star Oakland Raiders Bo Jackson-signed shadow box with jersey and photo. Considering the enthusiasm of so many football fanatics, these super-expensive items must be selling well, as Mvp.com has agreed to pay a minimum of $120 million in cash to SportsLine.com, Florida's largest Internet company. SportsLine initiated the partnership by selling Mvp.com to three retired superstar athletes.[23]

The National Football League Players Association (NFLPA) owns Players, Inc., which produces events, radio shows, and television programs and arranges with corporate clients for 1,000 athlete appearances per year. Blurring the lines between business and labor, Players, Inc., sells and/or endorses numerous products and arranges licensing deals that give the corporations the right to use players' names in their advertisements or on trading cards, memorabilia, or merchandise. The NFLPA is therefore a unique union. Unlike any other union, the NFLPA can sell its members. This cannot be done by the Teamsters or the Brotherhood of Electrical Workers, because no one would pay to see those union members work.

Players, Inc., grosses about $42 million in sales in a single fiscal year. The union sits on more than $100 million in assets. These resources are seen by the union as a financial reserve to be used in case of trouble such as the strike that occurred in 1993.[24]

Total Entertainment and Athletes Management (TEAAM) specializes in NFL contract negotiations, draft preparation, long-term financial management, and player marketing, which includes endorsements, personal appearances, and "image development." TEAAM represents Matt Turk of the Miami Dolphins, Stephen Davis of the Washington Redskins, Travis Taylor of the Baltimore Ravens, Robert Thomas of the Dallas Cowboys, and numerous other football players.

Until recently, the NFL enforced a ban on health care sponsorship and advertising. This ban was removed in 2003, thereby allowing the thirty-two NFL franchises as well as the league itself to make deals with prescription drug companies. The only limitation remaining is that advertising with NFL players or teams can be done only for individual products. This means that no drug company can bill itself as the representing sponsor of any one team. The NFL has also limited the products a drug company may advertise as football sponsors to eight categories: allergies, cholesterol reducers, dermatology, diabetes, erectile dysfunction, gastrointestinal, hair renewal and growth, and prostate medication.

The NFL allows players, coaches, owners, and team personnel to endorse these products without appearing in uniform or otherwise identifying with the NFL or a team. The drug companies can, however, use team and league insignia in their advertising. To insure compliance, all proposals must be submitted to the league office. In view of the problems all sports leagues have had with substance abuse, the league was reluctant to deal with drug companies. This was nevertheless achieved because the lure of money eventually overcomes all scruples.

As soon as the ban was lifted, drug companies literally inundated the NFL with advertising proposals. This response could have been foreseen if judged by the demographics alone. Nielsen Media Research announced in 2003 that total viewers per football game increased 5 percent in 2002, reaching 14.4 million. Nielsen also found that four of the fourteen top programs on network TV were football games.[25]

CONTRACT ADVISERS/AGENTS

A great deal of money is earned by the estimated 1,600 agents who represent football players and other athletes. On average, about six certified contract advisers are available to every college player selected. These agents succeed because the inexperienced college players have no idea how to get a professional contract and are usually too poor to spend much money on furthering their careers. The agents can therefore promote the careers of these novices or make idle promises that benefit only the agent.

Some agents complain that potential professional players who do not yet have a contract make outrageous demands when contacted by an agent. Even marginal players have been known to want expensive cars and other benefits in the belief that they can make such requirements before signing with any team. Yet, the NFLPA rule prohibits offering anything "of value" to entice a player to sign a contract.

Because the money is so tempting, numerous agents are anxious to sign a potential player. Some of these players are indeed successful and make their agents rich. Others are a disappointment. Many young men who dream of gaining access to the NFL believe that they will be successful because they receive so much attention from agents. Frequently, that attention is misplaced.[26]

The NFL union has certified too many agents. About 1,900 players are on the NFL rosters. Therefore, not even two players are available for every agent, thus the competition for players is immense. Consequently, the business is dominated by a few and superficially visited by many. An agent is known as a "contract advisor" by the NFLPA. To become certified a potential agent must pay $1,600 to apply. He or she can then attend a two-day seminar and must pass a written examination. A recent survey by the NFLPA revealed that 57 percent of agents had no clients. Only seventy-seven agents had more than eleven clients. In the 2003 season, forty-eight players represented themselves. One-fifth were represented by a total of thirty-two, or 2 percent, of all agents.[27]

The investment an agent must make in a player is considerable. It can cost an agent anywhere from $5,000 to $25,000 to provide a player with room and board and fly him around the country for workouts, interviews, and other activities needed to gain access to the NFL. In the spring of each year agents spend thousands of dollars preparing clients for the annual draft. A few of the players are indeed drafted high, sign big contracts, and receive large bonuses, of which an agent may collect no more than 3 percent.

The minimum rookie salary in the NFL is $225,000. Therefore, an agent's commission on that salary would be only $6,750. Obviously, an agent takes a huge risk representing a potential football player, since only a few players get large signing bonuses. Of course, if the risk pays off, the agent can earn immense sums, because some contracts run into the tens of millions. In addition, agents can earn 10 to 20 percent of endorsement money paid to players under contract to them.

An example of what an agent can do was the draft of Willis McGahee, Miami's All-American running back, by the Buffalo Bills as the twenty-third overall pick in 2003. In 2004 McGahee signed a five-year deal worth $15.53 million. This compares to the top 5 picks, who can command signing bonuses of $10 million each. Nevertheless, his agent, Drew Rosenhaus, did an excellent job in "selling" McGahee to the Bills because McGahee had a serious knee injury which he received during the Fiesta Bowl game against Ohio State in January 2003. McGahee tore three ligaments in his left knee in that game, making him a high-risk pick even after undergoing surgery.

Rosenhaus used a number of stratagems to make McGahee look desirable. He placed a number of phone calls to McGahee's cell phone during the draft telecast. This led some to believe that several NFL teams were on the line. He also let it be known that New England coach Bill Belichick had visited Miami earlier in the year just to see McGahee play, when in fact Belichick was looking at five other players.[28]

Other agents represent coaches rather than players. One of these is Robert La Monte, who handles only coaches out of his San Diego, California, office. His clients include five head coaches and a dozen coordinators who are looking for head-coaching jobs. He represents Mike Holmgren, head coach for the Seattle Seahawks; Marty Mornhinweg, senior offensive coordinator with the Philadelphia Eagles; Andy Reid of the Philadelphia Eagles; and John Fox of Carolina. Jon Gruden, head coach with the Tampa Bay Buccaneers, was appointed through the agency of La Monte. As one of the few head coaches to win the Super Bowl during his first year with his team, Gruden has been the target of numerous offers which will benefit him as much as his agent.[29]

Because there are so many agents and because there have been so many complaints about the conduct of some agents, a bill was passed by the New York Legislature in 2003 requiring sports agents to register. Twenty-eight states already have such laws. The aim of these requirements is to ensure that agents do not exploit players. The agents who are the targets of these laws have been accused of providing talented high school and college players with cash, cars, women, drugs, plane tickets, cell phones, dinners, tickets to sporting events, and other perks. Sports agents also employ "runners" who act for them.[30]

LAWYERS

Football is lawyer friendly. Numerous situations arise from playing the game that permit lawyers to earn considerable sums representing clients engaged in various disputes produced by the football culture. A good number of lawyers are hired by football players, coaches, teams, and others associated with the sport. These lawyers earn high fees for representing their clients in disputes resulting from football games, financial arrangements connected to football events, or criminal or aggressive conduct by players.

Some lawsuits connected to football are indeed spectacular. Among these was the lawsuit brought by Al Davis, owner of the Oakland Raiders, which asked a California judge to force the Tampa Bay Buccaneers and the Carolina Panthers to change their uniforms when playing in California. Davis argued that the uniforms of these teams violate the Raiders trademark rights because silver and black appear among other colors on these helmets and because they have a pirate on their helmet which resembles the Oakland pirate.

Davis is also suing the City of Oakland and Alameda County, California, because he believes he was the victim of lies when he was induced to leave Los Angeles and return to East Bay.[31] On April 15, 2003, lawyer Roger Dreyer alleged in Sacramento County Superior Court that "fraudulent misrepresentations" led the Raiders to sign an agreement to move out of Los Angeles and back to Oakland in 1995. James Brosnahan is the lawyer for the East Bay defendants. He argues that all statements about ticket sales were accurate and the team owners and the public were fully informed.[32]

Lawyers are also employed in disputes between the NFL and the NFLPA. A dispute over worker's compensation benefits was initially brought to the attention of the U.S. Senate by Senators Martin E. Williams of Rhode Island and Richard Saslaw of Virginia, both members of the Senate Commerce and Labor Committee. The senators sought to deal with the dispute by passing legislation concerning the rights of football players. However, Norman Chrite of the Redskins football team and Richard Berthelsen, lawyer for the players association, settled the dispute by introducing the issue during Super Bowl weekend in 2003, when it was settled. The issue at hand was the amount of compensation a player could expect by reason of injury.[33]

Lawsuits involving football are not limited to the professionals. Even parents of Pop Warner players have become involved in legal disputes. For example, a group of parents sued the board of the Fulton County, New York, Pop Warner Association over control of the equipment, the playing fields, uniforms, and fund-raising.[34]

Lawyers are also employed by football players to settle disputes between them. These can be the result of locker-room fights, confrontations over money, or events occurring on the playing field. An example is the lawsuit brought by Patrick Daley, an offensive lineman with the University of Wisconsin Badgers, against former teammate Ron Dayne, now a Giants running back. According to Daley, he suffered a broken nose and a broken orbital socket, requiring "very sophisticated . . . surgery" and running up $18,000 in medical bills, when Dayne punched him in the face on November 5, 1998. This, Daley claimed, ended his college football career and would probably prevent him from playing professional football. Daley is represented by lawyer Michael Fox and Dayne is defended by lawyer Stephen Hurley. Both lawyers are regarded as top trial lawyers, indicating that a large sum of money was involved in the settlement of the dispute. The sum was not made public.[35]

On August 3, 2001, Rashid Wheeler, a twenty-two-year-old safety on the Northwestern University football team, collapsed and died shortly thereafter. By the end of the month his mother had filed a wrongful death lawsuit against the university. Linda Will, Wheeler's mother, contended in the lawsuit that the university was negligent in failing to prevent her son's death. Although the official cause of death was bronchial asthma, the university lawyers tried to blame Wheeler's death on the use of banned substances.[36]

STADIUM CONSTRUCTION PROFITS

Considerable profits are made by construction companies who build football stadiums. An example is the new stadium built by Turner Construction for the Denver Broncos which was finished August 2001. The cost of the project, which took twenty-seven months, was $400 million. This project was particularly difficult because the land on which the stadium was built had not been entirely transferred to the new owners when the project began. In addition, two old stadiums were standing adjacent to the construction site and were not demolished until eighteen months into the project.[37]

With the entrance of the Houston Texans expansion team into the NFL, a new stadium was constructed there. The new Reliant Stadium seats 69,500 fans. The stadium also houses the Houston Livestock and Rodeo show. This new stadium features the first retractable roof in league history. The retractable roof is a compromise, because the Texans wanted to play in an open-air stadium while the rodeo needs an enclosed facility. The stadium extends over 1.9 million square feet and is divided into four segments, each with its own decor, design, and style. The stadium contains 165 luxury suites and some of the closest seating to the playing field in the entire NFL.[38]

Despite these innovations in Houston and in other new stadiums, profits from such construction are not necessarily assured. According to Fitch Ratings, a bond-rating agency, these new stadiums, despite heated seats, "have lost some of their cash flow potential and stability." The reason for this financial difficulty lies in the weak economy. This means that the community-owned assets backing these stadiums are performing poorly.

Fitch also reports that professional franchises are still performing well because the owners are obliged by the rules of the NFL to avoid risky or reckless decisions. Although in the 1990s a new franchise just about guaranteed a profit, both corporate and individual fans are less willing to pay for high-priced extras such as club seats and luxury boxes.

Recently, three new football stadiums opened. These were Gillette Stadium, used by the New England Patriots, the Seahawk franchise in Seattle, and the Texans.[39] Gillette Stadium opened in 2002 after the Patriots had used the old Foxboro stadium for forty-two years. This $325 million stadium was not financed by the taxpayers; instead, the fans are paying for the new stadium by means of ticket prices, which are the highest in the NFL. The average ticket price to see a Patriots game in 2004 is $160, and the average cost for four to see a game is $1,638, because blocks of seats are sold only for expensive sections.

A number of unanticipated expenses have accrued for the Patriots since the new stadium opened. Among these is the need for a separate training camp consisting of a new natural grass practice field directly adjoining the new stadium. In addition, the Patriots are renovating the practice bubble and constructing a 3,000-seat bleacher around the training field. The number of rest room facilities also needed to be increased. There is also a need for increased security, as team owner Robert Kraft seeks to change the rowdy conduct common in Foxboro to a "family atmosphere" in the new stadium.

In 2000 a new football stadium opened in Cincinnati. The stadium, for use by the Cincinnati Bengals, was financed by the public at a cost of $458 million. In addition to these construction costs, the taxpayers also spend $5 million a year to maintain the stadium. Since the stadium was built it is usually half full, because the Bengals are the poorest-performing team in the league, having finished the 2002 season with a dismal 2-14 record.

In 2003, when the stadium was seven years old, county commissioner Todd Portune of Hamilton County, Ohio, sued the owner of the Bengals franchise, Mike Brown, to get the public's money back, claiming that Brown "conspired to shake down" the citizens of the county by failing to deliver a winning team. Brown argued that he did not have enough money to hire excellent players. Portune claims that the NFL salary cap would have made it impossible for Brown to increase his payroll in any case.[40]

At issue is not only this lawsuit but also the financing of sports stadiums with public subsidies. Because the owners pocket all the profits, the taxpayers are usually the losers in these arrangements. According to Paul Weiler, author of *Leveling the Playing Field*, no city or municipality gets a good deal from financing a stadium.[41]

In San Diego the city council has begun negotiations with the Chargers concerning the building of a new football stadium to replace Qualcomm stadium. As usual, the team owners are hinting that they may leave San Diego if they don't get the new stadium at taxpayers' expense. They are supported in this demand by employees who fear losing their jobs if the team leaves the city. On the other side of the discussion concerning a new stadium is the cost to the taxpayer. Even the negotiations cost a good deal, as the city council has authorized spending $100,000 to retain a law firm, $50,000 to hire an accounting firm, and another $100,000 to hire consultants who may be needed later. The owners of the Chargers want the city to spend $400 million for the proposed new stadium, even though the city spent $78 million in renovations of the present stadium only five years earlier.[42]

Nearby Los Angeles has had no football team since 1994. Therefore, a number of investors are considering the possibility of building a new football stadium to replace the eighty-one-year-old Coliseum. One investment group has already developed a $500 million plan to redesign the eighty-two-year-old Rose Bowl, located in Pasadena.

Professional football teams are not alone in seeking to build new stadiums in the hope of greater profits. College football is so big in many universities that the major football schools collect millions in football revenues. The University of Tennessee has an annual football income of about $40 million. This is followed by Georgia, which gains about $37 million per year. Those who earn less, such as Louisiana State University, still produced an income of $27 million in 2002. Seeking to build a new stadium, LSU football fans are now confronted with an increase in ticket prices from $274 to $874 per year for a 50-yard-line seat. The university is supported by the "Tiger Athletic Foundation," which raises money from private donors, thereby bypassing the legislature.[43]

Even high school football teams participate in the building of new stadiums at great cost. An example is the new $19 million football stadium built for the Round Rock school district in Texas, near Austin. The new stadium seats 11,000 fans and has 2,700 parking spaces. Pepsi-Cola paid $250,000 to finance the scoreboard and big-screen equipment at this new high school stadium.

GAMBLING

Gambling on football games has been practiced as long as football has existed. In earlier years, betting on sports was also in vogue, as most ancient civilizations included betting and gambling.

There are those in American society who reject gamblers because they neglect their obligations to their families and because they do not perform the "normal" productive functions expected by the American work ethic. Furthermore, gambling is associated with criminality and particularly with organized crime and therefore is viewed with suspicion by the nongambling community. Because gambling produces a number of problems, such as failure to work regularly and failure to support spouses and children, it is discredited by those who view it as a vice. Yet, despite the condemnation of gambling by the general public, gambling in some forms is not condemned but even practiced by religious establishments in the form of BINGO and other games. Americans also play the stock market and take great risks when investing in stocks and bonds. This kind of investment is not called gambling, but it is gambling in reality. In fact, those who engage in futures trading are dealing in pure speculation and take as many risks as any sports gambler.[44]

The incentive to gamble is in part derived from the boring routine of everyday life. Many people feel that they are trapped in an unsatisfactory family life, a dull job, and a systematic rut. Gambling on football or anything else is therefore a possible way out of that misery—if one wins. Taking a chance destroys routine and adds excitement to life. Moreover, American culture is competitive in all its aspects, and competition and risk taking are part of the American culture base. Gambling is a great diversion, permitting the addict to live in the hope of gaining immediate riches and paying off all his or her debts.[45]

This is even true of football players with high salaries. Football is a risky occupation. Anyone who plays football is taking a risk. It is possible to die playing football. It is probable that any football player will be injured, and it is highly uncertain that young football players will ever enter the NFL or even gain football success in college. Therefore, football players are gamblers ipso facto.

Examples of gamblers in football are numerous. For instance, in 1963, Detroit Lion defensive tackle Alex Karras was suspended for one year by the football commissioner Pete Rozelle for placing bets on his own team. In that year, Green Bay halfback Paul Hornung was similarly suspended for betting on his own team, even as the Detroit Lions were fined for lack of supervision.[46]

In 1977 Art Schlichter signed with the Ohio State University football team as quarterback. Two years later he appeared on the cover of *Sports Illustrated,* having been a Heisman Trophy contender. In 1982 he was an All-American and the number one draft choice of the Balitimore Colts. He received a $350,000 signing bonus, which he gambled away. Prior to that gambling episode Schlichter was regarded as a straight arrow because he did not drink, did not use drugs, and never even touched a cigarette.

In 1983, Schlichter was suspended from the NFL for gambling but was reinstated in 1984. In 1987 he was arrested for bank fraud, unlawful gambling, and writing bad checks. By 1998 he filed for bankruptcy, listing $1 million in debts. Released from four years in prison, Schlichter played minor league football and was named most valuable player with Detroit in 1990. In 1993 he became a sports show host in Cincinnati. One year later, Schlichter was convicted of grand theft and served prison time in Terre Haute, Indiana, including treatment for compulsive gambling. During that treatment Schlichter continued betting and was sent to jail. Released, he continued his gambling, was then convicted in 2000 of money laundering and fraud and sent to prison for sixteen years with six years suspended and the final two to be spent at a day reporting program.[47]

Leonard Tose died on April 15, 2003, at age eighty-eight. He had been the owner of the Philadelphia Eagles football team, which he bought for $16 million. The son of Russian immigrants, Tose built up a trucking business of 700 vehicles. He accumulated immense wealth and gave away millions for medical research, playing fields for schools, and even bulletproof vests for the Philadelphia police.

However, Tose had a severe gambling problem, once losing as much as $50 million during a seventy-two-day losing streak in a casino that furnished him with free liquor. At his eighty-first birthday, Tose had lost his football team, his trucking business, and his Rolls-Royce. His fourth wife divorced him after he lost his mansion. He was forced to move into a modest hotel where his rent was paid by his friends. He drove an eight-year-old car and owned nothing else. He died penniless, the victim of a gambling addiction.[48]

One of the most-discussed football games ever played took place in 1958 when the Baltimore Colts beat the New York Giants 23-17 in overtime. The owner of the Colts was Carroll Rosenbloom, a notorious gambler. Rosenbloom had bet $1 million on the Colts to win by at least four points. After the regulation game ended with a 17-17 tie, the Colts had an opportunity to win the game with a field goal. However, owner Rosenbloom ordered coach Ewbank to try for a touchdown lest his bet be lost. The touchdown was achieved when Alan Ameche made it into the end zone and won the game for the Colts by six points and Rosenbloom saved his money.[49]

Adrian McPherson is another example of a football player ruined by gambling. McPherson was a nineteen-year-old quarterback for Florida State University, without doubt one of the principal teams in American college football, but, on November 25, 2002, his coach, Bobby Bowden, kicked him off the team. With that one of the most promising football careers came to an untimely end.

Two days later, McPherson was arrested for theft and gambling. He was tried on both charges. He pleaded no contest and was sentenced to thirty-months probation. McPherson was accused of betting on all of the Florida State games in 2002, in addition to stealing a $3,500 check from R&R Truck and Auto Accessories, a Tallahassee business. The check was cashed at a local bank with a forged signature. McPherson at first denied all of these charges but was nevertheless forced to resign from Murray State University in Kentucky because the controversy followed him there. Added to the criminal charges against McPherson were demands by bookie friends that he repay gambling debts he owed them. These "friends" also revealed that McPherson opened an account with SPG Global, an Internet gambling site.[50]

Gambling is big business in the United States, as is sports. The sports industry has about $213 billion in annual revenues, twice that of the auto industry. The gambling industry yields $800 billion per year and is therefore the largest industry in the United States. These statistics were reported by the National Gambling Impact Study Commission who found that $380 billion of that $800 billion derives from sports betting.[51]

Football players and owners are of course not the only Americans betting on the game. In fact, Super Bowl games invariably involve a great deal of betting, so much so that the NFL has prohibited the Las Vegas Tourism Promotion Board from running ads during Super Bowl games showing people making bets. This prohibition is, of course, ineffective.

SMALL BUSINESS CONTRACTS

When the Super Bowl was played in San Diego in 2003 the game had a $250 million impact on the business community in that city. The NFL awards about $1 million a day in contracts for services from Thursday through Sunday of Super Bowl weekend. For example, San Diego State and Lighting earned receipts of more than $400,000 on that weekend. The company did the lighting and scaffolding for six TV shows emanating from the Super Bowl.

Other companies that benefit from football games, and particularly the Super Bowl, are security firms, food suppliers, merchandisers, and a host of employees from parking lot attendants to cleaners.

In sum, the business of football is one of the most successful ever developed in the United States and appears to be growing all the time. That includes even the gambling business, which is viewed as a crime by some. If it is, then it is not the only criminal activity related to football. There is much more, which I will discuss in the next chapter.

SUMMARY

The NFL is the most successful sports enterprise in the United States, both in earnings and attendance, earning huge sums from television contracts, advertising, merchandise, and filming.

Advertising at NFL games is very expensive. Nevertheless, all television networks lose money on football events despite the fact that two-thirds of TV viewers watch football.

Football allows numerous nonplaying occupations to earn money. This includes advertising agencies and their employees, sponsors, endorsers, public speakers, contract advisers, lawyers, construction companies, and professional gamblers.

Gambling has led a number of football players into committing white-collar crimes. There are, however, other crimes committed by a good number of football players. That issue is the subject of the next chapter.

Chapter 9

Crime and American Football

THE BENEDICT-YAEGER RESEARCH

In 1998 Jeff Benedict and Don Yaeger published *Pros and Cons: The Criminals Who Play in the NFL*. The authors reviewed the criminal records of professional football players who had been charged with a variety of crimes from driving under the influence of alcohol to murder. The investigation by these authors revealed that 21 percent of NFL players have been charged with a serious crime.[1]

This book includes interviews with arresting officers and court records, as well as police reports. Included in these crimes are murder, rape, assault, robbery, burglary, grand larceny, and auto theft. All of these are felonies and are listed as class I offenses by the Uniform Crime Report issued annually by the Federal Bureau of Investigation.[2] In addition to these crimes, NFL players investigated by Benedict and Yaeger were also charged with kidnapping, false imprisonment, domestic violence, carrying concealed weapons, possession of stolen goods, criminal trespass, prostitution solicitation, possession of drug paraphernalia, fraud, vandalism, placing a bomb, shoplifting, and a host of drug-related offenses.[3]

Although the crimes of NFL players have been reported in the media for years, not much attention was given to this behavior until the trial of O. J. Simpson, who was acquitted in the 1994 deaths of his ex-wife, Nicole Brown and a waiter, Ron Goldman. Simpson had an illustrious career as a winner of the Heisman Trophy in 1968 and an All-Pro five times. After his football career ended, Simpson became a TV analyst and actor and was earning a considerable income endorsing a number of products when he was arrested. Subsequent to his acquittal on double murder charges he lost a wrongful death suit and was forced to make financial reparations to the families of his victims.[4]

Although the Simpson case became an international media sensation, the other innumerable crimes of NFL players have received little attention over the years. This inattention to football players' crimes extended to Cornelius Bennett, linebacker for the Buffalo Bills from 1987 to 1995, who was charged with rape and sexual assault. Bennett continued his football career with the Atlanta Falcons for three more years and played for the Indianapolis Colts in his final NFL appearance during 1999. Charges of rape and assault did not interfere with his NFL status. Likewise, Michael Irvin, wide receiver for Dallas, was charged with marijuana and cocaine possession; Nate Newton, Dallas Cowboys defensive lineman, was charged with sexual assault; Warren Moon, quarterback for Houston, was charged with domestic violence; Jake Plummer, who played quarterback with the Arizona Cardinals and Denver Broncos, was charged with sexual abuse; Andre Rison, wide receiver for a number of teams, was charged with aggravated assault; Bruce Smith, who was highly regarded as the best defensive end the Buffalo Bills ever had, was charged with driving under the influence; Deion Sanders, defensive back for Atlanta and other teams, was charged with aggravated assault and battery; and the Seattle Seahawks' Cortez Kennedy was arrested for domestic violence. These are only a few of the criminal cases uncovered by Benedict and Yaeger.

The author's writers explain these crimes by arguing that the pampering star players receive during their adolescence immunizes them in their minds from the consequences of their actions. Such an explanation may have its merits. However, there are more sophisticated explanations for violent and nonviolent crime. Since the publication of *Pros and Cons,* a great number of additional crimes have been committed by professional and college football players.

FELONIES AND MISDEMEANORS: THE FOOTBALL CULTURE OF CRIME

Murder

Ranger College is a small school in Eastland County, Texas. In Texas, as in many other states, colleges receive state funds based on enrollment. Therefore, Ranger College relied on an unusually large roster of athletes and gave them minimal supervision, just to keep enrollment high. Students, as I described previously, are more likely to enroll in a college with a winning football or basketball team than in one which does not emphasize athletics.

Included on the football team in 2003 was Devron Wadlington, who was jailed on March 30, 2003, for shooting and killing D'Waylon Jones with his AK-47 assault rifle after Jones and another man tried to rob him in his dormitory. Although the murder was evidently victim precipitated, the district attorney did not regard this killing as a self-defense action because Wadlington chased Jones outside and killed him there.[5]

This murder is viewed by criminologists as a victim-precipitated homicide. This does not mean that the killer can be viewed as innocent. It means that there are situations in which the victim contributes to the crime. This is particularly visible in cases of homicide, which often begin with an argument or fight between people who know each other. In about 12 percent of murders committed by men the murder is victim precipitated. For women the rate is far higher, as 60 percent of murders committed by women are precipitated by male victims.[6]

The study by Benedict and Yaeger includes three accusations of murder. These involved Brian Blades, a wide receiver for Seattle, who was acquitted of homicide after pleading guilty to a reduced charge; Derrick Fenner, a running back with Oakland who also plead guilty to a reduced charge after his murder charge was dropped; and Charles Jordan, wide receiver with Miami, whose murder charge was dismissed.[7]

Football players are also the victims of murder and attempted murder. Jo Jo Heath, who played nine seasons with the NFL, was stabbed to death in December 2002. Heath had been arrested for dealing drugs and charged with six counts of selling cocaine to undercover agents. He was also convicted of two robberies. In earlier years, Heath played running back, wide receiver, cornerback, and free safety for Cincinnati, Philadelphia, and the Canadian Football League.[8]

Dennis Weathersby was days away from starting a professional football career when he was shot in the back. He survived and made a full recovery. Nevertheless, he lost a good deal when he was drafted in the fourth round of the 2003 draft by the Cincinnati Bengals, the worst team in the NFL. Prior to the shooting he had a good chance of gaining a far better job. However, too many teams feared that his injuries would decrease his value.[9]

James Allen, a Southern University football player, was shot and killed minutes after he was kicked out of a club because of his part in a heated confrontation. The argument between Allen and other patrons of the club continued outside and ended when one of the men involved shot Allen once in the head at close range and then fled.[10] This kind of murder is not uncommon. In a study of 912 homicides, I found that fifty-one of 116 killings whose locations could be ascertained were conducted in or outside a bar.[11]

Former NFL running back Fred Lane was murdered by his wife, Deidra, in July 2000. Evidently, she ambushed her husband and killed him in the hope of cashing in a $5 million life insurance policy. The same woman had previously been convicted of bank robbery.[12]

It is common in murder cases involving a female killer and male victim, for the woman to claim domestic abuse drove her to the murder. Since domestic abuse is regarded as reason for self-defense actions by the potential victim who fears for her life, this defense is frequent. It is also frequently true. Thirty-one of the 126 football players studied by Benedict and Yaeger were charged with domestic violence.

Rape

Sexual abuse in the second degree is a class B felony. In Iowa that offense could result in a prison sentence of twenty-five years if convicted. In January 2003, two former football players for the University of Iowa, Royce Hooks and Brent Nash, both seniors majoring in exercise science, were indicted by a grand jury for committing sexual abuse against an eighteen-year-old woman whom they had met at a party. They were both suspended from the football team.[13]

On October 21, 2002, a three-member faculty committee at the University of Maine upheld the suspension of two football players, Paris Minor and Stefan Gomes, accused of sexual assault the previous June. The alleged victim said that she was held down by the two men and forced to have sex. This was investigated by the police, who turned over their findings to the district attorney. Thereupon a student conduct committee suspended the two football players, who appealed the decision to the faculty committee without success.[14]

Four Notre Dame University football players were formally charged with gang-raping a female student in March 2002. All four were accused of rape, conspiracy to commit rape, criminal deviant conduct, and sexual battery. Sexual battery is a class D felony in Indiana. The other three charges are class B felonies.[15]

In May 2001, Eric Knott, a tight end for Michigan State University, plead guilty to fourth-degree criminal sexual conduct. Earlier, Knott had been charged with criminal sexual conduct. A lengthy legal battle ended with Knott admitting to a lesser charge. Knott was accused of raping a thirteen-year-old Detroit girl, an offense that carries a life prison term in Michigan. It is mere speculation to believe that Knott was allowed to plead to the lesser charge and accept probation instead of any prison time because he was one of the most highly recruited high school football players in Michigan.[16]

On January 18, 2003, Jimmy Desmond Abram, a twenty-two-year-old senior defensive end at McNeese State College in Louisiana, was charged with sexually assaulting an Estonian woman studying at Lamar University in Beaumont, Texas.[17] In December 2001 two University of Minnesota football players, Steven M. Watson and Mackenzy Toussaint, were charged with rape for assaulting a woman in a campus apartment.[18]

In 1995 two members of the University of Nebraska football team were arrested for committing violent felonies at the outset of the football season. Tailback Lawrence Phillips, a strong contender for the Heisman Trophy that year, was arrested for assaulting his girlfriend, resulting in his temporary removal from the team. Because the prosecutor recommended probation, Phillips plead "no contest" and no further action was taken against him. Phillips's backup, Damon Benning, was arrested that same day for assaulting his former girlfriend. Benning defended himself against these charges by claiming that his former girlfriend had assaulted him and that he was only defending himself against this woman.[19]

Benedict and Yaeger list nine charges of rape or sexual assault among their sample of criminal football players, including Cornelius Bennett; Tony McCoy, defensive end for Indianapolis; David Meggett, kicker for New England; Nate Newton, offensive lineman for Dallas; Gerald Perry, offensive lineman for St. Louis; Christian Peter, defensive lineman for the New York Giants; Jake Plummer, Phoenix quarterback; Silvan Nilo, wide receiver for Tampa Bay; and William Moe, running back for Minnesota. It is noteworthy that none of these men were convicted of sexual assault or rape. In all cases the charges were dropped or the defendant plead guilty to a lesser charge or was found not guilty.

Sexual assault and rape are by no means confined to football players on the campuses of American colleges and universities. In 1987, Koss, Gidycz, and Wisniewski discovered that about 28 percent of college women had experienced an attempted or completed rape. Before the 1980s, little credence was given rape victims. This attitude gradually changed, so now victims receive more support than was true before that time.[20] Over the years, rape victims have been given more and more attention, so that in 1992 the Campus Sexual Assault Victims' Bill of Rights became law. According to that law, campus authorities must enforce the rights of victims and fully cooperate with them.[21]

Some unique features of campus life are conducive to rape. One of these is the sociocultural context of fraternity life in which the sexual coercion of women is expected and normative. The social organization of fraternities promotes the victimization of women as loyalty to the fraternity, group protection, the use of alcohol as a weapon, and emphasis on male superiority are all used to support rape-conducive conduct.[22] These values and this kind of rape conduct is frequently as much of the football team culture as it is a part of the fraternity culture since the same mechanisms operate in both environments. A football team is also a fraternity.

Assault

Assault is a class I felony and is listed as such in the Uniform Crime Reports of the Federal Bureau of Investigation.[23] Here too, football players make their mark. For example, John "Jumbo" Elliott, an offensive tackle for the Jets, assaulted a sixty-year-old limousine driver who had been hired to pick up several Jets players from a New Jersey steak house. Elliott was accused of picking up Donald Matinsky, who was dressed in a Santa suit, and throwing him to the pavement with such force that Matinsky suffered a fractured kneecap. Evidently Elliott was incensed when Matinsky asked him to get out of the cab. Elliott was also charged with public intoxication and harassment.[24]

Likewise, Iowa State University offensive lineman Sam Aiello was charged with assault in Iowa City in April 2003 after he poked a man in the eye with a pool cue. Aiello had been charged two years previous to this incident when he assaulted Jon Beurjer, the Iowa State quarterback, and gave him a concussion.[25]

Assault resembles murder. It has been called "the prototype of violent crime" because it is the most common of violent crimes and also the starting point for murder, rape, and all other types of violence. Assault represents potential lethal violence because the aggressor may in fact want to kill the victim or is unaware that it is not possible to predict the outcome of violent aggression. Assault, like murder, frequently targets friends, associates, and relatives. This is particularly true of female victims, as only 29 percent of female assault victims are attacked by strangers.[26]

University of Nebraska wingback Riley Washington plead not guilty when he was charged with attempted murder and the use of a weapon after he shot a man at a convenience store in 1995.[27]

Benedict and Yaeger list so many cases of assault and aggravated assault among their sample of criminal football players that I cannot review them all here. Suffice it to feature Deion Sanders, the two time All-American at Florida State, seven time NFL All Pro with Atlanta, Dallas, and San Francisco, and the only athlete to play in both World Series baseball and the Super Bowl. Deion Sanders is now a TV football analyst. Sanders also has the distinction of having been charged with aggravated assault, disorderly conduct, battery, trespassing, resisting arrest, and leaving an accident scene. Even longer lists of charges against other football players are reported by Benedict and Yaeger.

In April 1997, the St. Louis Rams selected Texas Christian University center Ryan Tucker in the fourth round of the NFL draft. At that time, Tucker was awaiting trial for an assault that left the victim paralyzed and brain damaged. When this was mentioned to his coach, Dick Vermeil, the coach replied that Tucker "can finish a fight and that is positive." Tucker eventually plead "no contest." [28]

When Baltimore running back Bryan "Bam" Morris missed a meeting with his probation officer, the owner of the Baltimore team,

Art Modell, persuaded the probation officer to let Morris play despite this. When Atlanta Falcons defensive back Patrick Bates was charged with assaulting his pregnant girlfriend and, three weeks after the child was born, kidnapping the child and beating the mother with a gun, he was let go by the Falcons, only to be signed by the Oakland Raiders.

Larceny

Football players are also well represented among nonviolent offenders. For example, in December 2002 Florida State defensive tackle Darnell Dockett was arrested for stealing $300 worth of merchandise from a sporting goods store. Although he was suspended from the January 1 Sugar Bowl game, he faced no criminal charges because the store owner, a former football player, would not press charges.[29]

In September 2001, University of Kansas freshman quarterback Mario Kinsey and sophomore running back Reggie Duncan were charged with the theft of a purse and the use of the credit card they found in it. Both football players had been convicted of other crimes in the past.[30]

Larceny is the most common American crime. In addition, it is the most common crime committed on college campuses.

Drug Offenses

Charges of drug possession and use are the most common of all accusations against football players. In April 2003, Jermaine Brooks, tackle for the University of Arkansas, was sentenced to ten years in prison for a felony drug conviction. Brooks was arrested in October 2002 for drug possession, drug distribution, and possession of numerous illegal weapons. At the time of his arrest, Brooks had 7.5 lbs of marijuana in his apartment together with such drug paraphernalia as plastic bags and scales.[31]

On April 7, 2003, Florida State wide receiver Talman Gardner was arrested and charged with marijuana possession and having a concealed loaded handgun. The gun charge was a felony and the drug charge a misdemeanor. He plead "no contest" to these charges and received one year of probation and 250 hours of community service.

Thereafter, the New Orleans Saints selected Gardner in the seventh round of the 2003 NFL draft.[32]

Michael Irvin, star wide receiver for the Dallas Cowboys, in 1996 plead "no contest" to second-degree felony cocaine possession. This plea permitted him to accept four years of probation and thereby avoid a prison sentence. Irvin, together with other Dallas football players, had rented a house where he and others took prostitutes and conducted drug parties. One of these prostitutes was the girlfriend of a Dallas police officer who therefore attempted to hire a hit man to kill Irvin for mistreating his girlfriend. However, the hit man was an undercover federal agent who arrested the officer, who was then charged with solicitation to commit murder and sent to prison.[33]

Drug abuse is a common offense in the United States. In 2000 an estimated 14.8 million Americans aged twelve or older were using illegal drugs. Marijuana is the most frequently used illegal drug and has been used by 75 percent of those using drugs other than alcohol. Those aged eighteen to twenty are the most frequent users of drugs, with a slight decline among those aged twenty-one to twenty-five and a larger decline in later years. Football players are members of those cohorts.[34]

Weapons Charges

University of Missouri defensive end Nick Tarpoff was charged on February 24, 2003, with a felony for possessing an illegal weapon. That is a class C felony punishable by a seven-year prison sentence. Tarpoff also made a false police report by claiming a would-be robber had shot him in an attempt to rob his home, when in fact Tarpoff had shot himself in the arm and needed medical attention.[35]

In August 1997, coach Barry Switzer of the Dallas Cowboys was arrested at the Dallas-Fort Worth International Airport for carrying a loaded .38 caliber revolver in his carry-on bag. Carrying a weapon into an airport is a third-degree felony punishable with two to ten years in prison and an up to $10,000 fine. Since Switzer was not licensed to carry a gun he also violated state law. According to Texas law, carrying a gun without a permit is a class A misdemeanor carrying a penalty of up to a year in jail and a $4,000 fine.[36]

In January 2002, Mushin Mohammad, Carolina Panthers receiver, was charged with carrying a concealed weapon and possession of marijuana. When àrrested, Mohammad had hidden two guns in his car. This was his second arrest on weapons charges. He had just been released from spending ninety days in jail on similar charges.[37]

A long list of football players who carry concealed weapons or are otherwise found guilty of weapons law violations can be easily constructed. Such a list includes James Whitley, Michigan co-captain, who plead guilty to carrying a concealed weapon in February 2002. Erik Williams, Cowboys offensive tackle, in 1997 was found possessing an Astra .44 revolver, a Glock semi-automatic pistol, and a Baretta. All guns were loaded at the time of Williams's arrest. Likewise, Brian Blades of the Seattle Seahawks, Leonardo Carson of the San Diego Chargers, Gerard Warren of the Cleveland Browns, and Damien Robinson of the Jets were all charged with illegal gun possession.[38]

A truly tragic case of self-destruction is the life of Bob Marshall, All-American football player at the University of Wyoming from 1956 to 1960. Marshall had a successful business career after his football days but then became involved in drug and gun possession, ending with a conviction for the acquisition of a kilo of cocaine in 2002. A long list of previous convictions on similar charges led to a life sentence for Marshall, now seventy years old.[39]

Drunken Driving

On October 6, 2002, Al Johnson, center for the University of Wisconsin offensive line, was arrested for his second drunk driving offense. Previously he had been convicted of drunk driving, paid a fine of $733, and lost his driver's license for seven months. This did not prevent the Dallas Cowboys from selecting Johnson in the second round of the 2003 draft.[40]

Bruce Smith, star player for the Buffalo Bills for fifteen seasons, was arrested for drunk driving in Virginia Beach, Virginia. Smith became a member of the Washington Redskins in 2000. Smith risked being fined $20,000 by the NFL had he been convicted, but he was instead acquitted in June 2003. The NFL's alcohol misconduct policy applies to players convicted of alcohol-related crimes.[41]

Numerous other incidents of alcohol abuse among football players can be cited. This offense is of course widespread and one of the most serious public health problems in the United States. These statistics reveal the extent of alcohol abuse in America today.

SUPER BOWL XXXIV

When Super Bowl XXXIV was played in Atlanta in 2000, the NFL lined up thirteen professional athletes who had been charged with twenty crimes among them. The ABP News reported that "one was convicted of involuntary manslaughter, a convicted thief was playing running back, a prostitute's john was in the defensive backfield, a drunken driver was on the field and a man convicted of negligent homicide was patrolling as linebacker."[42]

Of the 116 football players assembled in Atlanta that year to play the Super Bowl game, 11 percent had been arrested for one offense or another. Examples are St. Louis Rams linebacker Leonard Little, who plead guilty to involuntary manslaughter. He had been driving drunk and hit Susan Gutweiler, who died the next day. Little's blood alcohol content was twice the legal limit. He was therefore suspended from the NFL for eight games and then reinstated. He was also jailed for ninety nights but went free during the day. He was then given probation and ordered to serve 1,000 hours community service.

Steve Jackson, defensive back for the Tennessee Titans, was arrested in 2000 in Nashville for soliciting a prostitute. This led to his conviction and eleven months of unsupervised probation. He also paid court costs. Donald Walker, a teammate of Steve Jackson, plead guilty to the charge of assaulting his former girlfriend and was sentenced to probation.

St. Louis Rams linebacker Charlie Clemons was charged with carrying a concealed weapon into a school. He was attending the University of Georgia at the time. Not satisfied with these charges, Clemons proceeded to discharge a gun in a public street and was once more charged with carrying a concealed weapon. This time he was sentenced to a year probation and paid a fine of $1,150.

Rams wide receiver Tony Horne was charged in Richmond County, North Carolina, with the felony of distributing cocaine. He was fined

$285.50 and then committed assault, for which he was fined $2,006 and ordered to make restitution. The Rams's team, also included Ryan Tucker, whom I mentioned earlier in connection to beating Bobby McGhee, for which he was charged with aggravated assault and inflicting serious bodily injury.

Finally there is the case of Justin Watson, a 1994 Rams running back who was charged with burglary, theft, and grand theft, a felony. All this led to two years probation, two days in jail, and a fine of $815.[43]

We should ask whether professional football players are held to the same laws and punishments as nonathletes in American society. Evidently a double standard exists for athletes in the criminal justice system. This double standard could be eliminated if the NFL's collective bargaining agreement reduced the power of the independent arbitrators to overturn discipline imposed by the football commissioner for criminal conduct by football players.[44]

UNDERSTANDING CRIMINALITY AMONG FOOTBALL PLAYERS

Almost every week a football player or other athlete is accused of or charged with a crime. Many of these incidents involve violence, particularly violence against women. The charges are usually domestic violence, sexual assault, or rape. Therefore, college administrators and football coaches could be asked to screen recruits for past criminal behavior. That, however, would deprive many teams of winning players. Therefore, coaches and others shield players from the consequences of their crimes until the players conclude that the normal rules of conduct do not apply to them. This belief begins with the failure of many high school and college football players and other athletes to meet the usual academic requirements demanded of other students. It has been alleged that football players are so important to many colleges that they will do anything to keep an athlete playing and that therefore many college administrators do not want to know and do not ask about the conduct of athletes in their institution.

Violent behavior is a good deal more frequent among football players than other students. Todd W. Crossett, professor of sociology at the University of Massachusetts, found that 19 percent of sexual assaults on college campuses were committed by male student athletes, who constitute only 3.3 percent of the male student body.[45]

Failure of coaches and faculty to screen football players in colleges does not sufficiently explain the reasons for the considerable criminality of college and professional football players. Therefore it is necessary to seek the reasons for such conduct elsewhere.

Since 60 percent of college and professional football players are of African descent it is reasonable to discuss the origin of violence as a function of race in America. This means that the violent conduct of football players resembles the violent conduct of African-American young men who are not football players.

To illustrate this feature of the African-American community as compared to the Euro-American community we need only take a look at the homicide rates in both groups. According to the Bureau of Justice Statistics as published in 2003 concerning the years 1976-2000, 51.5 percent of all homicide offenders were black and 46.4 percent were white, the remainder, 2.1 percent, being attributed to persons of Asian descent. Since blacks constitute 12 to 13 percent of the American population, the black homicide rate is four times that of the white homicide rate. Similar differences can be found with reference to all crimes of violence.

Between 1976 and 2000 black killers were responsible for 94 percent of black victims of murder. It also noteworthy that 39.4 percent of all homicides committed by blacks involved family members. Similarly, 58.3 percent of white victims of homicide were family members of the killer.[46]

In 2001 the victimization rates for violent crimes committed by blacks exceeded that for whites, as had been true for a century or more. The white rate of victimization by violent criminals was 25.3 per thousand that year and the black rate 32, or 21 percent greater than for Euro-Americans. Simple assault, a crime quite prominent among football players, led to about 1,600 arrests per 100,000 blacks between the years 1980 and 2000. During that same twenty-year span, arrests of whites per 100,000 were about six hundred.[47]

If we are to explain the considerable violence exhibited by football players then such an explanation must rest first and foremost on an explanation of black violence. Football players exhibit behavior reflecting their culture, and violence is an integral part of the male black subculture in America.

The crime of slavery is the principal contributor to black violence even in 2003. Such a statement may seem far-fetched to those not acquainted with the long reach of history upon all human experience. Evidently, slavery has insured that the social, ethnic, and cultural experiences of African Americans differ from those of any other ethnic group represented in the population of the United States.[48]

The consequences of slavery did not end with Lincoln's Emancipation Proclamation of January 1, 1863. On the contrary. During the 140 years since then the African-American population has experienced poverty and economic deprivation and victimization by institutionalized discrimination. African Americans, like all Americans, live in a violent society originating with slavery and continued in numerous other fashions to this day. Slavery was of course brutal and violent. This began as soon as blacks were captured in Africa and then marched to the coast. It is estimated that one in three captives died during these marches. Then, another third died while at sea.[49] Violence against the slaves continued in this country in the form of lynchings, brutal beatings, murders, and mutilations. Between 1885 and 1921, 4,096 lynching were recorded in the United States. That constituted an average of 113 per year, or 9.5 per month for thirty-six years.[50]

The continued violence against African Americans after slavery was formally abolished in 1865 did not cease until World War II. During that eighty-year period, black people continued to be treated as social, civil, and political nonpersons without rights, without dignity, and without the guarantees reputedly encased in the American Constitution. The conflict between the ideals of American democracy and the daily reality of black life in the United States during the first half of the twentieth century was succinctly demonstrated by the Swedish economist Gunnar Myrdal in his epochal volume *An American Dilemma.*[51]

Race riots also contributed to the atmosphere of violence that confronted African Americans for years. Such riots led to the deaths of 500 African Americans between 1915 and 1919 alone. Such rioting continued thereafter, although later riots such as the Watts riot in 1965 and the Los Angeles riots in 1992 were initiated by black Americans themselves. These riots were sparked by perceived police brutality, which has a long history in this country.[52]

The death penalty is another source of violence directed at African-Americn men. These and many other oppressive conditions imposed on African Americans lead to a devaluation of black men's lives and a sense of hopelessness and lack of self-worth. Added to all these difficulties and assaults on their dignity and sense of powerlessness is the high unemployment rate among blacks, which makes it difficult for black fathers to support their families. This leads some men to leave their families, thereby leaving women behind who then become the heads of the black households. The absence of fathers is augmented by the high mortality rate among black males.

The consequences for black American boys are hopelessness and resignation to alcohol, crack cocaine, and other drugs, all available amid television and other media programs depicting wealth and material success. All of this leads to tremendous confusion, frustration, and emotional pain. That pain may be alleviated by entrance into violent occupations such as boxing and football. These sports permit black boys to escape poverty, earn respect, gain adulation, and achieve the American dream of money, power, and material comfort. Football and basketball are best suited to fulfill these dreams, albeit only a tiny minority of black men ever succeed in these sports.

GAMBLING AND DRUGS

Bernie Parrish, Dan Moldea, and Tim Green are authors of books that demonstrate the involvement of the NFL and its players, coaches, and owners in the most pervasive criminal enterprise in America, gambling.

In 1971 Bernie Parrish published *They Call It a Game.* Parrish played defensive cornerback for eight years, all but eleven games with the Cleveland Browns, from 1959 until 1967. Parrish announces on the first page of his book that he intended then "to drive Pete Rozelle, Arthur Modell, Carroll Rosenbloom, Tex Schramm, Clint Murcheson, Lou Spadia and the other so-called sportsman owners out of professional football."[53]

In addition to a severe indictment of the entire football hierarchy of that time, Parrish discusses the "fixing" of football games by organized gamblers, claiming that in 1965 alone over $13 billion was "made" by those who bet on football. According to Parrish there are four basic ways to "fix" a football game: (1) through a referee, (2) through an important player, (3) through the coaching staff and team management, and (4) by drugging a key player or a number of them.

Parrish explains at some length why so many football players take drugs. "The search for the magic potion leads into many dangerous situations," writes Parrish. For one, he claims that improper shots before games can lead to severe consequences and that he remembers two players who almost died because of such shots. Furthermore, he claims that players are given many experimental drugs before they come into general use. He is particularly concerned with Dexedrine, which may well have gone out of style more than thirty years after Parrish wrote his book.[54]

This is not to say that drugs are no longer used. Only the type of drug and competition from ever-newer drugs sometimes drive older drugs off the market. In the 1960s anabolic steroids were just coming on the market. These pills were used to increase the strength of the user and were used widely among all kinds of athletes. Parrish writes that "most players will try almost anything they believe might help improve their performance," including drugs but also hypnosis or even "the power of positive thinking."

Parrish claims that quarterbacks are the most vulnerable targets of gamblers who want to affect point spreads in their favor. Offensive tackles, according to Parrish, can miss blocks and get the quarterback sacked. His principal argument, however, is with the owners and their relationship to gambling. Parrish argues that owners can affect the game on the field in many ways. The owner can decide who is to be the starting quarterback and can therefore pick a man with little experience who will lose the game or affect the point spread in favor of the owner's bet. Since coaches are creatures of the owners, coaches, says Parrish, have to protect their careers by following the orders of the owners.[55]

Parrish also proposes that "gambling interests" will use an owner as a front for their activities. The "clean" owner then hires a cooperative head coach who then produces the desired results. Even TV is suspect, according to Parrish. He wants his readers to understand that a whole game could be nothing more than a prearranged TV production and no more truthful than a televised wrestling match.[56] This is unlikely. Parrish is probably wrong; such a conspiracy can hardly be carried out because too many people are involved who would have to keep silent concerning such a "fix" on so massive a scale.

In 1989, Dan E. Moldea published *Interference: How Organized Crime Influences Professional Football.* This book contains some of the most damning evidence concerning gambling and other crimes occurring in the NFL and influenced by the mafia. The book includes allegations of "fixing" games and revived the idea that Carroll Rosenbloom, owner of the Los Angeles Rams and the Baltimore Colts, was murdered.[57]

This book led to a furious controversy between the author and those who sought to deny his evidence and his book. Moldea begins by writing that "betting on pro-football games has become a veritable American institution—with individual gamblers averaging wagers of between $100 to $500 on a single sporting event."[58] Moldea also claims that numerous attempts have been made over the years to fix football games. He recollects how gambler Alvin J. Paris had been arraigned for his attempt to bribe Giants players Merel Hapes and Frank Filchok.[59]

Moldea makes five principal charges against the NFL by claiming that no fewer than twenty-one team owners have had documented personal and/or business ties with members of the organized crime syndicate. Furthermore, he suggests that no fewer than seventy NFL games may have been fixed; that no fewer than fifty legitimate investigations of corruption within the NFL have either been suppressed or killed as a result of the sweetheart relationship between NFL security, the internal police force within the league, and a variety of federal, state, and local law enforcement agencies; that the illegal gambling economy has become an adjunct to the First Amendment because of the insistence of the sports media to print and broadcast betting lines and hire oddsmakers and handicappers to predict the outcome of NFL games; and that the movement to legalize sports gambling by state jurisdictions will cause a proliferation of illegal bookmaking and organized crime activity.[60]

Interference was widely reviewed in various newspapers across the country. The most influential, *The New York Times Book Review,* printed a seriously disparaging attack by Gerald Eskenazi on September 3, 1989. The reviewer attacked the book and its author on the grounds that some names in *Interference* were misspelled and because the reviewer considered Moldea's work "sloppy journalism." None of the review's criticisms disputed the facts laid out by Moldea.[61]

Moldea sued *The New York Times* for defamation. This led editorial writers all over the country to invoke the First Amendment and claim that a Moldea victory threatened freedom of the press. The district court dismissed the case. The U.S. Supreme Court later "denied certiorari," meaning that Moldea lost his case.[62] Whatever the merits of Eskenazi's criticisms of Moldea's book may be, book reviews cannot alter the facts. The evidence presented by Moldea is overwhelming.

Titans is a novel concerning a football team. The author, Tim Green, used that name five years before the Houston Oilers became the Tennessee Titans in 1999. Tim Green is a former linebacker for the Atlanta Falcons. He is also an attorney, a best-selling author of a number of novels, and a football analyst for Fox Sports, *USA Today,* and National Public Radio.

Titans is the story of fictional football player Hunter Logan, who plays quarterback for the "New York Titans," an NFL team that has just won the Super Bowl. Like many professional athletes, Hunter is a gambler, which is good news for the mob, who learn from one of his friends that he has been betting on NFL games. This allows them to blackmail him, because his NFL contract for $16 million, his Nike shoe endorsement, and his career would all come to an immediate end if his gambling activities became known. The mob now demands that for its silence, Hunter take some points off the game. He rationalizes that this is okay since he has no intention of losing the game. The outcome in this novel is kidnapping and murder.[63] Although *Titans* is fiction, Green explains that he has seen players lose $5,000 while flying on a plane and that he saw the same person win back $10,000 rolling dice on the way home.

It has been alleged that gambling on football games is widespread on college campuses and in the NFL. An example of such involvement was the trial of Adrian McPherson, quarterback for Florida State University. That trial resulted in a hung jury in Tallahassee in June 2003 and dealt with the charge that McPherson gambled on the Internet, including games in which he played. McPherson was charged with betting large sums on every Seminoles game in 2002 until he ran out of his own money and therefore owed a professional gambler $8,000. McPherson was also charged with placing bets on basketball games, a sport in which he also excelled. In November 2002 McPherson was dismissed from the Florida State football team when he was charged with stealing a blank check from R&R Truck Accessories in Florida.[64]

Gambling is one of the principal sources of income for organized crime. In 1993 George Anastasia wrote that mob-related sports betting was as "pervasive as soft pretzels, and, in most cases, is considered as harmless as bingo."[65]

THE SOCIOLOGY OF CRIME

Criminal activity in America's most important form of entertainment, football, is to be expected. There are several reasons for this expectation. One of these is certainly the conflict of cultures which football and the whole sports world represents.

Sociologists have long held that at least one reason for crime is culture conflict. This means that there are different values among people with different orientations or views of the world, and therefore some clash with the expectations of others is likely. From the view of many football players, gambling is acceptable behavior. Likewise, assault, drug use, and excessive drinking of alcohol are viewed as normal and reasonable by some social groups and utterly condemned by others. Therefore, those in a position to make and enforce the laws create criminals by enforcing middle-class norms on many football players who come from a subculture that has different expectations from those of the middle-class legislatures and their agents, the police, the courts, and the media.[66]

Because this culture conflict exists in the United States, organized crime has benefited substantially. Gambling represents only one area in which this has been true, yet it is a major source of income for the mob, whose sole interest is the acquisition of money by any means.

Blocked opportunities and racial discrimination are also used as explanations for much of the crime that has invaded the NFL and its players. Indeed, football players earn huge salaries and have more money than most Americans will see in a lifetime. Nevertheless, the conduct of many football players reflects their origin in the minority community and the values and attitudes fostered there. This includes relative deprivation or the belief that one is prevented from attaining what others are given as a matter of course.

Violence is not caused by the absence of material goods. It is rather the feeling of inferiority and inequality that leads to violence. People who believe that they are always second class will compensate themselves by violating those who are weaker. This explains the excessive aggression of football players against others and particularly against women.[67]

Violence against women is unfortunately very common among football players. This is a crime that many nonviolent people cannot understand. Yet from the viewpoint of many violent men, including rapists and assaulters, violence on their part is caused by the behavior of the victim. A large number of the football players accused of violence have never learned to control their anger. It is of course an advantage for some football players to be angry and hence willing and able to direct that anger at an opponent in a football game. However, many angry players are equally angry in everyday life. There are those who cannot control their anger and therefore allow their anger to erupt into violence.

Violent offenders usually do not see themselves as criminals. Instead they generally see themselves as reacting in a justifiable manner to the behavior of others. This is particularly true of domestic abusers, who almost always accuse their victims of provoking them. Even mean drunks who engage in barroom brawls say that they did not intend to hurt anyone.[68]

Drug use in the NFL and by college players is also rooted in aspects of American life that spill over into the football culture. High school and even college football are played by adolescents, who frequently experience boredom, anxiety, and frustration as well as depression. Many adolescents don't know how to deal with all these feelings. They then use psychoactive drugs as a form of self-medication. The drug allows the user to avoid emotional pain. It is a form of hedonism for a young person who does not foresee the outcome of drug involvement.[69]

The National Institute of Drug Abuse has outlined some conditions that are associated with drug abuse. The first concerns families whose members have a history of alcohol abuse and/or a history of antisocial behavior or criminality. A second reason for drug use is the influence of friends who use drugs. This is certainly true of members of the NFL and of college football players. Third, drugs are often used by those who are involved in aggressive behavior, a criterion which certainly fits football players.[70]

In sum, criminal behavior among football players reflects criminal behavior in the United States in general. Like all American crime, football crime and its criminals are protected by politics, which permeate the entire football scene.

SUMMARY

It has been estimated that 21 percent of all NFL players are guilty of committing serious crimes. Until the O. J. Simpson trial little attention was given this phenomenon even though many of these crimes were committed by well-known players. Included in the criminal conduct of NFL players are the class I offenses as listed by the FBI, including murder, assault, rape, larceny, and others. Football players are also victims of murder and assault more often than is true of the general population.

The most common crime committed by football players is assault, including sexual and domestic violence. Much of this conduct is excused in the interest of winning football games. Drugs are frequently used, sold, and distributed by NFL players, many of whom carry loaded guns.

The reasons for this widespread criminality lies in the black experience in America and in the general American attitude toward crime. That includes the participation of football team owners in gambling.

Despite the involvement of many professional football players in crime, there can be no doubt that the National Football League is a great and enduring American achievement, both from economic and entertainment points of view. This achievement did not come about overnight nor by magic. It came about because the owners, and in particular the commissioners whom they appointed, recognized the need for a political organization called the NFL, which makes the teamwork and communal effort called professional football possible. Therefore the next chapter will be concerned with the NFL.

Chapter 10

The National Football League

The NFL's existence is dependent on two sources, both derived from an aspect of American values that permit high schools and colleges to serve as a pool or source of football enthusiasm. Without these values, which translate into the emotional and financial investment in football by millions of Americans, football could not exist. I first look at that region of the country that best exemplifies the football spirit in America. Next, I take one more look at college football and see how much influence and power college athletic departments have on the development of football players who make up the bulk of those who finally play in the National Football League.

FOOTBALL POLITICS AND THE SOUTH

Although football has generally replaced baseball as the national sport in America, some areas of the country have shown a greater affinity for the sport than others. Indeed, Pennsylvania, Kentucky, and Ohio have contributed a disproportionate number of football players to the college and professional ranks. However, Texas and other Southern states stand out, not only because they are the homes of many football players, but also because the intensity with which football is followed in the South is so much greater than anywhere else.

It has been said that in Alabama an atheist is someone who does not believe that coach Paul "Bear" Bryant was the epitome of Southern manhood. When the University of Alabama won the Sugar Bowl on New Year's Day in 1962 by defeating the University of Arkansas 10-3, U.S. Representative Frank Boykin of Mobile wrote a letter to coach Bryant, claiming that "your men stood like Stonewall Jackson."[1]

This letter was indicative of the widespread belief among Southerners in the 1960s that their way of life was threatened by the Civil Rights Movement and the voter registration drives then underway. Southerners were acutely aware of the negative image their section of the country portrayed. Therefore, they imbued the Alabama football team with the power to reverse that image in the belief that the whole world knew and admired their football achievements.

Because "The Crimson Tide" consisted of only white players, the team was viewed by some Southerners as a vindicator of white men's rights and accomplishments. Yet in 1961, Alabama was handed a political defeat when the Rose Bowl Committee had to withhold their invitation to the University of Alabama to play an integrated UCLA team that year. Evidently, the citizens of California viewed Alabama as the hotbed of racial animosity and hatred. Furthermore, many people believed that the Alabama team was especially brutal and that their level of aggression reflected Southern behavior generally. The failure of Alabama to receive an invitation to the Rose Bowl that year constituted the beginning of the increasing politicization of football.

By 1966 and 1967 Alabama had overcome some of the antagonisms that led to the Rose Bowl slight of 1961. The school played against integrated teams from the University of Nebraska, although Alabama still had no black players on its own team. However, by 1971 Coach "Bear" Bryant appointed two black players to his team. Because of his deification in the Southern community, Bryant was able to integrate the team despite widespread white hostility to this move.[2]

Although football is a Northern invention, it has become a rite of passage in the South. Football in the South is a testing arena, developing the qualities for soldiers later on. Virility, self-control, and daring courage are the qualities football reputedly teaches its practitioners. Leadership is also associated with the image of the Southern football player, although admittedly this quality is lacking in many football players today. Over 100 years ago such statements as the following were commonly believed: "[T]he greatest force in the university today contributing to sobriety, manliness, healthfulness and morality" is football.[3]

Integration created a different pattern of conduct and expectations concerning football in the South. In 1948 segregation was still so accepted and common in the South that the inclusion of black football players was seen as a challenge to the Southern way of life. The Sun Bowl management in 1950 would not permit halfback David Sowell to participate because he was black. Also in 1950, Loyola University of Los Angeles cancelled its scheduled game against Western Texas because black halfback Bill English had been barred by the Texans from playing there. Similar problems faced the Orange Bowl, which was not integrated until 1955. One year later, the Sugar Bowl finally allowed African-American Bobby Grier of the University of Pittsburgh to play against Georgia Tech.[4]

The integration of football followed the course of racial politics in the United States and became a true mirror of the political changes within the country as a whole. Until the end of the 1960s, Southern culture still included the values that had predominated that region since Reconstruction, specifically farming, poverty, racial segregation, and a one-party system. Together with these cultural phenomena, Southern middle- and upper-class men identified manhood with personal independence, including avoidance of working for someone else. Second was the belief in honor. Southern men derived their self-esteem from their communities and not from themselves; therefore, they had to prove again and again that they would tolerate no insult. Third was racism, which consisted of constantly exhibiting the power of white men over black men. Paternalism was a fourth feature of Southern masculinity, which consisted of a paterfamilias attitude in the home and at work. Finally, white Southerners called themselves "good ol' boys," meaning that they engaged in hedonistic drinking, fighting, and womanizing as final evidence of true machismo.[5]

Today, college football has taken the place of these five attributes, because the number of college-educated people in the South is so much greater than it ever was. Although at one time only a few "aristocrats" attended any college, more than 5 million Southerners do so now. College-level occupations, not farming, now predominate in the region. Many people therefore have a connection to one or more institutions of higher education. Furthermore, football is much more complex than it ever was. The playbook now resembles the textbook, and intelligence is attributed to quarterbacks and other players. The old personal independence is of course negated by football, which is played by a team according to the rules and dictates by the coach.

However, the old code of honor still exists in the football teams of today. Football players are viewed as unafraid fighters, similar to duelers of the nineteenth century. Most important, Southern men are offered a sense of regional identity by football even as the old criteria of Southern masculinity are slowly disappearing.[6]

COLLEGE FOOTBALL POLITICS

A second source of NFL success is the American college system. Recruitment of college players leads directly to the success of the NFL. Only a small percentage of college players ever reach the NFL, but almost all who do get there come from U.S. colleges and universities.

Recruitment of college football players has taken on political overtones because of the gap between academic skills and football prowess among so many potential recruits. The academic requirements for admission to such major football universities as Michigan would keep most of the Big Ten football players out of these universities. Therefore, these universities relax admission requirements for football players because the income from the football games staged by the eleven universities belonging to the Big Ten depends on winning and satisfying alumni.[7]

There is often little understanding between the athletic department and the university in the larger football schools in this country. This is due to the financial independence of the athletics department. The income from gate receipts at large football stadiums is so great that the athletic department becomes isolated from the university itself.

Some football coaches become so powerful and influential in big sports universities that they will be consulted by the board of directors regarding the appointment of the university president or other administrative officers. These officers may appear to be part of the academic profession but are in fact professional politicians in the same sense as elected officials in the public sector. Administrators must be able to convince alumni, board members, and sometimes a segment of the faculty that they should be president or provost or dean. That takes unusual political skills, both to attain such an appointment and to keep it.

Therefore, the distinction between the academic and athletic departments of large universities is considerable. Athletic departments usually report directly to the president of the university, while all other departments report to a dean, who in turn reports to a vice-president. Athletics departments usually avoid such a hierarchy and can do so because of their financial resources, the support they receive from alumni and the media, and the popular perception that football and other sports are the real reason for the existence of the university in the first place.

The most important political issue regarding football and other sports in any university is the issue of control. Coaches are convinced that they alone must control all aspects of their program and that they cannot tolerate outside interference of any kind. This is most reasonable from the point of view of head coaches, who must win football games if they are to stay on the job or remain in the profession. Yet football is only one part of the athletic department's responsibilities, and every university has an athletic director who is theoretically responsible for the coach's actions. In practice this is not the case, because coaches of the major football teams have a following in the media and the public knows their names and their reputations. Athletic directors have no such following, nor are their names of any consequence to the public or media. Coaches are highly paid celebrities. They live by publicity and are driven to win at any cost. Therefore, coaches value obedience from the team, because the coach must rely on the team members to play as they are directed. This contradicts the academic view, which emphasizes individuality and creativity. Coaches are often much more interested in furthering their careers than promoting the interests of athlete-students, who in turn are unlikely to be students of anything. In sum, it is a political reality that the purposes of the university and the purposes of the football coaches on many campuses are totally different.

Football coaches are independent of their universities because they are popular community figures. They are surrounded by loyal boosters and supporters. For that reason, university presidents are usually reluctant to "boss" any coach lest the coach's supporters weaken the good will the president needs to stay in his or her job. In many instances celebrity coaches can pressure the administration and faculty to do what, they want even if their wishes are opposed to ordinary university policy. This is very much in evidence when coaches pressure professors to hand athletes grades they do not deserve.[8]

College football coaches use their power and prestige not only to pressure professors regarding the grades of their athlete-students but also to overrule the college president. An excellent example was provided by James Duderstadt, former president of the University of Michigan. Citing Walter Byers, formerly director of the NCAA, Duderstadt tells how the former "legendary" football coach Fielding Yost defeated the president of the University of Michigan, James Angell in 1906-1907. Angell had organized the Western Athletic Conference by persuading several other college presidents to join this group and thereby keep college football from becoming altogether professional. The presidents wanted to limit the season to five games, restrict eligibility to three years for undergraduate students, cap student ticket prices, and prohibit special training tables and training quarters. They also wanted the football coach to be a full-time employee of the university. All this did not come to pass, largely because the coaches were interested in their own careers and the players were interested in gaining an opportunity to enter the NFL.

THE COMMISSIONERS

Aristotle wrote *Politics* in the fourth century B.C. as a guide to rulers and statesmen. He argued that the most important task of a politician is to give laws and frame a constitution that is enduring and based on universal legal principles.[9]

Keeping this in mind, the principal task of a sports commissioner is the development and enforcement of rules and regulations governing the sport. Such government should protect the participants, whether players or spectators, from unethical conduct; ensure that the games and their players are honest; and make certain that the league is justly compensated for the efforts of its players and the investments of its owners.

The first NFL commissioner was Jim Thorpe, who was elected by the owners in 1920 and served only a few months. At that time he was undoubtedly the greatest athlete America had produced, outstanding in any sport he attempted. As commissioner, however, he was a figurehead. The first truly active football commissioner was Joe Carr, who held that position for eighteen years, from 1921 to 1939. Carr had spent many years as a baseball and basketball organizer and served as first president of the American Basketball Association. He was also director of the National Baseball Association's promotional department. Carr had only five years of formal schooling. In 1904 he had organized a professional football team called the Columbus Panhandlers. Reorganized in 1907, that team functioned for twenty years.

In August and September 1920, Carr participated in the meetings in Canton, Ohio, that led to the formation of the American Professional Football Association. Carr was elected president of the association in 1921 and at once became effective in promoting the new sport. He established his authority by declaring that players under contract from the previous season could not be approached by another team unless first declared a "free" agent. He then introduced a standard player's contract resembling baseball contracts. He also appointed a committee to draft a constitution and by-laws to govern the association.

Carr enforced the rules created by that committee and saved football from disintegrating. The test came when the newly admitted Green Bay Packers were forced to leave the association because they had used college players in 1921. The Packers were reorganized under Curly Lambeau later that year when the name of the association was changed to National Football League.

Numerous other infringements of NFL rules by several teams led to their expulsion and to fines. Carr succeeded in giving the NFL the limits needed to maintain professional football and attract a greater number of fans. No sport can succeed if the rules are made up and change from week to week or from year to year. The public must know what to expect and must recognize that there is a level playing field if they are to be paying customers and loyal fans.

By 1927 Joe Carr recognized that football could not remain the small-town game it had been so far. He reduced the number of NFL teams from twenty-two to twelve. These remaining teams were principally located in large cities such as New York, Detroit, Chicago, and Cleveland.[10]

Joe Carr died in 1939 and was followed in the commissioner's position by Carl "Scummy" Storck. Storck, too, was one of the NFL's founding fathers and took part in the Canton meetings in 1920. Storck had been a league executive for twenty-one years, including his two-year term as president, as the commissioners were then called. Storck did little more than administer the daily needs of the NFL during his two years in office. The same may be said of Emer Layden, his successor. Layden had been one of the "four horsemen" of Notre Dame fame. He was the first to be called "commissioner," holding that job during World War II, when little could be accomplished by the league because the best players were in the service. The game was now played by those not eligible for the draft. Lacking manpower, several teams merged during these years. Layden resigned shortly after the war and entered the business world.[11]

For thirteen years thereafter, from 1946 to 1959, "Bert" Bell, the owner of the Pittsburgh Steelers, served as football commissioner. De Benneville Bell was a member of the "main-line" Philadelphia establishment.

Bell ranks with Carr and Rozelle as one of the truly great commissioners. His appointment came at a time when the NFL had to confront the then-wealthy All-America Football Conference. The AAFC had enrolled a good share of the best players after World War II and increased salaries considerably. The consequences for both the NFL and the AAFC were financially terrible. Both leagues lost a great deal of money, as the AAFC and the NFL played in the same communities and rivaled each other for fan support. For example, the Los Angeles Rams of the NFL were unable to gain the attendance of the rival AAFC's Dons.

Because the competition was so destructive, the AAFC repeatedly asked Bell to consider a common draft or dovetailing schedules and an annual "World Series." Bell refused all of these offers. Instead he used numerous political maneuvers to put an end to the AAFC. That end came in 1949, when Baltimore, Cleveland, and San Francisco joined the NFL and the other teams of the AAFC disbanded.[12]

Bell also made an effort to prevent gamblers from throwing games when he suspended two players in 1946, not for dealing with gamblers who had approached them, but for not reporting this to him.

Bell was also the first commissioner to deal with television. Television was a new experience for most Americans in 1950. Bell saw the advantage of television for the NFL and ruled at once that only road games could be televised to the home cities of each team. This ruling was under constant attack but served as the basis for the league's growth. Court cases, state and federal officials, and media moguls all pressured Bell to rescind this decree but he held fast. In 1973 Congress adopted legislation requiring any NFL game that had been declared a sellout seventy-two hours before kickoff to be made available to local TV.

Bell also was the first to recognize the NFL Player's Association, a move not at all to the liking of the owners. In addition, Bert Bell invented the annual college draft, which was adopted by the NFL in 1936. Bell died on October 11, 1959, while watching a football game between the Philadelphia Eagles and the Pittsburgh Steelers.

Austin Gunsel, treasurer of the NFL, served as interim commissioner from October 12, 1959, to January 26, 1960, when Pete Rozelle was elected to that position on the twenty-third ballot of the owners. Rozelle was then only thirty-three years old. He remained in that job until 1989, when he retired.

When Rozelle became commissioner, the NFL did not have a national following, nor did it have a history of success. In fact, baseball was America's favorite sport. Rozelle changed that and made football what it is today, that is, the sport which outranks all other sports combined as the number-one interest of the sports-minded public.[13]

Rozelle did this in several ways. First, he recognized the immense importance of a partnership with the television networks. Baseball was televised on a local basis but not nationally. Rozelle recognized the importance of reaching a nationwide audience through television. At that time football was televised only on weekends. Rozelle persuaded ABC to televise Monday Night Football. This not only helped the NFL immensely but also made ABC the third major television network, behind CBS and NBC, who had turned down the opportunity to televise weekday games.[14]

Second, Rozelle persuaded the NFL owners to share all revenues equally. That was indeed a move of business genius because it assured the followers of the game that they were viewing true competition between equal teams. This was never the case with baseball, which has always been dominated by the New York Yankees, solely because the Yankees have more money than any other team.

Football now began each season on a financially equal footing. Therefore, every team had a chance of reaching the Super Bowl, which helped ticket sales enormously. These two ideas would have been enough to make Pete Rozelle an immortal in football history. However, he did more. His business ability created the immense marketing strategies that made the NFL a true powerhouse. He invented the Super Bowl. It was Rozelle who first undertook to license team logos, and he was the one who built new stadiums all over the United States. He recognized the importance of NFL Films, founded with an investment of $3,000 by Ed Sobol, a Philadelphia amateur photographer. Rozelle hired Sobol to produce NFL films after the Sobols, father and son, had filmed the championship game between the New York Giants and the Green Bay Packers in 1962.

Today, Steve Sobol, son of the founder, generates more than $50 million in business not only for himself and his company but also for the team owners. This is of course small change compared to the NFL's $18 billion TV contract and its other revenues of $4 billion. However, in 1964 the NFL earned only $14 million in TV contracts, a sum now far outdistanced by NFL Films alone.[15]

The career of Pete Rozelle was indeed amazing. It was built on personal qualities permitting him to persuade rich men who were accustomed to getting anything they wanted to take less than they believed they deserved. He was also a master at preventing these same rich men from revolting against the authority he had gained from them. Rozelle did not profit very much himself. However, he created a new business in the same sense that Henry Ford and Andrew Carnegie had done in an earlier age. He was a business genius, which he demonstrated in particular in 1961.

In 1957 William Radovich sued the NFL under the provisions of the 1890 Sherman Anti-Trust Act. Radovich had been a professional football player from 1938 when he began his career with the Detroit Lions. In 1946 he asked to be traded to the Los Angeles Raiders to be closer to his dying father. This was refused. He therefore signed with the old Los Angeles Dons of the All-America Conference.

Years later he was offered a job coaching with the NFL after the All-America Conference had folded. The NFL front office blocked the appointment and Radovich contended that he had been black-listed from organized football by a conspiracy to monopolize football. Radovich's suit succeeded when the Supreme Court ruled that the Sherman Act applied to the football business.

In 1961 Pete Rozelle traveled to Washington to persuade Congress to exempt the NFL from the Sherman Anti-Trust Act. This was granted by Congress, so that thereafter the television networks could no longer deal with one team at a time but now had to deal with the entire NFL at once. This gave the NFL enormous bargaining power, leading to the promotion of the game from the new revenues available as a result of the establishment of this football cartel.[16]

The legislation permitting the NFL to negotiate a television contract jointly is called the Sports Broadcasting Act of 1961. In 1966 Congress enacted legislation approving the merger of the American Football League and the NFL. Then, in 1987, the issue of NFL antitrust violations came before Congress again. This was also the year in which the NFL Player's Association went on strike. The Subcommittee on Antitrust Monopolies of the Committee on the Judiciary of the 100th Congress held hearings on October 6 of that year. Pete Rozelle and his eventual successor Paul Tagliabue, the NFL counsel testified. The issue at hand was whether the NFL could show its games on cable and thereby force viewers to pay for watching games that would otherwise be free. Rozelle convinced the subcommittee that only a limited number of games would be shown on cable and that the subcommittee's fears were unfounded.[17]

These and many more achievements can be credited to Pete Rozelle, who retired as NFL commissioner in 1989. He was succeeded by Paul Tagliabue, no doubt the most knowledgeable man available for the job.

Tagliabue is credited with persuading the thirty-two owners to increase the percentage of revenue they share. Each of the league's owners share 60 percent of the league's revenues. He was able to do that because the owners trust his judgment and allow him to make decisions when no agreement between them can be reached.

In 1991 Tagliabue convinced the owners to expand the league by two teams, thereby apportioning the assets and income of the NFL among more participants. Tagliabue succeeded in persuading the owners that more would be earned and that they would gain rather than lose by this expansion policy. During the 1990s and the early 2000s the league expanded from twenty-eight teams to thirty-two by adding the Jacksonville Jaguars and Carolina Panthers and later the new Cleveland Browns and the Houston Texans.

Tagliabue also negotiated a salary cap for players. In return for the salary cap the 2,000 members of the player's association have free agency and share between 65 and 70 percent of some specified revenues. Tagliabue also provided the NFL with more profits and the most lucrative TV contract of any sports league anywhere.

THE NFL MACHINE

In 2002 the NFL had revenues of $4.8 billion. Four percent, or $200 million of this amount, came from Direct TV's Sunday Ticket, merchandise, film syndication fees, and sponsorships. It is divided equally, so that each team gets $6.2 million.

One billion dollars, or 21 percent, comes from local sponsorships, luxury suites, broadcasting, parking, and concessions. That money is kept by each club.

Another $1.1 billion, or 23 percent, comes from ticket revenues, and $350 million of that money is put into a visitors' pool and split evenly, so that each team gets $10.9 million. Another $2.5 billion, or 52 percent, comes from network and cable TV contracts and is split evenly among the 32 teams, giving each team $78 million.

Tagliabue estimates that revenues will grow by an additional $1 billion between 2003 and 2005.

The success of the NFL is demonstrated by the appointment of Steve Bornstein, who developed the sports broadcasting network ESPN. Bornstein is in charge of TV and all media contacts. In addition, Bornstein will be the CEO of a twenty-four-hour NFL-owned digital cable channel devoted to football, showing only classic games. Furthermore, the NFL has developed the NFL Network, consisting of around-the-clock talk shows, highlight reels, and tidbits for football junkies.[18] More income will be generated by the NFL by selling its footage archives through a video-on-demand service, allowing fans to watch old games for a fee. Tagliabue has also announced that he is negotiating with Time Inc. to produce an NFL magazine even as ESPN is negotiating with NFL films to produce two original movies.

Because NFL team ownership is restricted to twenty-five people with the principal owner holding at least thirty percent, NFL teams cannot be bought by large corporations. The NFL also has strict oversight rules. Therefore, each team receives about 63 percent of total revenues, so that the combined revenues of the top eight richest teams are only 28 percent more than the poorest eight teams. As a result, every team makes an operational profit. Compare that to baseball whose richest team, the New York Yankees, generated $218 million while the poorest baseball team, the Montreal Expos, earned only $9.7 million in 2001.

Because revenues are guaranteed in the NFL, the value of each franchise has risen over the years. This increase can be demonstrated by considering that in the early 1960s Jack Kent Cooke paid $300,000 for the Washington Redskins and then sold the team to Daniel Snyder in 2000 for $800 million. Likewise, Arthur M. Blank paid $545 million for the Atlanta Falcons in 2002. The previous owner, Rankin M. Smith, paid only $8.5 million in 1965.[19]

Rozelle as well as Tagliabue have also been instrumental in further strengthening football in this country by building or renewing football stadiums. To accomplish this, Tagliabue persuaded the owners to sell bonds to provide loans for the construction of football stadiums. So far $650 million worth of bonds have been sold, leading to the renovation or building of eight football stadiums.

URBAN WARFARE

One example of the manner in which football stadiums are built is the current drive to rehabilitate the Rose Bowl in Pasadena, California, in order to attract a future NFL franchise. Pasadena is only ten miles from downtown Los Angeles, so that a Pasadena team would in effect replace the Los Angeles Raiders who left there before the 1995 season. Since then the NFL has kept Los Angeles in mind as a possible expansion team site or as a revival of the old franchise. In 1999, when the Houston Texans became the thirty-second NFL team, Los Angeles appeared to have a chance. Presently, there is a possibility that the San Diego Chargers may be a viable candidate for a move to Los Angeles. Such a move would of course require a new stadium, as the Los Angeles Memorial Coliseum was built eighty years ago when the first football game was played there on October 6, 1923. Such an effort can be compared to the manner in which Baltimore succeeded in luring the Cleveland Browns to their city in 1995.[20]

There have been many moves of football teams from one city to another and back again. Examples of such moves are the Miami Seahawks, who moved to Baltimore in 1947, became the Colts, and then moved to Indianapolis in 1984. The Boston Redskins moved from there to Washington in 1937, and the Chicago Cardinals moved to St. Louis and from there to Arizona. The Cleveland Rams moved to Los Angeles and then to St. Louis, and the Portsmouth Spartans became the Detroit Lions in 1934. The Kansas City Chiefs had been the Dallas Texans until 1962, and the Oakland Raiders moved to Los Angeles and back again between 1982 and 1995. The Los Angeles Chargers became the San Diego Chargers in 1961, and the Houston Oilers turned into the Nashville Oilers or the Tennessee Titans in 1997. All of these moves and more were accompanied by a great deal of debate and some frustration, yet none resembled the outbursts of rage caused by the decision of Art Modell, owner of the Cleveland Browns, to move the team to Baltimore in 1995.[21]

The deal signed by Art Modell in October of that year obligated the state of Maryland to spend $200 million, of which the construction of a new 70,000-seat stadium was to cost $190 million. The remaining $10 million were allocated to land acquisition, a new training complex, and a parking deck. The team was authorized by this agreement to sell $80 million worth of seat licenses and would collect parking fees and share the naming rights with the state. It was also agreed that Modell would pay no rent. It has been estimated that as a result Modell added upward of $50 million to his fortune.

The cost to the taxpayer for the move of the Browns from Cleveland to Baltimore was huge. The $87 million worth of bonds sold carried interest of $92 million over thirty years. This was in addition to the $295 million in principal and interest already paid for stadium construction and another $130 million for the land under the stadium. The state therefore paid about $20 million for thirty years, which equaled the annual cost of running the entire Baltimore municipal library system.

THE INTERNATIONAL NFL

Tagliabue also developed a separate European football league.[22] In 1972, four football teams consisting entirely of soldiers belonging to NATO played the first American football tournament in Europe on the western coast of Italy. By 1976 individual teams began to play all over Europe. This led to the first European-American football club, founded in Austria on June 11, 1976. This club was called the First American Austrian Football Club (FAAC).

Later that year, an Italian team from Verona played a game against a U.S. Army team. The following year the first all-European game was played by two Italian teams, the Pink Panthers from Piacenza versus the Frogs from Bergano. This occurred in 1977. At the same time American servicepeople stationed in Germany were teaching the game to Germans. This led to the establishment of the Frankfort Lions football team in 1977 and the formation of the first German League in 1979. In 1980 the German Football Federation was organized. It is called *Der Amerikanische Fussball Verband Deutschland.*

In 1981 the first international game between two federation teams took place in Frankfurt and Cologne (Köln) between the Italian and German federations. The first game attracted only 4,500 spectators. The second game attracted 13,000 spectators.

On July 31, 1982, federations from five European countries formed the American European Football Federation (AEFF). Included were Austria, Finland, France, Germany, and Italy. These federations then played the first European championship in Castel Giorgio, Italy, where Italy defeated Finland 18-6 to become the first European football champions.

The league changed its name to the European Football League when Switzerland, the Netherlands, and Great Britain joined in 1985 and expanded the league to represent eight countries. By 1996 football federations representing fourteen European countries had evolved into the European Federation of American Football (EFAF). The additional federations came from the Ukraine, Sweden, Norway, Denmark, Belgium, and Spain. Since 1996 Russia and the Czech Republic also formed American football federations, bringing the total number of countries represented to sixteen.[23]

Today more than 45,000 players organized in 800 clubs participate in American football in Europe. Of these, Germany has the largest contingent of American football players, with 23,000 members. The Düsseldorf Panthers are the reigning European champions, having won the Eurobowl IX over the London Olympians.

An example of how the NFL succeeded in promoting American football in Europe is the manner in which the game was first introduced in Russia. Unlike other European countries that have American military bases, Russians did not have an opportunity to see Americans play the game. The NFL first introduced the game to Russian children by way of schools. This led to the establishment of a Children's League of American Football including about seventy players, all in Moscow. Then, in 1994, Harry Gamble, an NFL executive, visited Moscow and saw that the children playing the game had hardly any equipment. This visit led to an invitation by the NFL to the officials of the Russian children's league to visit the New York headquarters of the NFL, where the league provided not only equipment but also instructional videotapes. Then the NFL arranged for a Russian sportscaster to broadcast the Super Bowl to a Russian audience, a practice which continues to this day. In 1995 an adult team was created called the Moscow Patriots. This is not a professional team but consists of former members of children's teams.[24]

Another way in which several European countries have experienced American football has been the arrival of American football players in Europe. Americans who play in Europe do so because they view European American football as a stepping stone to an NFL contract. One example of such an effort relates to Kurt Warner. In 1998 Warner was living in Amsterdam, Netherlands, trying to keep his football career alive in a city that hardly noticed American football in its devotion to soccer. Since then, Warner led the St. Louis Rams as quarterback to their first Super Bowl victory when he was named the NFL's Most Valuable Player during the 1999-2000 season. Likewise, Brad Johnson quarterbacked the Tampa Buccaneers to their first Super Bowl championship in 2002 after playing in London, England, in 1995 just to keep in the running. After 2002 Johnson signed a contract worth $25 million over four years, including a $6 million signing bonus.

Jay Fiedler, quarterback for the Miami Dolphins, guided his team to a playoff spot in 2002. He too spent time in Europe, playing in Amsterdam earning a negligible salary, yet by 2002 he signed a five-year contract with the Dolphins yielding $24.5 million. Defensive tackle Brandon Noble is one of eight Dallas Cowboys who have played in Europe. Noble played in Barcelona, Spain, and was named NFL Europe defensive player of the week in 1998. By 1999 Noble was a defensive tackle in Dallas and started in all sixteen games for his team.

Those who play in Europe get minor league pay of about $11,000 to $15,000 a season. These players are hired by NFL Europe, giving them off-season experience and promoting the game internationally. NFL Europe was the idea of Paul Tagliabue, who started the league in 1991. Although attendance at these games cannot match the enthusiasm of Europeans for soccer, the league average attendance is 19,000 per game, except in Germany where attendance averages 30,000. Soccer attendance averages 100,000 fans per game in Europe.[25]

European football teams played in the World Bowl XI as their finale at the end of the 2002 season in Glasgow, Scotland. The winner was the German team from Frankfurt. Attendance included a crowd of 42,000 fans and a TV audience of 110 million watching in 140 countries.[26]

These European developments can be credited to both Pete Rozelle and his successor Paul Tagliabue and demonstrate how aggressive and farsighted management has made the NFL the powerhouse it is today.[27]

The latest effort to internationalize the NFL has been the trip taken by Chad Lewis to Asia. Lewis was a Brigham Young University tight end and played for the Philadelphia Eagles. Lewis speaks Chinese fluently because he did missionary work in China from 1990-1992.

FROM FOOTBALL TO POLITICS

Because football has the reputation of making "real men" out of its practitioners, politicians who have played football during their school years make an issue of that background in their campaigns. This was true of Dwight Eisenhower (1890-1969), who served as the thirty-fourth U.S. president. In his campaign for the presidency he made certain that potential voters heard over and over again that he had played tackle in high school and continued to play football when he entered the military academy at West Point in 1911. A knee injury prevented him from further play, but his football career, although short, was part of his campaign material. Even the superhero Eisenhower used football as a means of portraying himself in a heroic light.[28]

President Gerald Ford likewise had an impressive record as a football player, although he was unable to translate that record into winning the election of 1976, which made Jimmy Carter president. Ford had played football at South High School in Grand Rapids, Michigan, where he was named to the all-city and all-state football teams. During his years at the University of Michigan, from 1931 to 1935, Ford played on the university's national championship football teams in 1933 and 1934. He was voted the Wolverines most valuable player in 1934 and on January 1, 1935, played in the East-West College All Star game in San Francisco. In August of that year he also played in the Chicago Tribune All Star game at Soldier Field against the Chicago Bears. As a result Ford received offers from two professional football teams, the Green Bay Packers and the Detroit Lions, but chose instead to accept a position as assistant football coach at Yale where he entered law school and earned a law degree in 1941 while continuing as assistant football coach.[29]

Ronald Reagan, a former sportscaster with experience in radio and television announcing, became a famous movie actor by portraying the Notre Dame football star George Gipp in 1940. Reagan had played football before he was ten years old in neighborhood games in his home town, Tampico, Illinois. From neighborhood football Reagan graduated into high school football and played as a guard and end. After high school Reagan enrolled at Eureka College in Illinois. There he again played football. After graduating from college with mediocre grades Reagan began his sports broadcasting career in Davenport, Iowa. From there he moved to Des Moines and subsequently became one of the top football broadcasters in the country until he launched his movie and political career in 1937.

There can be no doubt that Jack Kemp launched his political career from his background as a professional football player. Kemp had been captain of the San Diego Chargers between 1960 and 1962 and then became captain of the Buffalo Bills. From 1962 to 1969 he played as quarterback for the Bills, who at that time were part of the now-defunct AFL. Kemp led the Bills to two AFL championships and was awarded the AFL's Most Valuable Player Award in 1965. He is also one of the co-founders of the AFL Players Association. From 1971 until 1989 Jack Kemp was a member of the U.S. Congress from western New York. He then became secretary of housing and urban development in the administration of President George H. W. Bush. In 1996 he was nominated Republican candidate for vice president of the United States.[30]

When Julius Caesar Watts retired from Congress in 2002 he had served four terms from Oklahoma's fourth district. Prior to his political career Watts served as an ordained minister after playing football as quarterback for his alma mater, the University of Oklahoma. He led that football team to two Orange Bowl victories and was twice named the Orange Bowl's Most Valuable Player. Thereafter he played for the Canadian Football League. Upon his retirement from congress he was named to several corporate boards. He has also formed a polling and public relations firm and is a frequent, highly paid speaker.[31]

Former University of Nebraska football coach Tom Osborne used his popularity in that state to gain a seat in the house of representatives in 2001. Osborne was head football coach from 1972 until 1997. During his career in football he led the team to three national championships in 1994, 1995, and 1997. Osborne holds three college degrees including a doctorate in educational psychology from the University of Nebraska. As a coach Osborne ranks among the most successful college coaches, in the company of such coaches as Joe Paterno of Penn State and Bobby Bowden of Florida State. Osborne appeared in twenty-five bowls during twenty-five years and ended his career 254-49-3.

Osborne was also credited with encouraging his players to do well in their studies. Over 70 percent of his players graduated, compared with only 53 percent nationally. This was accomplished by hiring 100 special tutors, holding practice exams, distributing laptops during road trips, and monitoring classroom attendance. Osborne even attacked the common delusion that college players will become professional superstars. In congress Osborne sits on the agriculture committee.

Two former football players have become famous for their achievements in the law. One was late Supreme Court Justice Byron R. White and the other Minnesota Supreme Court Judge Alan Page.

White was born in Wellington, Colorado, in 1917 and died in 2002. White played for the Pittsburgh Steelers in 1938 after graduating from the University of Colorado, which he had attended on a football scholarship. In 1939 he interrupted his football career and accepted a Rhodes Scholarship. The following year he played for the Detroit Lions but then joined the navy in 1942. Thereafter he went to the Yale Law School and practiced law in Colorado.

Although appointed to the Supreme Court by the liberal President Kennedy, White was no friend of civil rights. He opposed the Miranda decision, which demands that those arrested be told of their rights before police can question them. He was also opposed to *Roe v. Wade*, which established women's rights to abortion. Similarly, he wrote a decision arguing that homosexuals have no right to private sexual contact. He supported an employer's right to engage in racial discrimination as well as the right of individuals to sue newspapers that disclose the names of sources that they promised to hold secret. He upheld the right of the police to avoid getting a legal warrant before arresting a suspect.[32]

Alan Page became a judge on the Supreme Court of Minnesota in 1993. He played with the Minnesota Vikings and the Chicago Bears from 1967 to 1981. In 1971 he became the first defensive player to receive the Most Valuable Player award. While playing professional football he also attended the University of Minnesota Law School, graduating in 1978. He became Minnesota's assistant attorney general until nominated to the highest court in the state. In 1988 Page was inducted into the Pro Hall of Fame.[33]

THE NFL COMMUNITY

In July of every year the newsstands begin to sell football magazines and shortly thereafter training camps begins. It is then that the football season starts as fans speculate about the outcome and comment at length on radio sports shows concerning the players, the coaches, and the management. Debates rage as to whether the defense or the offense is more important and much is said about the incredibly bloated rule book. There is no end to predictions. One football magazine published in June 2003 "knew" that Philadelphia would beat Tampa Bay for the NFC championship and that Pittsburgh would do the same to Oakland in the AFC that year.[34]

July is also the month in which new talent is first tried out and introduced to the critical fans. Indeed, the names and stats of the new players were already known at the time of the draft, but until these men could actually be seen in training camp they were mere images in the media. In June the schedules of the coming season are published, as are the rosters of each team. The fans now study the statistics of the past season and make educated guesses as to the coming year's possibilities.

Beginning in June, but also continuing throughout the year, a number of football players exhibit their concern for the community that pays their big salaries. Those who have any understanding of their profession know that they may well have been hired by the coach and the manager but that in the end only community support makes their occupation possible. Therefore, a number of the players engage in visible charitable events. Donovan McNabb of the Philadelphia Eagles reads to children as part of Read Across America Day. In 2002 Brian Mitchell of the New York Giants received the "Unsung Hero" award for his community involvement.

The NFL has a Community Quarterback award, which recognizes community volunteers who "show leadership and commitment to improving their community." Every NFL team can participate in this competition and NFL Charities will then also select the national winner. Another charitable effort by the NFL is the annual "Hometown Huddle." Together with the United Way, players and other NFL employees build playgrounds for toddlers, host discussion forums, and bowl with seniors. This "Huddle" is part of the NFL's Tuesday program in which players, on their day off during the season, devote that day to community service. The NFL has participated in fund raising for the United Way for thirty years and has seen donations rise from $800 million annually to $3.77 billion.

The tragedy of September 11, 2001, in which 3,000 Americans were murdered, led the NFL to contribute money and blood, load supplies going to the World Trade Center site, and comfort victims.

The NFL also supports a player alumni fund. The cornerstone of that effort is the annual Charity Gold Classic Tour. This tour is used to support youth-oriented causes and is open to anyone who wants to enroll as an associate or corporate member.

In sum, the NFL is part of the American community. It is an institution in that it meets important needs for many Americans who love its action and its values and who support it with fervor and resolve.

SUMMARY

Football is not only a form of entertainment but also a business. That business depends on the support of a large number of American fans whose values are such that they coincide with the forms and conditions of football. In addition, the football business depends largely on the contribution of American colleges and universities, who are the "minor leagues" of professional football.

Professional football is organized in the National Football League, managed by a commissioner. There have been a number of commissioners, of whom Rozelle and Tagliabue stand out as most productive. This is particularly true of their ability to influence congress to exempt the NFL from the anti-trust laws of the United States and their immense achievements in the area of television rights, their development of the shared-income concept, and their building and rebuilding of football stadiums.

The international football leagues gaining strength in Europe and beginning in Asia are another example of the excellent manner in which the NFL has become one of the most successful business enterprises in America.

The NFL and its players are also community minded and support numerous charitable causes every year.

Epilogue

Football serves five functions in American life. The first, the *socioemotional function,* helps to maintain social-psychological stability. Human fighting has continued throughout the world for centuries. In Ireland, in Ceylon, in the Sudan, and in Serbia, citizens have fought one another over old wars lost or won, over revenge for this or that ancient feud, or over causes no longer in the memory of the combatants. The United States also fought its own Civil War. That, however, has been relegated to the history books. Instead, sports, and particularly football, is a means by which citizens can identify "the enemy" without mass killings and wars. Individuals who need to identify with power or conflict or both can lend their support to a football team without shooting their neighbor or persecuting another person because of his or her race or religion.

A second function of football in America is *socialization.* The socialization process inculcates members of any group with the values and mores of the society in which they live. Football participates in this process. Football is conflict, which is part of American life; however, rules limit the conflict permitted within the game, teaching Americans that competition and conflict are acceptable within the limits of "fair play."

A number of American cultural beliefs can be seen in any football game. Admiration for masculine strength and courage is only one of these. Agility, willingness to endure pain, stamina, and the "fighting spirit" are all part of football. But football penalizes "unsportsmanlike behavior," meaning excessive cruelty, unfair advantage, or deliberate effort to inflict more injury than necessary. The drive to earn as much money as possible in a short time is also part of American culture. Americans admire those who make a lot of money, and football emphasizes this value also. Football also celebrates youth, without a doubt an important value in our "youth culture."

Football also has an *ideological* and *political function.* Football promotes patriotism and the American Dream. Because football is truly American and not, like soccer, an international sport as yet, football prowess is American prowess and football achievements are American achievements. Football is a means of waving "Old Glory" and that is in fact done at all football games. Despite the need to emphasize teamwork in order to win a football game, individualism nevertheless receives a good deal of acknowledgment as the heroics of super-players are indeed rewarded and given wide publicity.

Innumerable football players have risen from utter poverty in the slums of our big cities and the coal mines of Appalachia. They have come from "rags to riches." Therefore, football functions as a means of *social mobility* which is so much a part of the American story. Indeed there are football players who waste their money on drugs and extravagance. There are however also many football players who have invested wisely, have become truly wealthy, and proved that the "land of unlimited opportunities" still exists.

Finally, football serves the function of *drawing diverse people together in a common cause.* Football integrates. It cements different people together because of their common interest. This is of great importance to Americans as diversity and willingness to give all an opportunity to succeed are essentials of the American democratic orientation. This is more evident in football than almost any other organization. Football players and now coaches as well are of all races, religions, ethnic origins, and economic backgrounds. Despite its violence, football is therefore an excellent example of racial integration at its best. Nothing is more instructive and supportive of the process of assimilation than the example of football, for even as the game is a form of conflict it welds us together. *Ubi concordia, ibi victoria.* Where there is harmony, there is victory.

Notes

Introduction

1. John J. Macionis, *Sociology,* Eighth edition (Upper Saddle River, NJ: Prentice-Hall, Inc., 2001), p. 67.

2. Larry Weisman, "Average salary tops $1M again: Veterans get the ax," *USA Today* (June 8, 2001), p. 613.

3. Allied Health Services, "Physicians salary surveys" (May 23, 2002), Allied Physicians Pub., Rehoboth Beach, DE.

4. Robin M. Williams, Jr., *American society: A sociological interpretation* (New York: Alfred Knopf, 1970), p. 417.

5. Charles H. Martin, "The tail that wags the dog: Football and the American university," *Reviews in American History,* 24(4) (December 1966): 629.

6. John M. Carroll, *Red Grange and the rise of modern football* (Urbana and Chicago: The University of Illinois Press, 1999), p. 11.

7. William Kornblum, *Sociology in a changing world* (New York: Harcourt College Publishers, 2000), p. 366.

8. Ryan Sanderson, "2000 NFL salaries," *Dawg Post* (June 10, 2001), available at <georgia.theinsiders.com>.

9. Edward T. Pound and Douglas Pasternak, "Money players," *U.S. News and World Report,* 132(4) (February 11, 2002): 30.

10. Fitzgerald Hill and John W. Murphy Jr., "The status of blacks as major college football coaches," *The Journal of Blacks in Higher Education,* 10(18) (Winter 1997): 122.

Chapter 1

1. Allison Danzig, *A history of American football* (Englewood Cliffs, NJ: Prentice-Hall, Inc., 1956), p. 5.

2. David Riesman and Reuel Denney, "Football in America: A study in cultural diffusion," *American Quarterly,* 3(4) (Winter 1951): 312.

3. Lawrence B. Angus, "Women in a male domain: Gender and organizational culture in a Christian Brothers college," in Lawrence B. Angus, *Inequality and social identity* (Washington, DC: Palmer Press, 1993).

4. "After football, White served on the Supreme Court," *espn.news services,* <msn.Espn.Go.Com/main.Html> (April 16, 2002).

5. Larry E. Craig, "The left's iron clad litmus test on abortion: Justice White could not be confirmed today," *U.S. Senate Republican Policy Committee* (April 25, 2002), p. 1.

6. Greater Buffalo Sports Hall of Fame, "Jack Kemp, quarterback Buffalo Bills," <www.buffalosportshallfame.com/Clall of 1992>.

7. Michael Messner, "Masculinities and athletic careers," in Michael Messner and Daniel Sabo eds., *Sport, men and the gender order: Crucial feminist perspectives* (Champaign, IL: Human Kinetic Books, 1990), p. 103.

8. Steven Schact, "Mysogeny on and off the 'pitch'," *Gender and Society*, 10(5) (1996): 550.

9. Garry Whannel, *Fields of vision: Televion sport and cultural transformation* (London: Routledge, 1992), p. 144.

10. G. MacLennan and H. Yeates, "Masculinity, class and sports in the nineties," *XY: Men, Sex and Politics*, 5(3) (March 1993): 22.

11. Myriam Miedzian, *Boys will be boys: Breaking the link between masculinity and violence* (New York: Doubleday, 1991); E. Dunning, P. Murphy, I. Waddington, and A. E. Astrinakis, *Fighting fans: Football hooleganism as a world phenomenon* (Dublin: University College Dublin Press, 2002).

12. Michael T. Maloney and Robert E. McCormick, "An examination of the role that intercollegiate athletic participation plays in academic achievement," *The Journal of Human Resources*, 28(3) (Summer 1993): 555.

13. Murray Sperber, *Onward to victory: The crisis that shaped college sports* (New York: Henry Holt and Co., 1998), p. 505.

14. Jeffrey Owings and Marilyn McMillen, *Who can play?: An examination of NCAA's Proposition 16* (Washington, DC: National Center for Education Statistics, 1995).

15. Paul M. Anderson, "Cureton v. NCAA," *You Make the Call*, 2(3) (Winter 2000): 1-11.

16. Maloney and McCormick, "An examination of the role," p. 569.

17. Allen Bodner, *When boxing was a Jewish sport* (Westport, CT: Praeger, 1997).

18. S. Karen Anderson, "The effect of athletic participation on the academic aspirations and achievement of African-American males in a New York City high school," *Journal of Negro Education*, 59(3) (1990): 507.

19. Fitzgerald Hill and John W. Murray Jr., "The status of blacks as major college football coaches," *The Journal of Blacks in Higher Education*, 10(18) (Winter 1997): 122.

20. Richard E. Lapchick, "Black college football coaches lose yardage," *Sport in Society*, (June 7, 2002), available at <www.sportsinsociety.org>.

21. "Pop Warner little scholars," <www.dickbutkus.com>.

22. National Alliance for Youth Sports, "Time out for better sports for kids" (July 2001), <http://www.timeoutforbettersportsforkids.org/news/main/.htm>.

23. Dana P. O'Neill, "Open season on discord," *The Philadelphia Daily News* (August 12, 2002): 1.

24. Dan McGraw, "Winning is the only thing," *U.S. News and World Report*, 129(8) (August 28, 2000): 46-48.

25. O'Neill, p. 1.

26. Herbert G. Blumer, "Collective behavior," in Alfred McClung Lee, ed., *Principles of sociology*, Third edition (New York: Barnes and Noble Books, 1969), p. 65.

27. Rick Reilly, "Not your typical tear jerker," *CNN Sports Illustrated* (June 12, 2001): 1.

28. Edward Wong, "Giant Stadium imposes a ban on bottled drinks," *The New York Times* (December 19, 2001): S5.

29. "Russian soccer fans riot in central Moscow, one reported dead," *Peoples Daily* (June 10, 2002): 2.

30. Bill Buford, *Among the thugs* (New York: Norton and Co., 1992).

31. Richard Lacayo, "Blood in the stands," *Time,* 125(23) (June 10, 1985): 38-41.

32. Information on Korea, Seoul, Korea, available at <http://www.koreain fogate.com>.

33. Konrad Lorenz, *On aggression* (New York: Harcourt, Brace and World, 1966). Originally published as *Das Sogenannte Böse* (Wien: Schoeler Verlag, 1963).

34. Jeffrey H. Goldstein and Robert L. Arms, "Effects of observing athletic contests on hostility," *Sociometry,* 34(1) (March 1971): 83.

35. Bernard Lefkowtiz, *Our guys: The Glen Ridge rape and the secret life of the perfect suburb* (Berkeley: The University of California Press, 1997), p. 113.

36. Lorraine Adams and Dale Russakoff, "Columbine jock culture probed," *The Washington Post* (June 12, 1999), p. A1.

37. "Texas teen dies after football practice," *CNN.com* (August 18, 2001), available at <www.cnn.com/2001/us/>.

38. Amy Shipley, "Pushing the limits on every level," *The Washington Post* (August 31, 2001): A1.

39. Robert C. Cantu and Frederick O. Mueller, "Fatalities and catastrophic injuries in high school and college sports, 1982-1977," *The Physician and Sports Medicine,* 27(8) (August 1999): 1.

40. Vincent G. Stilger and Charles E. Yesalis, "Anabolic-androgenic steroid use among high school football players," *Journal of Community Health,* 24(2) (1999): 131-145.

41. *Board of Education of Independent School District No. 92 of Pottawatomie County v. Earls,* 01-332, June 24, 2002.

42. Mark H. Beers and Robert H. Berkow, *The Merck manual of diagnois and therapy* (Whitehouse Station, NJ: Merck and Co. (1999), Section 22, Chapter 35.

43. Everett C. Hughes, "Dilemmas and contradictions of status," *American Journal of Sociology,* 50 (1945): 353.

44. Frederick Jackson Turner, *The frontier in American history* (New York: H. Holt and Co., 1920).

45. Murray Sperber, *Onward to victory: The crisis that shaped college sports* (New York: Henry Holt and Co., 1998), p. 507.

46. *General social surveys 1973-1998, cumulative codeboook* (Chicago: National Opinon Research Center, 1999), p. 1223.

47. Conrad C. Vogler and Stephen E. Schwartz, *The sociology of sport: An introduction* (Englewood Cliffs, NJ: Prentice-Hall, 1993), p. 197.

48. Murray Sperber, *Beer and circus* (New York: Henry Holt and Co., 2000), p. xiii.

49. Michael Oriad, *King football* (Chapel Hill: The University of North Carolina Press, 2001), p. 71.

Chapter 2

1. George Juergens, *Joseph Pulitzer and the "New York World"* (Princeton, NJ: Princeton University Press, 1966), p.viii.

2. Robert W. McChesney, "Media made sports: A history of sports coverage in the United States," in Lawrence A. Wenner, ed., *Media, sports and society* (Newbury Park, CA: Sage Publications, 1989), p. 54.

3. Tim Considine, *The language of sport* (New York: Facts on File, 1982).

4. Henri Taifel, "Social psychology of intergroup relations," in *Annual Review of Psychology* (Palo Alto, CA: Annual Reviews, 1982), p. 1.

5. Murray Sperber, *Beer and circus: How big-time college sports is crippling undergraduate education* (New York: Henry Holt and Co., 2000), p. 71.

6. Burton Clark and Martin Trow, "The organizational context," in Theodore M. Newcomb, ed., *College peer groups: Problems and prospects for research* (Chicago: Adline Publishing Co., 1966), p. 20.

7. Edward Wong, "There's no stoppping athletes misbehavior," *The New York Times* (December 23, 2001):1:3.

8. Sally Jenkins, "A course without credit: Hooliganism 101," *Pipe Dream* (April 12, 2002): 6.

9. Dave Campbell, "Record chaser's headline 2002 magazine," *Texas Football* (June 14, 2002), available at <texasfootball.com>.

10. Frank Demarzo, "Tobias changes mind, wants out of Arkansas," *Miami Herald* (May 4, 2002): 10D.

11. Marissa Silvera and Susan Miller Degnan, "Canes reward Coker," *Miami Herald* (February 6, 2002): 1D.

12. Robert Lipsyte, "Life in the Santa Claus zone: Who has been naughty or nice?" *The New York Times* (December 23, 2001): S8, 11.

13. Lee Sigelman, "It's academic—or is it—admissions standards and big-time college football," *The Social Science Quarterly,* 76(2) (June 1995): 247.

14. Donald F. Sabo and Joe Panepinto, "Football ritual and the social reproduction of masculinity," in Michael Messner and Donald Sabo, eds., *Sport, men and gender order* (Champaign, IL: Human Kinetics Books, 1990), p. 117.

15. Michael Oriard, *Reading football: How the popular press created an American spectacle* (Chapel Hill: The University of North Carolina Press, 1993), p. 189.

16. Hutton Webster, *Primitive secret societies: A study in early politics and religion* (New York: Octagon Books, 1968), pp. 36-47.

17. Michael Oriard, *King football* (Chapel Hill: The University of North Carolina Press, 2001), p. 330.

18. Mac E. Barricks, " Racial riddles and the Polack joke," *Keystone Folklore Quarterly,* 15(1) (Spring 1970): 11.

19. Shantae Goodloe, "Missed basket not as bad as missed opportunity," *USA Today* (July 14, 2002): 1.

20. John Richard Betts, *America's sporting heritage, 1850-1950* (Reading, MA: Addison-Wesley, 1974), p. 126.

21. Reed Harris, *King football: The vulgarization of the American college* (New York: Vanguard Press, 1932), p. 113.

22. Oriard, *King football,* p. 117.

23. Wes Smith, "The selling of Albert Means," *U.S. News and World Report* (September 10, 2001): 25.

24. Sperber, *Beer and circus,* p. 241.

25. Gale Lang, Roger G. Dunham, and Geoffrey P. Alpert, "Factors related to the academic success and failure of college football players: The case of the mental dropout," *Youth and Society,* 20(2) (December 1988): 209.

26. Robert Lipsyte, "In college athletics, you have to follow the money," *The New York Times* (January 27, 2002): VIII, 11.

27. Arthur Padilla and John Boucher, "On the economics of intercollegiate athletic programs," *Journal of Sports and Social Issues,* 11 (1988): 61.

28. Matthew P. McAllister, "College bowl sponsorship and the increased commercialization of amateur sport," *Critical Studies in Mass Communication,* 15(4) (December 1998): 357.

29. J.L. Fizel and R.W. Bennett, "Telecasts and recruiting in NCAA Division I football: The impact of altered property rights," *Journal of Sports Management,* 10(4) (October 1996): 359.

30. John C. Weistart, "College sports reform: Where are the faculty?" *Academe,* 12, (July-August 1987): 12.

31. John Consoli, "Buyers: Not a bust," *Media Week,* 12(1) (January 7, 2002): 2.

32. Arthur Padilla and David Baumer, "Big-time college sports: Management and economic issues," *Journal of Sports and Social Issues,* 18(2) (May 1994): 123.

33. Kelly Whiteside, "Football stats face a change," *USA Today* (August 27, 2002): C1.

34. Tom Dienhart, "NCAA only cares about bottom line," *The Sports News* (March 25, 2002): 1.

35. J. Douglas Toma and Michael Cross, "Intercollegiate athletics and student college choice," paper presented at the International Sociology of Sport Association, July 28, 1998, Montreal, Canada.

36. Tim Layden, "The lonliest losers," *Sports Illustrated,* 97(20) (November 18, 2002): 69.

37. Bill Benner, "The anatomy of a losing football program," *Indianapolic Business Journal,* 22(41) (December 17, 2001): 18.

38. Tommy Perkins, "Southern Heritage Classic revenue decreases by 42 percent," *Memphis Business Journal,* 23(30) (November 23, 2001): 1.

39. Laura Newpoff, " Ohio stadium suites put corporate fans in luxury," *Business First,* 18(12) (November 9, 2001): B3.

40. Brad Young, "Backbreaking Buckeyes," *Time,* 154(24) (December 13, 1999): 58.

41. Greg Netzer, "The Ken and Joey show," *Oregon Business,* 24(11) (November 2001): S29.

42. Edward Wong, "SUNY athletics experience growing pains in Division I," *The New York Times* (Febraury 7, 2002): D1, D7.

43. Ibid., p. D7.

44. "Undefeated, untied and uninvited: The 1951 USF football team celebrates its 50th," *USFNews,* 11(2) (October 23, 2001): 1.

45. Rick Telander, *The hundred yard lie* (Urbana: The University of Illinois Press, 1996), p. 2.

46. Daniel J. Garland and John R. Barry, "The effects of personality and perceived Division I: The leader behaviors on performance in collegiate football," *Psychological Record*, 38(2) (Spring 1988): 237.

47. Arnold LeUnes and Jack R. Nation, "Saturday's heroes: A psychological portrait of college football players," *Journal of Sports Behavior*, 5(3) (September 1982): 139.

48. Allen L. Sack and Robert Thiel, "College football and social mobility," *Sociology of Education*, 52(1) (January 1979): 60.

49. John J. Macionis, *Sociology*, Eighth edition (Upper Saddle River, NJ: Prentice Hall, 2001) p. 274.

50. Hanah Cho, "Friedgen, Williams take home pay tops highest paid state employees," *Capital News Service* (April 19, 2002): 1.

51. "UM gives Coker a new deal," *St. Petersburg Times* (February 5, 2002): 1.

52. "Where there is a Willingham," *Sports Illustrated* (January 1, 2002): 1.

53. "South Carolina boosts salaries for Holtz, assistants," *Sporting News* (March 30, 2002): 1.

54. Mike Celizik, "Bowden's salary is latest ugly lesson," *The Sports News* (October 21, 2001): 1.

55. Larry Copeland, "Title IX: Public get a chance to sound off," *USA Today* (August 27, 2002) C1.

56. Bill Pennington, "Want to try out for college sports? Forget it!" *The New York Times* (September 22, 2002): 1: 28.

57. Robert Lipsyte, "Lesson 1: Mixed messages part of curriculum," *The New York Times* (January 20, 2002): S8 11: 2.

58. Frederick O. Mueller and Jerry L. Diehl, *Survey of football injuries* (Waco, TX: The National Center for Catasrophic Sport Injury Research, 2002), p. 1.

59. Ibid., p. 7.

60. Brian Vastag, "Football brain injuries draw increased scrutiny," *JAMA*, 287(4) (January 30, 2002): 17.

61. Ibid., p. 18.

62. Gordon O. Matheson, "Can team physicians buy credibility?" *The Physician and Sports Medicine*, 29(12) (December 2001): 1.

63. Oriard, *King football*, p. 175.

64. Cheerleaders of America, available at <www.coacheer.com/college>.

65. *American Cheerleader Magazine*, <www.kable.com/pub/ancr/newssubs.asp?>.

Chapter 3

1. Michael Oriard, *King football* (Chapel Hill: The University of North Carolina Press, 2001), p. 5.

2. Robert W. Peterson, *Pigskin: The early years of profootball* (New York: The Oxford University Press, 1996), p. 13.

3. "NFL-AFL merger creates a sports industry giant," *Discovering U.S. History* (May 19, 2002): 6.

4. "Despite NBC pledge," *Communications Daily* (March 15, 2001): p. 1.

5. Ibid., p. 67-147. See also Howard Fendrich, "Death of a league: XFL's short rise, rapid fall," *SLAM FOOTBALL* (May 14, 2001), available at <www.canoe.ca/FootballXFL>.

6. Women's Pro Football League, available at <http://www.womensprofootball.com/history.cfm>.

7. Frank Pastor, "Ex-Buc QB Milanovich joins Storm," *St. Petersburg Times* (March 14, 2002): 1.

8. Pro Football Hall of Fame, available at <www.profootballhof.com>.

9. Justin Bachman, "High priced Super Bowl ads make cheap hits," *Financial News* (February 1, 2004): 1.

10. Bloomberg News, "Entertainment/Media," *Los Angeles Times* (Janurary 31, 2002): Part 3, p. 2.

11. David Morris and Daniel Kraker, "Rooting the home team," *The American Prospect Magazine* 40 (September-October 1998): 38-43.

12. Ibid., p. 39.

13. Mairin Burns, "Era of stadium financing ends: But sports finance teams still have steady flow of related deals," *The Investment Dealer's Digest* (April 8, 2002): 12.

14. Jim Lehrer, "Playing for dollars," *Online NewsHour* (January 29, 1999), available at <http://www.pbs.org/newshour/newshour_index.html>.

15. U.S. Senate, Committee on the Judiciary on the Stadium and Franchise Relocation Act of 1999, "Written testimony of Andrew Zimbalist" (Washington, DC: United States Government Printing Office, June 15, 1999): 1.

16. Bureau of Labor Statistics, "2000 national occupational employment and wage estimates" (Washington, DC: U.S. Department of Labor, 2001): 1.

17. Micheal Hiestand, "Baldinger brings passion to booth," *USA Today* (August 9, 2002): 2C.

18. Peggy Panosh, "Westwood One/CBS Radio Sports and National Football League renew agreement," *Business Wire* (April 9, 2002): 1.

19. "Pro-Football 2001 Salaries," <www.usatoday.com/football/nfl/salaries/afceast.htm>.

20. Hilary Cassidy, "Coors' NFL deal is huge, but brewer fails to get the whole nine yards," *Brandweek,* 43(13) (April 1, 2002): 11.

21. Robert Sullivan, "Paid to play games," *Time Magazine for Kids,* 6(22) (March 30, 2001): 1.

22. Matthew Grimm, "Grid lock: NFL Goliaths signed for seasonlong Coke blitz," *Brandweek,* 34(26) (June 28, 1993): 1.

23. Sean Wood, "Despite economic woes, athletes' endorsements are a smash hit," *Fort Worth Telegram* (August 22, 2002): 1.

24. Anthony Schoettle, "Colt stars poised to make success pay," *Indianapolis Business Journal,* 20(45) (February 7, 2000): 5.

25. Rick Maloney, "Flutie attracts endorsement opportunities," *Business First-Buffalo,* 16(17) (January 17, 2000): 5.

26. Len Pasquarelli, "NFL cracking down on supplement endorsements," *ESPN. com* (June 5, 2002).

27. Loren Steffy, "Roger Staubach, CEO," *Bloomberg Markets* (May 2002): 4.

28. Cynthia L. Gramm and John F. Schnell, "Difficult choices: Crossing the picket line during the 1987 National Football League strike," *Journal of Labor Economics,* 12(1) (January 1994): 55.

29. Lawrence Hadley, Marc Poitras, John Ruggiero, and Scott Knowles, "Performance evaluation of National Football League teams," *Managerial and Decision Economics,* 21(2) (March, 2000): 63-70.

30. Thomas G. Smith, "Outside the pale: The exclusion of blacks from the National Football League, 1934-1946," *Journal of Sport History,* 15(3) (Winter 1988): 255.

31. Ibid., p. 261.

32. Ibid., p. 275.

33. Thomas George, "NFL pressured on black coaches," *The New York Times* (October 6, 2002): 8:9.

34. Mark Sappenfield, "Football's last race barrier crumbles," *The Christian Science Monitor* (January 5, 2001), pp. 1-2.

35. Sheila Moran, "The football fan—What drives him?" *Los Angeles Times* (September 21, 1977): 92.

36. Jeffrey O. Segrave, "Sports as escape," *Journal of Sports and Social Issues,* 24(1) (February 2000): 61-77.

37. Daniel L. Wann, "Aggression among highly identified spectators as a function of their need to maintain positive social identity," *The Journal of Sports Medicine,* 17(2) (August 1993): 135-143.

38. Pro Football Hall of Fame, <http://www.profootballhof.com>.

39. Wann, "Aggression," p. 76.

40. Ibid., p. 135.

41. Ibid., p. 141.

42. Carolyn Sachs and Lawrence D. Chu, "The association between professional football games and domestic violene in Los Angeles County," *Journal of Interpersonal Violence,* 15(11) (2000): 1192-1201.

43. Michael Welch, "Violence against women by professional football players," *Journal of Sports and Social Issues,* 21(4) (November 1997): 392-411.

44. Steven M. Ortiz, "Traveling with the ball club: A code of conduct for wives only," *Symbolic Interaction,* 20(3) (August 1997): 226.

45. Ibid., p. 241.

46. "Violence against women," p. 395.

47. Associated Press, "Maryland's Perry out 4-8 weeks," *The Charlotte Observer* (August 23, 2002): 6C.

48. Tom Jackman, "Phillips and ex-girlfriend settle lawsuit," *The Kansas City Star* (September 26, 1996): D1.

49. "Phillips faces DWI charges," *The New York Times* (June 18, 1996): B14.

50. Mike Ulmer, "It's a violent game off the field," *SLAM Football* (January 26, 2001): Sports section.

51. Bob Becknell, "Felicia Moon testifies her husband choked her," *The San Angelo Standard Times* (February 17, 1996).

52. Associated Press, "NFL rookies learn the hard knocks," *The Augusta Chronicle* (June 30, 2002): Sports.

53. Securities and Exchange Commission, "Litigation release no. 17218" (November 2, 2001): 1. Available at <www.sec.gov//litigation/lr17218.htm>.

54. Edward C. Pound and Douglas Pasternak, "Money players," *U.S. News and World Report*, 132(4) (February 11, 2002): 30-36.

55. Deion Sanders, *Power, money and sex* (New York: W. Publishing Group, 1998).

56. Reuters Health Information, "Concussions come back to haunt football players," <http://www.doctorbob.com> (May 10, 2000).

57. David Riesman and Reuel Denney, "Football in America: A study in cultural diffusion," *American Quarterly*, 3(4) (Winter 1951): 309-325.

58. Ibid.

Chapter 4

1. John J. Macionis, *Sociology*, Eighth edition (Upper Saddle River, NJ: Prentice-Hall, 2001), p. 248.

2. Ibid, p. 248.

3. Rick Horrow, "Model of consistency: NFL sets pace for all sports leagues," *CBS SportsLine.com* (September 4, 2002).

4. William J. Rudman, "The sport mystique in black culture," *Sociology of Sport Journal*, 3 (1986): 305.

5. Kevin J. Matthews, "2001 racial and gender report card," (Boston: Center for the Study of Sport in Society, 2001), p. 1.

6. John R. Woodward, "An examination of a National Football League college draft publiction: Do racial stereotypes still exist in football?" *Sociology of Sport Journal*, 5(2) (November/December 2002): 1.

7. Richard E. Lapchick, "Black college football coaches lose yardage," *Sports Business Journal* (January 1, 2001): 1.

8. William I. Thomas, *The unadjusted girl* (Boston: Little Brown and Co., 1923), pp. 1-40.

9. Michael Messner, "The meaning of success: The athletic experience and the development of male identity," in Harry Brod, ed., *The making of masculinities: The new men's studies* (Boston: Allen and Unwin, 1987), p. 193.

10. William M. Leonard and John M. Reyman, "The odds of attaining professional athlete status: Refining the computations," *Sociology of Sport Journal*, 5 (1988): 162.

11. Michael Messner, "Boyhood, organized sports, and the construction of masculinities," in *Men's lives*, Second edition (New York: Macmillan Publishing Co., 1989) p. 160.

12. Celia S. Heller, *On the edge of destruction* (New York: Schocken Books, Inc., 1994), p. 3.

13. Jerome Karabel, "Status-group struggle, organizational interests, and the limit of institutional autonomy," *Theory and Society*, 13(1) (1984): 1.

14. Ibid., p. 2.

15. Robert Slater, *Great Jews in sports* (Middle Village, NY: J. David Publishers, 2000) p. 189.

16. U.S. Department of Commerce, Bureau of the Census, 1999.

17. H. G. Bissinger, *Friday night lights: A town, a team, and a dream* (Boston: De Capo Press, 2000).

18. J. Brent Clark, *Third down and forever* (New York: St. Martin's Press, 1993).

19. Larry McMurtry, *The last picture show* (New York: Scribner's, 1999).

20. Gary Shaw, *Meat on the hoof: The hidden world of Texas football* (New York: St. Martin's Press, 1972).

21. Don DeLillo, *End zone* (New York: Houghton Mifflin, Inc., 1982).

22. Douglas Terry, *The last Texas hero* (Garden City, NY: Doubleday, 1982).

23. "96 million sports fans watch football," *www. sportsfansofamerica.com* (February 8, 2003).

24. Branch Johnson, "Football: A survival of magic?" *The Contemporary Review,* 135(1929): 228.

25. William Arens, "The great American football ritual," in William Arens and Susan Montague, eds., *The American dimension: Cultural myths and social realities* (Port Washington, NY: Alfred Publishing Co., 1975), pp. 3-14.

26. David Kopay and Perry Dean Young, *The David Kopay story* (New York: Arbor House, 1977), p. 53.

27. Gerhard Falk, *Stigma: How we treat outsiders* (Amherst, NY: Prometheus Press, 2002), p. 11.

28. Ursula A. Falk and Gerhard Falk, *Ageism, The aged and aging in America* (Springfield, IL: Charles C Thomas Publishers), p. 78.

29. M.A. Milhovilovic, "The status of former sportsmen," *International Review of Sport Sociology* 3 (1968): 73.

30. Personal interview by the author with Mike Hamby, July 16, 2003.

31. Len Pasquarelli, "A player's nightmare: The price of pro football," *The Atlanta Constitution* (January 28, 1994): E2.

32. Henry Blitz, "The drive to win: Careers in professional sports," *Occupational Outlook Quarterly* (Summer 1973): 3.

33. Bob Martin, "Concussions come back to haunt football players," *Health News* (May 8, 2001): 1.

34. Pasquarelli, "A player's nightmare: The price of pro football," p. E3.

35. Ibid., p. 3.

36. Falk, *Stigma,* p. 129.

37. "Thomas runs with idea of helping others," *The Buffalo News* (February 6, 2003): F1.

38. Art Sricklin, "Pat Summerall," *A New Voice* (March 2002): 2.

39. "Retired players get major pension increase," *NFL News* (May 21, 2002): 1.

Chapter 5

1. John W. Wright, *The American almanac of jobs and salaries* (New York: Avon Books, 2000), p. 163.

2. Emile Durkheim, *The rules of the sociological method* (Glencoe, IL: The Free Press, 1938 [originally 1898]), p. 257.

3. Dave Kindred, "Woody and Hero suffer same fate; Hayes' tantrums worry his friends," *The Washington Post* (December 31, 1978): H1.

4. Mike Bobo and Spike Dykes, *Principles of coaching football* (Boston: Allyn and Bacon, 1998), p. 26.

5. David Sabino, "Scouting reports," *Sports Illustrated,* 97(9) (September 2, 2002): 98.

6. Peter King, "Shop right," *Sports Illustrated,* 97(9) (September 2, 2002): 50-53.

7. Lisa Zimmerman, "Iso breaks ground for female trainers," *NFL.com* (August 16, 2002).

8. E. Adamson Hoebel, *Anthropology* (New York: McGraw-Hill Book Company, 1966), p. 26.

9. "Becoming an official," <http://members.tripod.com/refereestats/career.htm>.

10. "League and officials agree," *The New York Times* (September 18, 2001): C18.

11. Michael L., "NFL officiating theoretically a full-time job," *Behind the Football Stripes* (January 5, 2002): 1.

12. "The Northwestern game today," *Ariel, The University of Minnesota Student Newspaper,* 22 (1898): 127.

13. Katherine Jellison, "Book review of *Go! Fight! Win! Cheerleading in American Culture* by Mary Ellen Hanson," *Journal of Sports History,* 24(2) (Summer 1997): 243-244.

14. Ibid., p. 244.

15. Marida Walker, "10 questions with Herkie," *American Cheerleader,* 8(5) (October 2002): 48.

16. Alyssa Roenigk, "Partner up," *American Cheerleader,* 8(6) (December 2002): 38.

17. Erik Brady, "Cheerleading in the U.S.A.: A sport and an industry," *USA Today* (April 26, 2002): 8.

18. Tom Farrey, "Turn your head and scoff," *ESPN.com* (September 12, 2002): 1.

19. Don Colburn, "The rule of hard knocks," *Washington Post Health* (April 1, 1997): 7.

20. "Sports: Pro football player dies of heatstroke; other developments," *World News Digest* (August 9, 2001): 1.

21. Michael S. Bahrke and Charles Yesalis, *Performing enhancing substances in sport and exercise* (Champaign, IL: Human Kinetics, 2002), p. 10.

22. Arnold Mandell, "The Sunday syndrome: From kinetics to altered consciousness," *Federation Proceedings* (1981) 40: 2693-2698.

23. Bill Gilbert, "Drugs in sport," *Sports Illustrated* (June 23, June 30, and July 7, 1969): 30-42.

24. Dan Vergano, "NFL doctors, players face off over painful choices," *USA Today* (January 31, 2002): 1.

25. Victoria Staff Elliott, "Today's football players may see longer, healthier lives," *AMNews* (November 11, 2002): 1.

26. Brad D. Hatfield, Jerry P. Wren, and Michael Bretting, "Comparison of job responsibilities of intercollegiate athletic directors and professional sport general managers," *Journal of Sport Management* 1(2) (1987): 129-145.

27. Bill Pennington, "Countdown to the Vagabond Bowl," *The New York Times* (Janaury 28, 2001): D1,3.

28. Jacob Horowitz, "Leader of the Patriots," <http://www.jewsweek.com/society/216lhtm>.

29. Richard Sandomir, "The Jets fill one opening: New owner at $635 million," *The New York Times* (January 12, 2000): A1,5.

30. The discussion of the owners of football teams is based on numerous Web sites available on the Internet. These may be accessed by finding each team on the NFL roster and then seeking some background information about the owner's business and payment for the team.

Chapter 6

1. "Visa Hall of Fame," (October, 1998), available at <http://www.cardweb.com/cardtrak/news/1998/october/7j.html>.

2. "Premier NFL fan recognition program celebrates its fifth anniversary at Super Bowl XXXVII," *Global New Wire* (Janaury 17, 2003): 1.

3. Mary Kathryn Craft, "Football not just a boys club anymore," *The Sun News* (Myrtle Beach, SC): Lifestyles section (January 24, 2003): K6469.

4. Ibid.

5. Heidi Knapp Rinella, "Women proving they are football fans, too," *Las Vegas Review Journal* (January 26, 2003): Final Edition, p. 13.

6. Stephanie Harvin, "Football fan frenzy," *The Charleston Post and Courier* (September 8, 2002): G1.

7. Charles Horton Cooley, *Human nature and the social order* (New York: Schocken Books, 1964 [org. 1902]): 5.

8. Alan Nevill, "Football fans make referees dance to their tune," *New Scientist* 174(2342) (May 11, 2002): 18.

9. F. Ishu Ishiyama, "On self-validation," *The Trumpeter* 10(4) (December 1993): 5.

10. William Kornblum, *Sociology*, Fifth edition (New York: Harcourt College Publishers, 2000), p. 235.

11. Robert B. Caldini, "Basking in reflected glory," *The Journal of Personality and Social Psychology* 34 (1976): 366.

12. Charles E. Kimble and Brian P. Cooper, "Association and disassociation by football fans," *Perceputal and Motor Skills* 75 (August 1992): 303.

13. Eric M. Leifer, "Pervese effects of social support: Public and performance in major league sports," *Social Forces* 74(1) (September 1995): 81.

14. Joe Baird, "Few FAN-atics," *The Salt Lake Tribune* (November 17, 2002): Final p. 8A1.

15. John Eisenberg, "The future of fandom," *The Baltimore Sun* (December 15, 2002): 1D.

16. Jim Herron Zamora, "Raiders haters aplenty in Bay Area," *San Francisco Chronicle* (January 23, 2003): A6.

17. Konrad Lorenz, *On aggression* (New York: Harcourt, Brace, and World, 1967), p. 261.

18. Fran Golden, "Football heaven," *The Boston Herald* (October 27, 2002): O52.

19. Carl Nolte, "Raider Nation hits the rails," *San Francisco Chronicle* (November 2, 2002): A1.

20. Ibid.

21. Paul Swiech, "Pigskin pigout: As the scores add up on game day, so do the calories," *The Bloomington Pantagraph* (November 18, 2002): D1.

22. Kornblum, *Sociology*, p. 164.

23. Mark Bradley, "Out of control? Behavior of football fans takes an ugly turn in the South," *Atlanta Journal Constitution* (November 6, 2002): 1F.

24. Kornblum, *Sociology*, p. 209.

25. Jeff Barker, "Just who is home team?" *The Baltimore Sun* (December 28, 2002): 1C.

26. Mike Klingaman, "Notre Dame leaves few fans on fence," *The Baltimore Sun* (November 9, 2002): 1C.

27. Tony Perry, "Pro football: Uniform response to Raider rooters," *Los Angeles Times* (December 8, 2002): Part 4, p. 6.

28. Jamie Kritzer, "Are you ready for some football?" *Greensboro News and Record* (September 12, 2002): City Life p. 2.

29. Kornblum, *Sociology*, p. 231.

30. Stewart Mandel, "Surviving Super Bowl Sunday," *Sports Illustrated* (January 27, 2003): 1.

31. David Barron, "Welcome to the city of tough love," *The Houston Chronicle* (September 29, 2002): Pt. 2,1.

32. Perry, "Uniform response."

33. Tom Archdeacon, "When the whole tale is told," *Dayton Daily News* (November 15, 2002): G3.

34. Scott Rabalais, "LSU letter warns fans of behavior in Tiger Stadium," *Baton Rouge State Times* (November 9, 2002): 3D.

35. Gustave LeBon, *The crowd: A study of the popular mind* (New York: Viking, 1960 and 1895).

36. Ralph Turner and Lewis M. Killian, "The field of collective behavior," in Russell L. Curtis and Beningo Aguerre, eds., *Collective behavior and social movements* (Boston: Allyn and Bacon, 1993), p. 5.

37. Jonathan B. Cox, "Fantasy football grows to multi-million dollar industry," *Knight-Ridder Tribune Business News* (September 19, 2002): 1.

38. Michael Watt, "A new on-line biz: Feeding fantasy football's fanatics," *Long Island Business Week* 49(39) (September 13, 2002): 20A.

39. Rachel A. Einwohner, "Gender, class and social movement outcomes," *Gender and Society*, 13(1) (February 1999): 56.

40. Edward O. Wilson, *Sociobiology* (Cambridge, MA: Belknap, 1975).

41. Susan Brownmiller, *Against our will: Men, women and rape* (New York: Bantam Books, 1976), p. 6.

42. Sylvia Levine and Joseph Koenig, *Why men rape* (Toronto: Macmillan, 1980), pp. 28, 42, 56, 72.

43. Joseph H. Pleck, "Prisoners of manliness," *Psychology Today* (September 1981): 68.

44. Robert L. Arms, Gordon W. Russell, and Mark J. Sandilands, "Effects on the hostility of spectators of viewing aggressive gports," *Social Psychology Quarterly* 42(3) (September 1979): 275.

45. Ibid., p. 279.

46. Adam Brown, *Fanatics: Power, identity and fandom in football* (New York: Routledge, 1998), p. 274.

Chapter 7

1. Ronald A. Smith, *Play by play: Radio, television and big time college sports* (Baltimore, MD: The Johns Hopkins University Press, 2001), p. 33.

2. Benjamin G. Rader, *In its own image: How television has transformed sports* (New York: The Free Press, 1984), p. 138.

3. Brad Schultz, *Sports broadcasting* (Boston: Focal Press, 2002), p. 17.

4. Ibid., p. 154.

5. "Frank Gifford—Pro football hall of fame," *Sports Stars U.S.A. Home* <www.sportsstarsusa.com/sportscasters/gifford-frank.html>.

6. "Pat Summerall: NFL on FOX play by play announcer," <foxsports.lycos.com/shows/index.Adp?>.

7. CBS Sportsline (2002), available at <SportsLine.com>.

8. John J. Macionis, *Sociology* (Upper Saddle River, NJ: Prentice-Hall, Inc., 2001), p. 74.

9. Allen Wilson, "Bills' draft class of 2002 made significant contributions," *Buffalo News* (January 8, 2003): C1.

10. Buster Olney, "Garcia deflated Giants, now charges loom," *The New York Times* (January 7, 2003): D2.

11. Howard Liss, *Football talk* (New York: Arch Paperback, 1973); Joseph Olgin, *Illustrated football dictionary for young people* (New York: Simon and Schuster, 1978); David S. Porter, *Biographical dictionary of sports* (Westport, CT: Greenwood Publishing Group, 1992).

12. Editorial, *Arizona Daily Wildcat*, November 24, 1997.

13. *The Magazine*, September 16, 2002.

14. *Sporting News*, December 22, 2002.

15. *Sports Illustrated*, 97(2) (September 2. 1002).

16. Kelley King, "Willis McGahee," *Sports Illustrated* 97(4) (December 16, 2002): 8.

17. Elsa Myers, ed., *Subject guide to books in print* (New Providence, NJ: R.R. Bowker, 1998), p. 4954.

18. Sally Pont, *Fields of honor: The golden age of college football and the men who created it* (New York: Harcourt Brace, 2001).

19. Mark F. Bernstein, *Football: The Ivy League origins of an American obsession* (Philadelphia: The University of Pennsylvania Press, 2001).

20. Murray Sperber, *Shake down the thunder* (New York: Henry Holt & Co., 1993).

21. Ray Robinson, *Rockne of Notre Dame* (New York: Oxford University Press, 1999).

22. Robon Lester, *Stagg's university: The rise and fall of big-time football at Chicago* (Urbana and Chicago: The University of Illinois Press, 1995).

23. John M. Carroll, *Fritz Pollard: Pioneer in racial advancement* (Urbana and Chicago: The University of Illinois Press, 1998).

24. John M. Carroll, *Red Grange and the rise of modern football* (Urbana and Chicago: The University of Illinois Press, 1999).

25. Jon Morgan, *Glory for sale: Fans, dollars, and the new NFL* (Baltimore, MD: Bancroft Press, 1997).

26. Chris Crutcher, *Running loose* (New York: Greenwillow Books, 1983).

27. Jan Cheripko, *Initate the tiger* (New York: St. Martin's Press, 1996).

28. Robert Brancato, *Winning* (New York, Alfred Knopf, Inc., 1977).

29. George Plimpton, *Paper lion* (New York: Harper Row, 1966).

30. Robert F. O'Brien, *School songs of America's colleges and universities: A directory* (New York: Greenwood Press, 1991).

31. Macionis, *Sociology,* p. 156.

Chapter 8

1. Doug Lesmerises, "In sports, NFL means business," *The Wilmington News Journal* (January 24, 2003): S1.

2. Ibid., p. S1.

3. Tom Lowry, "The NFL machine," *Business Week* (January 27, 2003): 1.

4. Doris Hajewski, "Green Bay Packers tops in football merchandise marketing, say vendors," *Tribune Business News* (February 26, 2003): 6

5. David Barron, "With new building, NFL films a booming business," *The Houston Chronicle* (October 6, 2002): 12.

6. "Yale Bowl," <http://www.yale.edu/athletic/Facility/Bowl/history.htm>.

7. Bob Doughty, "College bowl games," *American Mosaic* (December 28, 2001): 2.

8. Scott Dupre and Larry Novernstern, "College bowls are filling up," *Mediaweek* 5(43) (November 13, 1995): 4.

9. Kenneth Hein, Todd Wasserman, and Mike Beirne, "Big brands still the superstars: Names dominate again, as others mull $2 million price tag," *Adweek Southwest* 24(48) (December 2, 2002): 2(1).

10. Joe Mandese, "Super Bowl glitter for less gold," *Advertsing Age* 65(3) (January 17, 1994): 4.

11. Stefan Fatsis, "US networks calling time out on soaring sports fees," *The Wall Street Journal* (March 27, 2003): 1.

12. Joe Concha, "NBC's arena deal forward thinking," *NBC Sports.com* (April 19, 2003): 2.

13. Penelope Patsuris, "A wide world of TV sports," *Forbes* (December 12, 2002): 12.

14. Margot Suydam, "The big game," *Business and Company* 41(5) (February 4, 2000): 21.

15. Ed Klein, "TV commercials are over the edge," *Westchester County Business Journal* 42(3) (January 20, 2003): 45.

16. Dan Trigoboff, "Squeeze play in Pittsburgh," *Broadcasting and Cable* 131 (46) (November 5, 2001): 14.

17. Hajewski, "Green Bay," p. 7.

18. "Marketing revival for America's team," *Retail Merchandiser* 43(2) (February 2003): 16.

19. Karen Benezra and Kenneth Hein, "NFL wrap: Gruden's got that GQ look; Basics, Nike broaden their reach," *Brandweek* 44(5) (Februrary 3, 2003): 14.

20. Paul King, "On the menu," *Nation's Restaurant News* 37(6) (Februrary 10, 2003): 52.

21. "Super Bowl is prime snacking time for Americans," *MMR* 20(3) (February 10, 2003): 38.

22. Ted Jackovics, "Florida based cigar firm's NFL related product aims for end zone," *Tampa Tribune* (March 16, 1999): 13.

23. John Dorschner, "Fort Lauderdale based online sports site forms high profile team," *The Miami Herald* (December 22, 1999): S1.

24. Richard Alm, "Sports unions blur the line between business and labor," *The Dallas Morning News* (March 16, 2000): 11.

25. Rich Tomaselli, "NFL revokes ban on drug company sponsorship," *Advertising Age* 74(11) (March 17, 2003): 3.

26. Ron Borges, "NFL Draft '03—The union has created certified mess," *The Boston Globe* (April 25, 2003): E1.

27. Kevin Acee, "Small fry sinking in NFL agent pond," *The San Diego Union Tribune* (April 22, 2003): C1.

28. Mark Gaughan, "Bills weren't tricked, Rosenhaus says," *The Buffalo News* (April 29, 2003): D1.

29. Kevin Lynch, "La Mote makes his big deals," *San Francisco Chronicle* (January 27, 2003): C1.

30. Joel Stashenko, "Bill in works to require registration of sports agents," *Sports News* (February 7, 2003): 9.

31. Ron Borges, "In Pirate suit, Davis looks like corporate raider," *The Boston Globe* (April 20, 2003): C4.

32. Rick DelVeccio, "Raiders, Oakland collide in court," *The San Francisco Chronicle* (April 15, 2003): A13.

33. Greg Edwards, "Redskins, players group will talk," *Richmond Times Dispatch* (January 28, 2003): A5.

34. Fred A. Mohr, "Parents look to revamp Pop Warner," *The Post Standard* (April 4, 2003): B1.

35. Mike Miller, "Dayne, Daley settle law suit," *Madison Capital Times* (February 24, 2003): 2A.

36. Mindy Hagen, "Northwestern U. football players used supplements" (January 27, 2003): 1.

37. Joe Gyan Jr., "New stadium naming rights could give state bigger profit," *The Baton Rouge Advocate* (January 17, 2003): 4B.

38. "Reliant Stadium," *Texas Construction* 10(12) (December 2002): 35.

39. Christopher DeReza, "Box seats no longer promise profits," *Asset Scrutinization Report,* N.Y. Asset Securitization Report, February 2003.

40. Stephanie Simon, "Not so easily thrown for a big loss; suit demands millions the public has paid to bankroll a big stadium," *Los Angeles Times* (April 27, 2002): A30.

41. Paul C. Weiler, *Leveling the playing field: How the law makes sports better for fans* (Cambridge, MA: Harvard University Press).

42. Caitlin Rother and Noberto Santana Jr., "Council ok's talks with Chargers on new facility," *The San Diego Union Tribune* (March 19, 2003): B1.

43. Mike Triplett, "Critical plan," *Times Picayune* (March 9, 2003): 8: 1.

44. T. J. Lears, *Something for nothing: Luck in America* (New York: Viking, 2003).

45. Ibid., p. 219.

46. "Athletes who have it all can lose it all to gambling addiction," *Times Union (Albany)* (January 14, 2003): A7.

47. Scott McGregor, "Art Schlichter: Bad bets and wasted talent," *The Cincinnati Enquirer* (July 2, 2000): S1.

48. "Leonard Tose, a big spender died on April 15, 2003, aged 88," *The Economist* (Apirl 24, 2003): 1.

49. Mort Olshan, "The best game ever played," *Gambling Times* 26 (October-November 2002): 2.

50. Roger Mooney, "The fall of Adrian McPherson," *The Bradenton Herald* (May 2, 2003): S1.

51. Jeff Shain, Stephen F. Holder, and Susan Miller Degnan, "Campus gambling? You can bet on it—Wagering part of college experience," *The Miami Herald* (December 29,2002): S1.

Chapter 9

1. Jeff Benedict and Don Yeager, *Pros and cons: The criminals who play in the NFL* (New York: Warner Books, 1998).

2. Federal Bureau of Investigation, *Crime in the United States* (Washington, DC: United States Government Printing Office, 2001).

3. Benedict and Yaeager, *Pros and cons,* p. 263.

4. Gregg Lanotte, "Simpson judge OKs jury prospects who admit bias," *U.S. News* (September 25, 1996): 3.

5. "Ranger college football player jailed on murder charge," *Associated Press State and Local Wire* (April 11, 2003).

6. Frank Schmalleger, *Criminology today,* Third edition (Upper Saddle River, NJ: Prentice-Hall, 2002), p. 292.

7. Bendedict and Yaeger, *Pros and cons,* p. 263.

8. Lori Shontz, "Former Pitt player found stabbed to death," *Pittsburgh Post Gazette* (December 21, 2002): B8.

9. Akillah Johnson and Monte Morin, "Shooting clouds future for NFL draft prospect," *Los Angeles Times* (April 22, 2003): 2: 1.

10. Josh Noel and Joseph Schiefelbein, "SU football player killed outside a bar," *State Times Morning Advocate* (Janaury 25, 2003): 1B.

11. Gerhard Falk, *Murder, its forms, conditions and causes* (Jefferson, NC: McFarland Publishers, 1990), p. 31.

12. "Woman awaiting trial in slaying of husband," *The Associated Press* (March 18, 2003).

13. Jill Swederstrom, "Former Iowa State U. football players indicted," *Iowa State Daily* (January 24, 2003).

14. Jerry Lauzon, "Suspension of players upheld at U. of Maine," *Portland Press Herald* (October 22, 2002): 1A.

15. John Jackson, "Notre Dame four formally charged in rape case," *Chicago Sun Times* (May 25, 2002): 112.

16. Kevin Tuczek, "Michigan Sate recruit pleads guilty to lesser charge," *The State News* (May 25, 2001): 28.

17. "Louisiana football player accused in rape," *Morning Advocate* (Baton Rouge) (January 18, 2003): 7B.

18. Jeff Shelman, " School as well as courts, must rule," *Star Tribune* (August 17, 2001): 8C.

19. "Sports: College football champions charged," *World News Digest* (September 21, 1995): 1.

20. M. P. Koss, C. A. Gidycz, and N. Wisniewski, "The scope of rape," *Journal of Consulting and Clinical Psychology,* 55 (1987): 162-170.

21. Public Law 102-325, Section 486 (c). Higher Education Amendment of 1992.

22. Patricia Y. Martin and Robert A. Hummer, "Fraternities and rape on campus," *Gender and Society* 3(4) (1989): 462.

23. Federal Bureau of Investigation, *Uniform crime reports.*

24. Ken Berger, "Grand jury hears Jets versus Santa case," *Newsday* (February 11, 2003): A68.

25. "Iowa's lineman suspended from team on assault charge," *Associated Press Sports News* (April 11, 2003).

26. Bureau of Justice Statistics, *Criminal victimization in the United States* (Washington, DC: U.S. Department of Justice, Office of Justice Programs, 2000), p. 172.

27. "Sports: College football champions charged," p. 1.

28. Karen Goldberg Goff, "NFL's tarnished heroes," *Insight on the News* 14(46) (December 14, 1998): 37.

29. "Police probing FSU football player," *Times-Picayune* (December 24, 2002): 2.

30. Ric Anderson, "KU trouble: DA files charges against football players," *Topeka Capital Journal* (September 12, 2001): 2.

31. Scott Cain, "Razorbacks report," *Arkansas Democrat Gazette* (April 13, 2003): 36.

32. Josh Robbins, "Trial date set for McPhersons's alledged bookie," *Sun Sentinel* (May 8, 2003): S3.

33. "Sports: NFL Cowboys' Irving gets probation; other developments," *World News Digest* (August 29, 1996): 1.

34. Substance Abuse and Mental Health Services Administration, *National household survey on drug abuse, 1999* (Washington DC: U.S. Government Printing Office, 2000).

35. Bill Coats, "MU football player faces weapons charge," *St. Louis Post Dispatch* (February 25, 2003): D1.

36. Robert Ratcliffe, "Cowboys' Switzer arrested," *Houston Chronicle* (August 5, 1997): 1.

37. Luke Cyphers and Michael O'Keefe, "Are jocks gunning for trouble?" *Daily News* (March 3, 2002): 4.

38. Ibid., p. 4.

39. John L. Smith, "At 69, misguided team player gets ready for another sentence," *Las Vegas Review-Journal* (December 17, 2002): 18.

40. Lee Sensenbrenner, "Athlete faces criminal charge; Johnson arrested for drunk driving," *Capital Times* (November 8, 2002): 2A.

41. Mark Maske and Greg Sandoval, "Smith Faces $20,000 fine if convicted," *The Washington Post* (April 30, 2003): DO2.

42. <http://slicker-productions.com/comp/cornerarchive/corner27.html>.

43. Ibid., p. 5.

44. Matthew McKelvey, "Separating sports and real life: How professional sports leagues keep ahtletes out of criminal procedures," *New England Journal on Civil and Criminal Confinement* 27(1) (2001): 91.

45. Todd W. Crosset, Jeffrey R. Benedict, and Mark A. McDonald, "Male student athletes reported for sexual assault: A survey of campus police departments and judicial affairs offices," in Michael S. Kimmel and Michael A. Messner, eds., *Men's lives* (New York: Allyn and Bacon/Longman 2001), pp. 144-145.

46. Bureau of Justice Statistics, *Homicide trends in the U.S.: Trends by race* (Washington, DC: U.S. Government Printing Office, 2003), p. 2.

47. H. Snyder, *Juvenile arrests 2002* (Washington, DC: Office of Juvenile Justice and Delinquency Prevention, 2003), p. 1.

48. Anthony E. O. King, "Understanding violence among young African-American males: An Afro-centric perspective," *Journal of Black Studies* 28(1) (September 1997): 79.

49. Nathan I. Huggins, *Black odyssey: The Afro-American ordeal in slavery* (New York: Vintage, 1990).

50. Langston Hughes, *Fight for freedom: The story of the NAACP* (New York: Norton, 1962).

51. Gunnar Myrdal, *An American dilemma* (New York: Harper Row, 1944).

52. Robert Staples, "Masculinity and race, the dual dilemma of black men," *Social Issues* 34 (Winter 1978): 169.

53. Bernie Parrish, *They call it a game* (New York: The Dial Press, 1971), p. 11.

54. Ibid., p. 81.

55. Ibid., p. 195.

56. Ibid., p. 199.

57. Dan E. Moldea, *Interference: How organized crime influences professional football* (New York: William Murrow and Co., Inc., 1989), p. 352.

58. Ibid., p. 21.

59. Ibid., p. 57.

60. Dan E. Moldea, *Moldea vs. New York Times: The untold story* (Moldea.com and Investigating Journalism), p. 7.

61. Gerald Eskenazi, *Interference: How organized crime influences professional football* (September 3, 1989): 8.

62. Christopher Hansen, "Playing 'chicken' with the First Amendment," *Columbia Journalism Review* (May/June 1994): 1.

63. Tim Green, *Titans* (New York: Turner Publishing, 1994).

64. "Nole no more: FSU boots McPherson amid blank check investigation," *Sports Illustrated* (November 26, 2002): 1.

65. George Anastasia, *Blood and honor: Inside the Scarfo mob* (New York: Morrow), p. 268.

66. Frank Schmalleger, *Criminology today* (Upper Saddle River, NJ: Prentice-Hall, 2002), p. 212.

67. Elliott Currie, "Crime and social inequality," in Ronald Weitzer, ed., *current controversies in criminology* (Upper Saddle River, NJ: Prentice-Hall, 2003), p. 16.

68. Ronald D. Hunter and Mark L. Dantzker, *Crime and criminality* (Upper Saddle River, NJ: Prentice-Hall, 2002): 15.

69. Howard Abadinsky, *Drug abuse: An introduction* (Chicago: Nelson-Hall, 1989), p. 120.

70. National Institute on Drug Abuse, "Cocaine use in America," *Prevention Networks* (April 1986): 1-10.

Chapter 10

1. Andrew Doyle, "An atheist in Alabama is someone who doesn't believe in Bear Bryant," in Patrick B. Miller, ed., *The sporting world of the modern south* (Urbana and Chicago: The University of Illionis Press, 2002), p. 217.

2. Ibid., p. 270.

3. Patrick B. Miller, "The manly, the moral and the proficient: College sport in the new south," in Patrick B. Miller, ed., *The sporting world of the modern south* (Urbana and Chicago: The University of Illinois Press, 2002), pp. 17-56.

4. Charles Martin, "Integrating New Year's Day," in Patrick B. Miller, ed., *The sporting world of the modern south* (Urbana and Chicago: The University of Illinois Press, 2002), p. 175.

5. Wilbur J. Cash, *The mind of the south* (New York: Vintage Books, 1941), p. 52.

6. Ted Ownby, "Manhood, memory and white man's sports in the American south," in Patrick B. Miller, ed., *The sporting world of the modern south* (Urbana and Chicago: The University of Illinois Press, 2002), p. 327.

7. James J. Duderstadt, *Intercollegiate athletics and the American university* (Ann Arbor: The University of Michigan Press, 2000), p. 48.

8. Ibid., p. 109.

9. Aristotle, *The politics*, Carnes Lord, translator (Chicago: The University of Chicago Press, 1984), p. 10.

10. Joe Horrigan, "Joe Carr," *The Coffin Corner* VI(6) (Huntingdon, PA: Professional Football Research Association, 1984).

11. "Elmer F. Layden (1903-1973)," available at <http://www.sportsecyclopedia.com/nfl/comish/layden.html>.

12. "Bert Bell: The commissioner," *The Coffin Corner* (Huntington, PA: Professional Football Researchers Association, 1996), p. 2.

13. David Harris, *The league: The rise and decline of the NFL* (New York: Bantam Books, 1986), p. 11.

14. Ibid., p. 18.

15. David Lidsky, "Innovators: This is NFL films," *Fortune Small Business* (August 22, 2002): 7.

16. Michael Lewis, "High commissioner Pete Rozelle," in *Time 100: Builders and titans* (New York: Time Inc., 2003), p. 1.

17. Committee on the Judiciary of the United States Senate, Hearing before the subcommitte on antitrust monopolies and business rights (Washington DC: U.S. Government Printing Office, 1966), p. 33.

18. Ronald Grover, "Is this an end run by the NFL?" *Business Week* (October 27, 2003).

19. Tom Lowry, "The NFL machine," *Business Week* (January 27, 2003): 86.

20. "NFL may soon return to Los Angeles," *SLAM Sports* (Janurary 25, 2003): 1.

21. Jon Morgan, *Glory for sale* (Baltimore, MD: Bancroft Press, 1997), p. 368.

22. Manny Topol, "A super commish," *Newsday* (January 26, 2003): FO6.

23. Megan Merrill, "Russia's big gamble on American football," *The Moscow Times* (April 7, 2003): Sec. 2653.

24. Ibid., p. 1, Sec. 2653.

25. Rick Cantu, "European imports," *The Austin American Statesman* (Janurary 11, 2002): C1.

26. Ian S. Bruce, "Gridiron grip," *The Sunday Herald* (June 15, 2003): 15.

27. Ibid., p. 27.

28. Carlo D'Este, *Eisenhower: A soldier's life* (New York: Henry Holt and Co., 2002), p. 14.

29. Bud Vestal, *Jerry Ford up close* (New York: Coward, McCann and Geoghegan, 1974), p. 57.

30. Gil Nielsen, "IDT corporation appoints Jack Kemp to its board of directors," *Business Wire* (April 4, 2003): 1.

31. Eddie Hall, "Congressman speaks at Kansas State U. about the future of America," *Kansas State Collegian* (April 29, 2002): 9.

32. Gwen Florio, "Byron R. White, 1917-2002: Retired Justice made state proud," *The Denver Post* (April 16, 2002): A-O1.

33. "The Honorable Alan Page, Minnesota Supreme Court Justice," National Public Radio <www.npr.org/programs/npc/2001/>.

34. "2003 NFL predictions," *Athlon Sports* (2003): 47.

Index

Abram, Jimmy Desmond, 203
Academics
   anti-intellectualism, 23, 28-29
   deficiency overlooked in
      recruitment, 41-42
   failure, football players and, 43-44
   players, achieving at, 12-17
   unimportant, 23
Achieved status, 27-28
Achievement, as value, 2
Active crowd, 146
Activity, as essence of football, 3
Adams, K.C. Bud, 125
Adams, Lorraine, 23-24
Adultery culture, 77-78
Advertising
   college bowl games, 179
   and commercial artists, 181-182
   and health care sponsorship, ban on,
      186
   the Super Bowl, 179-181
Against Our Will (Brownmiller), 150
Agents, 186-189
Aggression, 19-25. *See also* Violence
   sexual, 78
   and spectator identification, 76
   theories of, 75
Aggressive crowd, 144
Aiello, Sam, 205
Alexander, Kermit, 102
All-American Football Conference
   (AAFC), 62
Allen, James, 202
Allen, Paul G., 131
American Cheerleader, 59, 116, 118
American Football League (AFL), 9, 62
American Open Partner Stunt title, 118

American Professional Football
   Association, 61-62
American Professional Football
   Conference, 61
America's Recruiting Magazine, 36
Amphetamine use, 121
Anderson, Elizabeth, 164
Anderson, Mike, 38
Andrews, Matt, 133
Anti-intellectualism, 23, 28-29
Any Given Sunday, 172
Arena Football League (AFL), 63-64,
   157
Arens, William, 99
Arms, Robert, 21
Arrington, Jill, 161
Ascribed status, 27
Assault, football players and, 204-206

Baldinger, Brian, 67
Banks, Carl, 101
"Basking in reflected glory," 137
Battles, Cliff, 96
Bauman, Charlie, 111
Beausay, William, 73-74
Beebe, Don, 102
Belichick, Bill, 165
Bell, "Bert," 228-229
"Bench warmer," 34
Benedict, Jeff, 199-200, 201, 203, 205
Benner, Bill, 48-49
Bennett, Cornelius, 200
Benning, Damon, 203
Benson, Tom, 129
Bernstein, Bonnie, 67
Bernstein, Mark F., 167

Bidwell, William, 131
Biletnikoff, Fred, 94
Bissinger, H.G., 19, 96
Black athletes. *See* Ethnicity
"Black Athletes: Fact or Fiction?", 52
Black Sunday, 171
Blades, Brian, 201
Blanda, George, 94
Blank, Arthur, 130
"Blindside," 34
Bornstein, Steve, 232-233
Bowden, Bobby, 54
Bowlen, Pat, 126
Bradshaw, Terry, 1-3
Brallier, John K., 61
Brancato, Robert, 170
Brooks, Aaron, 73
Brooks, Jermaine, 206
Brown, James E., 80
Brown, Mike, 125
Brown, Paul, 66, 72
Brown, Ruben, 3
Brownmiller, Susan, 150
Buckwalter, Ronald J. (Judge), 13
Buford, Bill, 21
Burris, Jeff, 3
Business, football as a, 86-87, 232-233
    advertising, 179-182
    agents, 186-189
    gambling, 194-197
    lawyers, 189-191
    merchandise, 182-186
    NFL Films, 178-179
    small business contracts, 197
    stadiums, construction of, 191-193
    ticket sales, 177-178

Caldwell, Jim, 17
Cameron, Cam, 48-49
Campbell, Don, 37
Campus Sexual Assault Victims' Bill
    of Rights, 204
Cancer, death due to, 105-106
Carr, Joe, 227-228

Carroll, John M., 168
Carruth, Rae, 78
Carter, Leonard, 25
Casual crowd, 19
Cattell, Raymond, 52
Chappel, Dave, 103
Charitable events, football and, 241-242
Charity Gold Classic Tour, 242
Cheerleader Supply Company, 117
Cheerleaders
    American Cheeleader, 59, 116, 118
    college football, 58-59
    competitions, 118
    Dallas Cowboys Cheerleaders, 156
    National Cheerleaders Association
        (NCA), 117
    pom-pom, 117
    scholarships for, 119
Cheerleaders of America, 59
Choyinski, Joe, 15
Chu, Lawrence, 76
Clark, Burton, 36
Clemons, Charlie, 209
Clinton, Bill (President), 13-14
Coaches, 109-112
    college football
        power of, 224, 225-226
        as role model, 53-56
        salary, 46-47
    discrimination against black, 72. *See
        also* Ethnicity
    recruitment of, 110
    salary, 109-110
    and violent outbursts, 111-112
Coker, Larry, 38, 54
College football
    advertising and, 50, 179
    bowl games, 46, 59, 98
        advertising and, 179
    cheerleaders, 58-59
    coach
        power of, 224, 225-226
        as role model, 53-56
        salary, 46-47
    corporate sponsors, 45, 46
    ethnicity and, 51-52

College football *(continued)*
  media and, 45-46
  money and, 44-51
  players, 52-53
  politics, 224-226
  recruiting players, 35-44
  as subculture, 33-35
  team violations, 48
  television and, 45
  "Top Six," 56
  twelve-game season, 47
"Collegiate subculture," 36
Columbine High School, 23-24
Commercial artists, 181-182
Commission for Opportunity in
    Athletics, 55
Commissioners, NFL, 226-232
Committee on Fair Employment
    Practices, 72
Community Quarterback award, 241
Concussion, 120
Conduct, gender and, 149-152
Considine, Tim, 34
Conspicuous consumption, 8
Contract
  advisors, 186-189
  one-sided, 14-15
Control, as political issue, 225
Controlled violence, 76
Conventionalized crowd, 20
Cooper, B.P., 137
"Cornerback," 34
Corporate sponsorship, 45, 46
Crime, football players and, 210-213.
    See also Violence
  assault, 204-206
  Benedict-Yaeger research, 199-200,
      201-203, 205
  drug offenses, 206-207
  drugs and, 213-217
  drunk driving, 208-209
  gambling and, 213-217
  inattention to, 200
  larceny, 206
  murder, 200-202
  rape, 202-204

Crime, football players and *(continued)*
  and sociology, 217-219
  weapons charges, 207-208
Criminality, football players and,
    210-213
Crossett, Todd W., 210-211
Crowd, The (LeBon), 147
Crutcher, Chris, 169
Csonka, Larry, 96
Culpepper, Daunte, 73
Culture, football, 135-137
Cummings, Von C., 80
Cureton, Tai Kwan, 13
Curry, Bill, 142

Daley, Patrick, 190
Dallas Cowboys Cheerleaders, 156
Davis, Al, 126-127, 189
Dawson, Len, 96
Deference to Male Authority, 40
DeLillo, Don, 97
Denney, Reuel, 82
DFJItalia, 80
Dictionary, football, 163
Dierdorf, Dan, 159
Diet, football fans, 141
DiFonzo, Luigi, 80
Disproportionate importance, 34-35
Ditka, Mike, 103
Dockett, Darnell, 206
Doctor, team, 120
Domestic life, players, 76-79
Dooley, Vince, 142
Dorsett, Tony, 184-185
Douglas, Terry, 97
Draper, Marion, 58
Drug offenses, football players and,
    206-207
Drug overdose, death from, 106
Drug testing, mandatory, 27
Drug use, 121, 213-217, 219
Drunk driving, football players and,
    208-209
Dungy, Tony, 73

Dunning, Eric, 12
Durkheim, Emile, 111

"Eagles Court," 145
Early death, fear of, 105-106
Edwards, Herman, 73
Edwards, Terrence, 142
Efficiency, 4
Eisenhower, Dwight (President),
    237-238
Eligibility rules, and academics, 12
Elliott, John "Jumbo," 204-205
Ellis, William Webb, 7
Elway, John, 185
Emmert, Mark, 146
End Zone (DeLillo), 97
Endorsements
    players, 69-70
    as revenue, 183-184
Engberg, Dick, 159
Equity in Athletics Disclosure Act of
    1994, 55
Esiason, Norman J. "Boomer," 67, 159
Ethnicity, 4, 15-17
    in college football, 51-52
    and criminality, 210-213
    in the NFL, 71-73, 87-91
European Federation of American
    Football (EFAF), 235-236
Existential deprivation, 136
Exploitation, athletes, 14
Expressive crowd, 20, 144
Extreme Football League (XFL), 63

Fanatics, fans as, 73-76
    Andrews, Matt, 133
    "basking in reflected glory," 137
    diet, poor, 141
    and existential validation, 136
    and fantasy football, 147-149
    and football culture, 135-137
    generational differences, 137-139
    in-groups, 34, 141-144

Fanatics, fans as *(continued)*
    Joseph, Deborah, 135
    loyalty and, 143
    and militant enthusiasm, 139, 140
    out-groups, 34, 141-144
    regional differences, 137-139
    and relative deprivation, 136-137
    and tailgate parties, 139-141
    Vice Hall of Fans, 133-134
    and violence, 20-21, 37, 139-140,
        144-147
Fantasy football, 147-149
Fantasy Football Guide, The, 149
Fatalities, football, 25-27, 56-58. *See
    also* Injuries, football
Females. *See* Women
Fenner, Derrick, 201
Fiedler, Jay, 41, 93, 105, 237
Fields of Honor (Pont), 166-167
Fighting Fans (Dunning), 12
Financial advisor, 107
First American Austrian Football Club
    (FAAC), 235
Fiscus, Lason, 61
Fitch Ratings, 191
Flutie, Doug, 70
Food, football and, 184
Football
    and aggression, 19-25
    "birth" of, 7
    books, 166-170
    as a business. *See* Business, football
        as a
    cheerleaders. *See* Cheerleaders
    children's, 17-19
    coaches. *See* Coaches
    college. *See* College football
    commissioners, 226-232
    culture, 135-137
    doctor, 120
    fanatics, 73-76
    fatalities, 25-27, 56-58
    general managers, 122
    history of, 61-64
    ideological function of, 243-244
    injuries. *See* Injuries, football

Football *(continued)*
    integration and, 244
    jokes, 174-175
    language, 162-163
    magazines, 164-166
    and masculinity, 7-8, 10-11
    movies, 170-173
    newspapers and, 161-163
    officials, 114-116
    owners, 123-132
    players. *See* Players, football
    political function of, 243-244
    race and. *See* Ethnicity
    referees, 115
    scouts, 112-113
    and social class, 81-82
    social mobility and, 24
    social psychology of, 7-12
    and socialization, 243
    socioemotional function of, 243
    songs, 173-174
    in the South, 221-224
    stadiums, 65-66
        construction profits, 191-193
    as status system, 27-32
    televised, 64-71, 155-161
    trainers, 113-114
    as warfare, 12
*Football: The Ivy League Origins of an
    American Obsession*
    (Bernstein), 167
Football Hall of Fame, 74-75
    Vice Hall of Fans, 133-134
Football language, 162-163
Ford, Gerald (President), 238
Ford, William Clay, 128
Foster, DeShaun, 36
Fox Television, 65
Fraud, football players as victims of,
    79-81
Free agency, 113
Freedom, as value, 4
Friday Night Lights (Bissinger), 19, 96
Friedgen, Ralph, 53-54
Frontiere, Georgia, 131
Frustration-aggression hypothesis, 75
Frykholm, Linda, 80

Galloping Ghost, The, 171
Gamble, Harry, 236
Gambling, 194-197, 213-217
Gardner, Talman, 206-207
Garland, Daniel, 52
Gender, influence on conduct, 149-152.
    See also Masculinity
General managers, 122
Gennarelli, Chris, 181
Gent, Peter, 170
George, Eddie, 49
German Football Federation, 235
Gibbs, Joe, 67
Gibson, Chris, 181
Gidycz, C.A., 204
Gifford, Frank, 158
Glazer, Malcom, 129
Glen Ridge High School, rape, 22
Global Sports and Entertainment, 80
Glory for Sale (Morgan), 169
Goldstein, Jeffrey, 21
Goldstein, Rube, 15
Gomes, Stefan, 202
Grange, Harold Edward "Red," 2, 3
Green, Tim, 216
Green Bay Packers, and merchandise
    marketing, 183
Greenberg, Hank, 71
Greene, Jonathan, 24
Griese, Bob, 103
Griffin, Archie, 49
Gruden, Jon, 183
Gunsel, Austin, 229

Hadley, Lawrence, 70-71
Halas, George, 62, 128-129
Hamby, Mike, 101-102
Harris, Eric, 23, 24
Harrison, Marvin, 69
Hay, Ralph, 61
Hayes, Wayne "Woody," 49, 111
Health care sponsorship, advertising
    ban on, 186
Heath, Jo Jo, 201

Heffelfinger, William W. (Pudge), 61
Heisman Trophy, 49
Henry, Wilbur, 96
"Herkie" jump, 117
Herkimer, Lawrence, 117
Hess, Leon, 123
Hierarchal, sports as, 89-90
Hofschneider, Rocky, 24
Hogan, James, 41
Hogenson, Sherlyn, 141
Holtz, Lou, 54
"Hometown Huddle," 241
Horne, Tony, 209-210
Hornung, Paul, 195
Horween, Ralph, 92
Housel, David, 142-143
Hughes, Roger, 41
Huizenga, H. Wayne, 123
Hunt, Lamar, 127
"Husker Power," lyrics, 173

Ideological function, football, 243-244
Imitate the Tiger, 169-170
Income, players, 3
Individualism, as value, 2
"In-group," 34, 141-144
"Initiates," 39
Injuries, football, 26. *See also*
          Fatalities, football
   concussion, 120
   health problems, retired players, 121
   punch-drunk syndrome, 81, 105
   second-impact syndromes, 58, 120
Instinctual view of aggression, 75
Integration, football and, 244
*Interference: How Organized Crime
          Influences Professional
          Football* (Moldea), 215-216
Irsay, Jim, 125
Irsay, Robert, 125
Irvin, Michael, 207
Iso, Ariko, 114
Izo, George, 103-104

Jackson, Steve, 209
James, Edgerrin, 69
Jenkins, Sally, 37
Jewish football players, 91-93
Jim Thorpe—All American, 171
"Jock culture," 23-24
Johnson, Al, 208
Johnson, Brad, 236-237
Johnson, Branch, 99
Johnson, Traver, 112
Jokes, football, 174-175
Jones, Darnell, 80
Jones, Jerry, 128
Jordan, Barry, 81
Jordan, Charles, 201
Joseph, Debroah, 135-137

Kaplan, Louis "Kid," 15
Karras, Alex, 194-195
Kelly, Jim, 95
Kemp, Jack, 8, 9-10, 238-239
Kemp, Ray, 71
Kimble, C.E., 137
King, Phil, 92
King, Shaun, 73
Kinsey, Mario, 206
Klebold, Dylan, 23, 24
Knott, Eric, 203
Knowles, Scott, 70-71
Knute Rockne: All-American, 171-172
Kopay, David, 99-100
Koss, M.P., 204
Kraft, Robert, 65, 123

La Monte, Robert, 188
Lambert, Jack, 96
Lane, Fred, 202
Lang, Gale, 43-44
Lang, Lynn, 42-43
Language, football, 162-163
Language of Sports, The (Considine),
   34
Lapchick, Richard E., 17, 88

Larceny, football players and, 206
Last Picture Show, The (McMurtry), 97
Last Texas Hero, The (Douglas), 97
Lawyers, 189-191
Layden, Emer, 228
LeBon, Gustave, 147
Lefkowitz, Bernard, 22-23
Legal advisor, 107
Leonard, Benny, 15
Lerner, Alfred, 124-125
Levine, Israel, 92
Levy, Marv, 110-111
Lewis, Chad, 237
Liberty, as value, 4
Licensed goods, revenue from, 182-183
Lillard, Joe, 71
Little, Leonard, 209
Locker room, women in, 163-164
Lombardi, Vince, 10
London Football Association, 7
Longest Yard, The, 172
Looney Jr., Joe Don, 97
Lorenz, Konrad, 21, 139-140
Losing, importance of, 10-11
Loyalty, fan, 143. *See also* Fanatics, fans as
Luckman, Sid, 71, 92
Lujack, Johnny, 93
Lukens, Donald, 80
Lurie, Jeff, 127

Madden, John, 67, 158-159
Magazine, The, 164-165
Magazines, football and, 164-166
Male initiation ritual, football as, 99
Maloney, Michael T., 14
Mandell, Arnold, 121
Manley, Dexter, 41
Manning, Peyton, 69
Mara, Tim, 127
Marino, Dan, 95, 160
Marshall, Robert, 71
Mascots, 156
Masculinity, 7-8, 10-11, 39, 98-100

Material comfort, 3
Matson, Ollie, 51
McCloskey, Michael, 129
McCombs, Billy Joe "Red," 128
McCormick, Robert E., 14
McGahee, Willis, 188
McGonagle, W. Brad, 41
McMahon, Vince, 62-63
McMonigle, Sean, 146
McMurtry, Larry, 97
McNabb, Donovan, 73, 241
McNair, Robert, 126
McPherson, Adrian, 196, 217
Means, Albert, "selling of," 42
Meat on the Hood (Shaw), 97
"Megadosing," 27
Memphis Business Journal, The, 49
Mentors in Violence Prevention program, 37
Merchandise, football, 182-186
Mesick, James, 148
Michaels, Al, 159
Milhovilovic, M.A., 101
"Militant enthusiasm," fans and, 139, 140
Minor, Paris, 202
Mitchell, Brian, 241
Mix, Ron, 92-93
Modell, Arthur, 124
Mohammad, Mushin, 208
Moldea, Dan E., 215-216
Monarchy, presidency as, 14
Money. *See* Business, football as a; Salary
"Monsters of the Gridiron," 69
Montana, Joe, 94-95
Moon, Warren, 78-79
"Moral density," 111
"Moral holiday," 144
Morgan, Jon, 169
Morgan, Mindy, 163
Morris, Bryan "Bam," 205-206
Motley, Marion, 72
Moulds, Eric, 70
Movies, football, 170-173
"Mr. Touchdown USA," lyrics, 173
Murder, football players and, 200-202

Namath, Joe, 94
Nandi boys, 40
Nantz, Jim, 67
National Assessment of Educational
    Progress, 31
National Center for Catastrophic Sport
    Injury Research (NCCSIR),
    56
National Cheerleaders Association
    (NCA), 117
National Collegiate Athletic
    Association (NCAA), 13, 44
National Football League (NFL), 1, 62
    and charitable events, 241-242
    commissioners, 226-232
    community, 240-242
    international, 235-237
    as revenue source, 232-233
    and Southern states, 221-224
    and urban warfare, 233-235
National Football League Players
    Association (NFLPA), 185
National Indoor Football League, 157
National Institute of Occupational
    Safety and Health, 106
National Opinion Research Center
    (NORC), 30, 53
National Signing Day, 38
National Trainers' Association, 114
Newsome, Ozzie, 122
Newspapers, football and, 161-163
NFL. *See* National Football League
    (NFL)
NFL Films, 178-179, 230
NFL Sunday Ticket, 144
Noble, Brandon, 237
North Carolina Triad, 143-144
North Dallas Forty (Gent), 170
North Dallas Forty (movie), 170-171
"Notre Dame Victory March," lyrics,
    174

Occupational prestige, 29-30
"Offiant," 39

Officials, 114-116
Ohio, football and, 96
O.J. Simpson Story, The, 172-173
O'Leary, George, 38-39
Olson, Lisa, 164
On Aggression (Lorenz), 21, 139-140
One-sided contract, 14-15
Orange Bowl, 59
Oriard, Michael, 39-40
Orr, Terry, 80
Ortiz, Steven, 77-78
Osborne, Tom, 239
Our Guys (Lefkowitz), 22
"Out-group," 34, 141-144
Outing, 39
Owners, 123-132

Page, Alan, 96, 240
Pain, acceptance of, 11-12
Paper Lion (Plimpton), 170
Parrish, Bernie, 213-215
Pederson, Paul, 141
Pennsylvania, football and, 93-95
Personal Seat License, 66
Peter, Christian, 78
Phillips, Lawrence, 78, 203
Place, Craig, 24
Players, football, 52-53
    and adultery, 77-78
    black. *See* Ethnicity
    and cancer, death due to, 105-106
    and charitable events, 241-242
    crime and. *See* Crime, football
        players and
    and domestic life, 76-79
    drug overdose, death from, 106
    early death of, 105-106
    endorsements, 69-70
    jewish, 91-93
    masculinity and, 7-8, 10-11, 39,
        98-100
    from Ohio, 96
    from Pennsylvania, 93-95
    politicians who were, 237-240

Players, football *(continued)*
   retired, 100-107
   as revenue, 184-186
   salaries, 3, 68
   and social stratification, 85-86
   from Texas, 96-97
   as victims of fraud, 79-81
   wives of, 77-78
Play-off games, television and, 157
Plimpton, George, 170
Poitras, Marc, 70-71
Pollard, Fritz, 71, 168
Pom-pom, 117
Pont, Sally, 166-167
Pop Warner Little Scholars, 17-18
Pop Warner Youth Football League, 17
Portrait of America, 98
Position scheduling, 157
Pros and Cons: The Criminals Who Play in the NFL (Benedict/Yaeger), 199-200, 201-203, 205
Prototype of violent crime, assault, 205
"Punch drunk" syndrome, 81, 105
"Pyramiding," 27

Race, football and. *See* Ethnicity
"Racial stacking," 73
Radio, and football, 67-68, 156
Radovich, William, 230-231
"Raiders Nation," 139
"Rambling Wreck from Georgia Tech, The," lyrics, 174
Rape, football players and, 202-204
Reagan, Ronald (President), 238
Recruitment
   college football players, 35-44
   NFL coaches, 110
Red Grange and the Rise of Modern Football (Carroll), 168
Referees, 115
Relative deprivation, 136-137
Renfro, Mel, 104
Retired football players, 100-107
   health problems, 121

Richardson, Jerry, 130
Riesman, David, 82
Riots, crowd, 20-21, 37
Robeson, Paul, 71
Robinson, Ray, 167
Rockne of Notre Dame (Robinson), 167
Rogers, Sam, 3
Rooney, Dan, 124
Rose Bowl, 46, 59, 98
Rosenbloom, Carroll, 131, 196
Rosenblum, "Slapsie" Maxie, 15
Rosenhaus, Drew, 188
Ross, Barney, 15
Rozelle, Pete, 229-230
Rudman, William J., 88
Ruggiero, John, 70-71
Running Loose (Crutcher), 169
Russakoff, Dale, 23-24
Ryan, Chris, 181

Sachs, Carolyn, 76
Salary
   college football coaches, 46-47
   NFL coaches, 109-110
   players, 3, 68
Salary cap, 113
Sanders, Deion, 81, 160, 205
Schlister, Art, 195
Scholarships, athletic, 15
School Ties, 92, 171
Schramm, Tex, 119
Schwartz, Issy, 15
Schwartz, Stephen, 30
Scouting Combine, 112
Scouts, 112-113
Scranton, Pierce, 121
Second-impact syndromes, 58, 120
Sex appeal, as recruitment device, 40-41
Sexism, 11
Sexual aggression, football players, 78
Sexual symbolism, football as, 99
Shake Down the Thunder (Sperber), 167
Shaw, Gary, 97

Sherman Anti-Trust Act, 230, 231
Sigelman, Lee, 39
Simmons, Bob, 17
Simpson, O.J., 79, 199
Sixteen Personality Factor
    Questionnaire, 52
Slater, Fred, 71
"Slave trade," 16
Small business contracts, 197
Small World Fantasy Professional
    Football League, 148
Smith, Bruce, 208
Smith, Musa, 165
Snyder, Dan, 127-128
Sobol, Ed, 230
Sobol, Steve, 230
Soccer, 7
    violence at events, 20-21
Social class, football and, 81-82
Social learning theory, 75
Social mobility, football and, 244
Social stratification, 85-86
Socialization, football and, 243
Socioemotional function, football, 243
Sociology, crime and, 217-219
Solar ritual, football as, 99
Songs, football, 173-174
Sonnenfeld, Stefan, 181
Southern Methodist University, "slush
    fund," 48
Southern states, football and, 221-224
Spanos, Dean, 126
"Special admissions," 43. *See also*
    Academics
Spectator identification, 75-76
Sperber, Murray, 43, 167
Sporting News, The, 165-166
Sports Broadcasting Act, 231
Sports Illustrated, 59, 166
Sportscasters, 67, 156, 158-161
Sportsline, 148
Spurrier, Steve, 109, 110
"Stacking," drugs, 26
"Stacking," racial, 88
Stadiums, 65-66
    construction profits, 191-193

Stagg, Amos Alonzo, 2, 167-168
Stagg's University, 167-168
Stark, Melissa, 160-161
State University of New York (SUNY)
    at Buffalo, 50-51
Staubach, Roger, 70
Stern, Bill, 156
Steroid use, 26-27, 121
Storck, Carl "Scummy," 228
Stringer, Korey, 120
Subcultural language, sports, 34
Summerall, Pat, 67, 158
Super Bowl, 98, 135
    advertising and, 179-181
    first televised, 157-158
    XXXIV, crimes against players of,
        209-210
*Superrep: America's Recruiting
    Magazine*, 35
Switzer, Barry, 207

Tagliabue, Paul, 231-232
Tailgate party, 139-141
Tarpoff, Nick, 207
Taylor, Steven, 25
Television, football and, 64-71, 155-161
Texas, football and, 96-97
Texas Football (Campbell), 37
They Call It a Game (Parrish), 213-215
Third Down and Forever (Looney Jr.),
    97
Thorpe, Jim, 61, 62, 74-75, 226-227
Ticket sales, 177-178
Tisch, Preston Robert, 127
Titans (Green), 216
Tobias, Brandon, 38
Toler, Burl, 51
Tomlin, Joe, 17
Tose, Leonard, 195-196
Total Entertainment and Athletes
    Management (TEAAM),
    185-186
Toxic cascade, 58
Trainers, 113-114

"Trench coat mafia," 23, 24
Trow, Martin, 36
Tucker, Ryan, 205
Turner, Frederick Jackson, 28
Twelve-game season, college football, 47

United Nations Trade Honduras Project, 80

Values, 1
Veblen, Thorsten, 8
Vice Hall of Fans, 133-134
Violations, college football teams, 48
Violence. *See also* Crime, football players and
   and aggression, 19-25
   catharsis, 152-153
   in children's sports, 18
   domestic, 78
   fan, 20-21, 37, 139-140, 144-147
   men against other men, 151
   at sporting events, 20-21, 37
Visser, Lesley, 160
Vogler, Conrad, 30

Wadlington, Devron, 201
"Walk-on," college teams, 55-56
Wann, Daniel, 75
Warfare, football as form of, 12
Warfield, Paul, 96
Warner, Glenn "Pop," 17
Watson, Justin, 210
Watts, Julius Caesar, 239
Wauford, Jon, 112
Weapons charges, football players and, 207-208

Weathersby, Dennis, 201-202
Weaver, Wayne, 125-126
Welch, Michael, 79
WestwoodOne, 67-68
Wheeler, Rashid, 190-191
White, Byron R., 240
White, "Whizzer," 8-9
White Men Can't Jump, 51-52
Wild card games, television and, 157
Williams, Brandon, 78
Williams, Jay, 71
Williams, Ricky, 165
Williams, Robin M., 2
Willingham, Tyrone, 52, 54
Willis, Bill, 72
Wilson, Ralph, 124
Winfield, Antoine, 81
Winning (Brancato), 170
Winning, importance of, 10-11
Wisniewski, N., 204
Wives, football players, 77-78
Women
   college athletic programs, 55
   as football fans, 134-135
   in the locker room, 163-164
   male athlete isolation from, 39
   sportscasters, 160-161
   trainer, 114
   violence against, 78, 218
   wives of football players, 77-78
Women's Professional Football League (WPFL), 63
Wood, Andrea, 26

Yaeger, Don, 199-200, 201-203, 205
York, Denise DeBartolo, 130-131

Zimbalist, Andrew, 67